Attainment's
Early Reading Skills Builder
Teacher's Guide

Diane Browder
Lynn Ahlgrim-Delzell
Leah Wood

ERSB

Win/Mac CD

The CD contains printable PDF files of ERSB.
PDF reader software is required to view the PDFs.
Acrobat® Reader® Software is included on the CD.

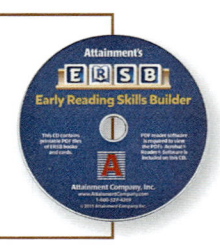

Early Reading Skills Builder
Teacher's Guide

By Diane Browder, PhD • Lynn Ahlgrim-Delzell, PhD • Leah Wood, PhD

Edited by Linda Schreiber • Graphic design by Elizabeth Ragsdale

An Attainment Company Publication
©2015 Attainment Company, Inc. All rights reserved.
Printed in the United States of America
ISBN: 1-57861-907-6

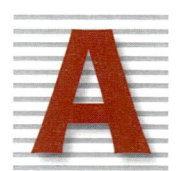

Attainment Company, Inc.

P.O. Box 930160
Verona, Wisconsin 53593-0160 USA
1-800-327-4269
www.AttainmentCompany.com

Reproducible resources within this material may be photocopied for personal and educational use.

Contents

About the Authors 4

Preface 5

Early Reading Skills Builder Inventory 7

Overview of Early Reading Skills Builder 8

How to Use ERSB 18

Development of ERSB and Research Support 23

Scripted Lessons 25

    Level 1 26

    Level 2 36

    Level 3 46

    Level 4 56

    Level 5 66

    Level 6 76

    Level 7 86

    Level 8 96

    Level 9 106

    Level 10 116

    Level 11 126

    Level 12 136

    Level 13 146

    Level 14 156

    Level 15 166

    Level 16 176

    Level 17 186

    Level 18 196

    Level 19 206

    Level 20 216

    Level 21 226

    Level 22 236

    Level 23 246

    Level 24 256

    Level 25 266

    Level 26 276

Appendixes 287

    Appendix A: Decision Tree 288

    Appendix B: How to Complete ERSB Activities without the Software 289

    Appendix C: Guide to Pronunciation of Phonemes Using the International Phonetic Alphabet 292

    Appendix D: Characters by Name 293

    Appendix E: Data Collection Form 294

References 296

About the Authors

Diane Browder, PhD, is the Lake and Edward P. Snyder Distinguished Professor of Special Education at the University of North Carolina, Charlotte. Dr. Browder has over two decades of research and writing on assessment and instruction for students with severe developmental disabilities. She was the 2009 recipient of the Distinguished Researcher Award from the AERA Special Education SIG and the 2009 First Citizens Bank Scholar at the University of North Carolina, Charlotte. In 2011, Dr. Browder was recognized by the state of North Carolina with the O. Max Gardner Award for research that has made a contribution to humanity.

Lynn Ahlgrim-Delzell, PhD, is an Associate Professor of Research at the University of North Carolina, Charlotte. Lynn has over 30 years of experience working with individuals with severe developmental disabilities. She began her career as a school psychologist. She was a research associate at the university for 16 years prior to becoming a faculty member. Her research interests include literacy instruction, assessment of individuals with developmental disabilities, and research methods for low-incidence populations.

Leah Wood, PhD, is an Assistant Professor at California Polytechnic State University, San Luis Obispo. She earned her PhD from the University of North Carolina, Charlotte, with an emphasis on special education of students with moderate-to-severe disabilities. She is a Board Certified Behavior Analyst (BCBA-D) and specializes in the application of systematic instruction to teach academic content and skills to students with intellectual disabilities and autism spectrum disorder. Dr. Wood's research focuses on examining academic interventions for students with developmental disabilities in the area of text comprehension across content and formats, with and without the application of technology.

Preface

Early Reading Skills Builder was created through federal funding for research (ED-IES-11-C-0027) received as a subcontract with Attainment Company. Our goal was to create an early reading program for students who use assistive technology either because they are nonverbal or because they need visual referents to augment their use and understanding of speech and language. It was developed for students who have developed early literacy skills, like print awareness and the phonemic awareness needed to begin decoding. *Early Reading Skills Builder* creates a path towards becoming an independent reader. While students may continue to rely some on their listening skills to access text from their grade level, some can also learn to be fully literate if given the chance to learn phonics. This curriculum offers that opportunity especially for students with developmental disabilities, including intellectual disabilities or autism spectrum disorders.

Our journey in discovering how to teach students with developmental disabilities to read began in 2001 with the authorization of the No Child Left Behind Act (NCLB, 2001). Up until this point in educational history, many students with developmental disabilities were not expected to learn to read and did not receive reading instruction. This point was well-articulated by Kliewer, Biklen, and Kasa-Hendrickson (2006), who described how a lack of attention to literacy contributed to the culture of disability. This lack of emphasis was also illustrated empirically in a comprehensive literature review of reading instruction for students with moderate-to-severe disabilities. This review found a predominance of research regarding sight-word instruction, with little attention paid to other elements of reading, such as phonemic awareness, phonics, and reading comprehension (Browder, Wakeman, Spooner, Ahlgrim-Delzell, & Algozzine, 2006). In particular, phonemic awareness and phonics skills, deemed necessary for learning to read by the National Reading Panel (2000), received very little attention and were the target of only 18 studies between 1975 and 2003 (Browder et al., 2006). Therefore, we had few models for developing a beginning reading program for students with moderate-to-severe developmental disabilities.

We began our work in literacy in 2004 with what we knew through the literature review, and we blended it with seminal works on teaching reading for typical readers, referring to programs such as *Beginning to Read: Thinking and Learning about Print* (Adams, 1990), *Put Reading First: The Research Building Blocks for Teaching Children to Read* (Armbruster, Fehr, & Osborn, 2003), and work on shared stories (e.g., Bus, van IJzendoorn, & Pellegrini, 1995; Justice, McGinty, Piasta, Kaderavek, & Fan, 2010; Skotko, Koppenhaver, & Erickson, 2004). This resulted in the development of a task analysis (Browder, Trela, & Jimenez, 2007) for teaching students to access adapted grade-level text. The task analysis teaches early literacy skills, pointing to text, turning pages, and anticipating repeating storylines, so students could access age-appropriate text. We continue to encourage the use of read-alouds of grade-aligned text (appropriate to students' chronological age) with resources like *Building with Stories* (Zakas and Schreiber, 2010) or *Teaching to Standards: English Language Arts* (Mims, Lee, Zakas, & Browder, 2013).

Using both what we had learned about interactive read-alouds and the skills that build towards reading, we developed a curriculum called *Early Literacy Skills Builder* (ELSB; Browder, Gibbs, Ahlgrim-Delzell, Courtade, & Lee, 2007). This curriculum blended what we knew about systematic instruction to teach students early reading skills such as the alphabetic principle, phonemic awareness, and vocabulary. Once students completed ELSB, it was designed to lead into traditional remedial phonics instruction curricula such as *Reading Mastery* (Engelman & Bruner, 2003) or *Corrective Reading* (Engelmann, Carnine, & Johnson, 1988). But even then we knew there was going to be one difficulty with this link to traditional phonics curricula. Traditional phonics curricula, even the remedial versions, require students to respond verbally to the instruction. Verbal pronunciation of phonemes (sounds) requires fairly sophisticated verbal skills that many students with developmental disabilities, particularly those with severe disabilities, do not possess. As students successfully complete ELSB in school systems all over the country and internationally, there was a growing demand for a next step curriculum.

So with the help of the Attainment Company, we created a phonics curriculum for students unable to access traditional phonics instruction. We began by examining phonemic sequences of traditional remedial phonics instruction and consulting with reading experts. New technology in the development of iPad apps and software with text-to-speech features was available to provide the verbal element nonverbal students needed. *Early Reading Skills Builder* (ERSB) is a culmination of more than three years of work and innovation between the Attainment Company and the research team at the University of North Carolina, Charlotte. Like all of our prior curricula, each step was field-tested by teachers with real students in schools in the Charlotte, NC region.

These teachers and students in the research studies using ERSB were significant contributors to the final product. We could not have designed ERSB without their assistance and feedback. Our work on ERSB was only possible with the cooperation of Charlotte-Mecklenburg Schools (CMS) and Gaston County Schools (GCS). We would like to thank Gina Smith, Assistant Superintendent for Exceptional Children Programs at CMS; Tracie-Lynn Zakas, Program Specialist for Extended Content Standards at CMS; Sadie Broome, Executive Director Exceptional Children at GCS; Karen Miller, Program Facilitator/Autism at GCS; and Barb Puceta, retired Program Facilitator, Speech-language Pathologist, Augmentative Communication/Assistive Technology at GCS, for extending access to teachers and students. We would also like to acknowledge the teachers who were very generous with their time and feedback. The CMS teachers were Mary Allen, Jennifer Caldwell, Shelby Hazelip, Elizabeth Goins, Robin Portlock, Jennifer McDonald, Kim Muhich, Kaitlyn Kingston, Lora Caudill, Barbara Putnam, Elizabeth Jue de Vine, and Yolanda Macon. The GCS teachers were Tosha Owens, Rebecca Holt, Jennifer Simpson, Amber Hay, Pam Martin, Anna Allen, Kim Harmon, Joanne Hare, Jennifer Besser, and Heather Piercy. We would also like to thank all of the students and their parents for the trust they afforded us in providing the opportunity to try our ideas.

Finally, we would like to acknowledge financial support from the contract awarded to Attainment Company in collaboration with the University of North Carolina, Charlotte, from the US Department of Education, Institute of Education Sciences, Small Business Innovation Research (ED-IES-11-C-0027), and the leadership of Carol Stanger, the Principal Investigator of the research project at Attainment Company. Also, thank you to Scott Meister (Lead Programmer), Julie Denu (Software Manager), Cherie Godar (Assistant Editor and Narrator), Heidi Barnhill (Graphic Designer), Jon Karbo (Narrator), Elizabeth Ragsdale (Graphic Designer), and Linda Schreiber (Project Manager/Senior Editor).

Early Reading Skills Builder Inventory

Early Reading Skills Builder (ERSB) comes with everything you need to get started teaching reading.

ERSB Teacher's Guide

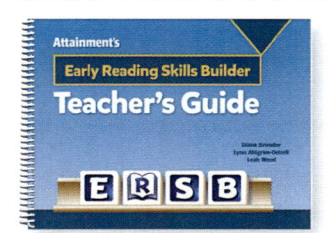

This *Teacher's Guide* describes the curriculum, provides the Scope and Sequence, and summarizes the research outcomes of ERSB. It also provides an overview of each level (including the letter/sounds, phonemic awareness, phonics, sight words, generalization words, level of connected text, and objectives of the level), a detailed description of how to use the curriculum, and the scripted lessons for teaching ERSB. Evidence-based strategies and procedures are embedded in the teaching scripts.

ERSB software/iPad app

ERSB is a blended curriculum in that the software/app is integrated with print materials. The ERSB software is Win/Mac compatible. For iPad users, a redemption code is provided to allow downloading of the ERSB app from the App Store. A software *User Guide* is included in the software/app and should be reviewed or printed for best use of the software/app.

Champion Reader books

Two sets of four *Champion Reader* books are provided for students who would like additional reading practice beyond the software lesson. The passages from the *Champion Readers* are also provided electronically within the lessons on the software.

Champion Writer

Four copies of the *Champion Writer* are provided. The *Champion Writer* is a consumable product; all students require their own copy. Additional books may be purchased.

Card sets

Cards representing the sight words and capital and lowercase alphabet letters are provided for additional practice. Cards can be organized in the storage case provided.

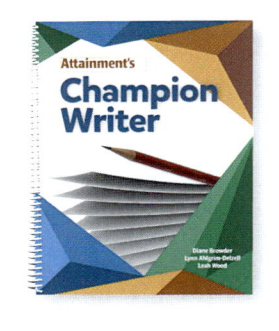

Dry-erase board

A dry-erase board is provided for instructional use. The board is two-sided; the blank side can be used for providing students with response options or pointing out new sounds/letters being learned. The lined side can be used by students who want to practice forming letters and words.

Electronic files

PDF files of various teaching materials are provided on the Win/Mac CD with a Classroom License for printouts:

- The characters—by name and photo—who appear in the reading passages
- The four *Champion Readers*, in the event you want a student to practice reading an individual passage
- Sight Word Flashcards and Alphabet Cards for additional practice
- Pictures to use for the decoding activity
- The *Champion Writer*, should you wish to print individual pages for students
- The words for The Unscrambler activity in the *Champion Writer*

Overview of Early Reading Skills Builder

Early Reading Skills Builder (ERSB) is a multi-year reading curriculum for students who have acquired early foundational literacy skills (i.e., conventions of print, early stages of phonological awareness, some letter-sound correspondence, some sight word vocabulary) but are unable to access traditional reading curricula, especially phonics curricula. For these students, some of whom are nonverbal, there is a need for systematic instruction and text-to-speech software to augment voice during instruction. While the need for a phonics curriculum for students with developmental disabilities (e.g., intellectual disabilities, autism spectrum disorders) initially prompted this work, the curriculum has grown to be one that addresses a wider range of literacy skills with a wider range of students. ERSB teaches early reading skills to the start of second grade.

It is important students have been introduced to precursor literacy skills, such as those taught in the **Early Literacy Skills Builder** curriculum (ELSB; Browder, Gibbs, Ahlgrim-Delzell, Courtade, & Lee, 2007). (See Appendix A for a description of precursor literacy skills.) Using ERSB following ELSB is highly recommended since the instructional approaches are very similar and some of the content overlaps. While ERSB was created to follow ELSB, it is not a prerequisite to have completed the ELSB curriculum specifically. The systematic instruction often needed by students with developmental disabilities found in ELSB is also present in ERSB. Because students may begin ERSB after a couple of years in the ELSB curriculum, the characters and story themes are age-appropriate for older beginning readers (e.g., preteens or teens). For example, the character Zack can drive and plays guitar in a band.

A unique feature of ERSB is the software and professionally recorded phonemes that serve as the student's voice. Individual phonemes can be spoken and blended together, and words can be segmented using the software to say the sounds. Another unique feature is that instruction follows the systematic prompting and fading procedures that are evidence-based practices for this population (Browder, Ahlgrim-Delzell, Spooner, Mims, & Baker, 2009; Spooner, Knight, Browder, & Smith, 2012). ERSB is based on multiple years of research at the University of North Carolina, Charlotte (see p. 23 for a summary).

Underlying principles

The National Reading Panel (NRP; 2000) identified five critical components in learning to read that include vocabulary, phonemic awareness, comprehension, phonics, and fluency. ERSB strategically teaches four of the five components (vocabulary, phonemic awareness, comprehension, and phonics), while fluency is embedded in the repeated reading practice. There are a number of different pedagogical approaches to teaching reading. Armbruster, Fehr, and Osborn (2003) found systematic and explicit phonics instruction is effective for typically developing students across varying social and economic backgrounds, especially students at risk for developing reading problems. There are different systematic and explicit approaches to teaching phonics. ERSB uses the synthetic phonics approach. In this approach, students learn letter sounds, pair them to the written letters, then combine them to form known words. This approach has been demonstrated to be successful in teaching phonics to students with developmental disabilities (Armbruster et al., 2003).

In ERSB, using the synthetic phonics approach, the basic principles of both direct and systematic instruction are embedded. Direct instruction is a procedure that teaches a discrete set of skills through guided practice. It has been found effective in teaching a variety of reading skills (Carnine, Silbert, Kame´enui, & Tarver, 2004). Systematic instruction includes a variety of different procedures based on the principles of applied behavior analysis (Wolery, Bailey, & Sugai, 1988). The forms of systematic instruction found in ERSB include the time-delay procedure, least intrusive prompting, and fading of prompts.

Time-delay procedure

The time-delay procedure promotes learning a desired response with few or no errors on the part of the student. Errors are prevented at first by providing a prompt of the correct answer concurrently with a directive, so the student responds correctly. For example, as the directive to find a letter that makes the /m/ sound is given, the letter m is also highlighted or pointed to. This is 0-seconds time delay and students are praised for touching the correct response, even though the teacher has shown the student which item to touch. This prompt is faded by gradually inserting more time delay (e.g., 4 seconds) between the instructor's (or software's) presentation of a directive and the prompt to allow the student to respond independently. If the student has not responded in the set amount of time, the answer is provided for the student. Through this teaching method, students learn the skill while making as few errors as possible. In ERSB, in every level, the first six activities of Lesson 1 are provided at 0-seconds time delay (this is automatic in the software/app). Lessons 2–5 are set to provide a 4-seconds time delay (the time delay can be adjusted within the software by the instructor).

Least intrusive prompting

Least intrusive prompting is a hierarchy of increasing assistance that instructors use to promote the correct response. By giving no more assistance than necessary, students are encouraged to initiate correct responses. Although least intrusive prompting has often been used for motor tasks in daily living, recent research applications have shown how to modify this intervention for text comprehension (Browder, Hudson, & Wood, 2013; Mims, Hudson, & Browder, 2012) by reading progressively smaller passages of text until the student can locate the answer.

ERSB uses least intrusive prompting for answering comprehension questions (Activity 8) after reading connected text. The idea is to provide the least amount of assistance needed in order to get the student to respond correctly. This is the ERSB least intrusive prompting (LIP) hierarchy for comprehensive questions:

- The instructor asks a comprehension question and waits for the student to respond.
- If the answer is not correct, the instructor rereads the sentence containing the answer aloud.
- If still not correct, the instructor rereads the sentence and provides the answer.

Prompt fading

Fading involves gradually removing a prompt so the student does not become dependent on the prompt to respond. In ERSB, a prompt fading sequence is used to teach students how to read silently. In this fading sequence, the levels are adjusted as shown:

1 The passage is read aloud while pointing to the text.

2 The passage is read with a whisper while pointing to the text.

Although not included in the software, the instructor can continue to add increments to the fading sequence of prompts by:

3 Pretending to read by moving his or her mouth without making sounds while pointing to the text to be read.

4 Pointing (only) to the text to be read.

Finally, no prompts are provided as the student reads silently. This fading sequence occurs gradually over several levels and ends at Level 4.

Curriculum components

ERSB is a blended curriculum, meaning that the software and the print materials can be used interchangeably. There are nine activities in the curriculum emphasizing nine goals. Table 1 presents the activities, goals, and a description of the tasks for ERSB.

Table 1 ERSB activities, goals, and tasks

Activity	Goal	Description of task	Instructional procedure
Letter/sound identification	Identify letters and sounds.	The student selects the grapheme (letter) that corresponds to the phoneme (sound) spoken, "What letter says /m/?" or "Which of these says /m/?"	Lesson 1: 0-second time delay Lessons 2–5: 4-second time delay
Blending	Blend sounds to form words.	A word containing the letter/sounds learned (or being reviewed) is segmented for the student. The student blends the sounds together and then chooses the corresponding word.	Lesson 1: 0–second time delay Lessons 2–5: 4-second time delay
Segmenting I	Segment the first, middle, or last sounds in words.	A word containing the letter/sounds learned (or being reviewed) is spoken and the student begins to learn to segment by identifying the first sound(s) of the word. Later levels require the student to listen for the last sound(s), and eventually, for the middle sound(s) in a word. **Note that this is a listening task**, rather than a spelling task, and the student is simply choosing the letter(s) of the sound heard.	Lesson 1: 0-second time delay Lessons 2–5: 4-second time delay
Segmenting II	Segment the individual sounds in words.	This is a true segmentation task. The student "sounds out" a word by choosing the letters that correspond to the sounds he or she hears in the word spoken. The student must choose the letters corresponding to the sounds heard in the word in the correct order. • The student **does not** need to correctly spell the word; the software will automatically spell the word correctly (e.g., adding a silent e when needed, doubling the consonants, using s when /z/ is the sound in the word, capitalizing proper nouns) when the correct letter/sounds are chosen. • The student **does** need to choose the letter/sounds in the correct sequence. When all letters/sounds have been chosen in the correct order, the sounds are blended together by the instructor (software) and the blended word is spoken. • Early levels begin with CVC words but the word patterns get progressively more difficult by including words with consonant blends, silent letters, and r-controlled vowels as the student advances through the levels.	Lesson 1: 0-second time delay Lessons 2–5: 4-second time delay

(Table continues)

Activity	Goal	Description of task	Instructional procedure
Decoding	Decode words and identify their meanings.	The student decodes the written word given and then selects the picture that represents the word. This activity begins by naming each picture. **It is crucial that the student knows the name of each picture before beginning** so decoding of the text is the focus. • For Levels 1 and 2, decoding (sounding out) is modeled. Each letter in the word is highlighted (or pointed to) and the corresponding sound is spoken. • In Level 3, decoding prompts begin to be faded. The letters in the word are highlighted and the letter's sound is whispered as a reminder to sound out the word. • In Level 4, the decoding model is completely faded and the student reads the word silently.	Lesson 1: 0-second time delay Lessons 2–5: 4-second time delay
Sight words	Read sight words.	Sight words are irregular words that are not decodable. In early levels, the sight words may include some "decodable words" because the words contain some sounds that have not been taught yet, but are needed to create the passage. The student selects the word that corresponds to the spoken word.	Lesson 1: 0-second time delay Lessons 2–5: 4-second time delay
Reading text	Read connected text.	Each level is accompanied by a short passage to read. One page is read at the culmination of every lesson. The passages increase in length as the student advances through the levels. As in the decoding objective, prompts are faded to teach silent reading. • In Levels 1 and 2, the student touches the word to read it; upon touching a word, it is fully voiced. • In Level 3, this prompt begins to be faded and the student is told to read silently in his or her head. When the student touches the word to read it, the words are whispered. • Beginning in Level 4, the student should not be touching the words to hear them read unless they miss the comprehension question. For remaining levels, the student reads the passage silently (in his or her head) without touching the words.	Least intrusive prompting • In Levels 1 and 2, if the student does not begin to read by touching the words or stops reading, the least amount of guidance needed to prompt the student to continue to read is used. • Error correction includes interrupting touching (reading) words in the incorrect sequence, followed by guiding the student to words in the correct sequence.

(Table continues)

Table 1 ERSB activities, goals, and tasks (continued)

Activity	Goal	Description of task	Instructional procedure
Comprehension questions	Answer comprehension questions about connected text.	The student answers a literal question about the passage just read. If the student does not respond with the correct answer to the question, the sentence containing the answer is highlighted and the student can read it again. If the student does not respond correctly after the second reading, the correct answer is modeled. Error correction includes interrupting choosing the incorrect response, followed by guiding the student to the correct answer.	Least intrusive prompting
Writing	Write responses to activities that review the level's objectives.	The student completes activities that review the lesson's objectives.	Assistance and adaptations as required.

The software/app includes eight of the nine activities. The ninth activity—the writing task—is a print-only activity and is completed outside of the software/app activities.

The software/app uses text-to-speech technology to augment the student's voice when working through the activities. The software also collects data on the student's performance so progress can be monitored and level of difficulty adjusted.

Scope and sequence

ERSB includes 26 levels and each level has five lessons. Each level has its own unique connected text passage that has students apply the information they learned in the level's activities. Passages included for reading connected text are provided in both an electronic form (in the software/app) and a print version. Each level builds upon earlier levels by reviewing previously learned letter/sounds and sight words and increasing length and complexity of the connected text. ERSB is designed to take a student to the end of a first-grade reading level. The following illustrates the Scope and Sequence of the ERSB curriculum; specific objectives for each level are provided at the start of each level.

ERSB Scope and Sequence

Level	Focus	New sight words	Lexile	ATOS	Word count	Mean sentence length	Word patterns	Compound words	Dialog
Level 1	Ss, Mm, short Aa	boy, I, a, is, see	1 = −240L 2 = −200L	1 = 0.2 2 = 0.2	1 = 26 2 = 23	1 = 3.7 2 = 3.3	VC, CVC		
Level 2	Rr, Tt/tt, short Ii, ss	girl, my, friend, on, the	1 = 100L 2 = 0L	1 = 1.6 2 = 0.6	1 = 50 2 = 43	1 = 3.8 2 = 3.9	CVC		
Level 3	Ff, Nn, short Oo	no, do, me, yes	1 = −80L 2 = −110L	1 = 0.6 2 = 0.3	1 = 72 2 = 79	1 = 2.8 2 = 3.6	VC, CVC		
Level 4	Gg, Dd, short Uu	has, they, where, and, dog, he	1 = −90L 2 = −120L	1 = 0.2 2 = 0.3	1 = 79 2 = 83	1 = 3.4 2 = 3.3	CVC		
Level 5	Ll/ll, Hh, Kk/c/ck	we, have, she, to, log	1 = 0L 2 = 0L	1 = 0.6 2 = 1.4	1 = 93 2 = 90	1 = 4.4 2 = 4.3	CVC		
Level 6	Bb, Ww, short Ee	like, go, his, does, too	1 = −50L 2 = 10L	1 = 0.3 2 = 0.3	1 = 139 2 = 134	1 = 4.5 2 = 4.2	CVC		
Level 7	Jj, Pp, Yy	eat, bee, of, want, as, be	1 = 90L 2 = 40L	1 = 0.5 2 = 0.3	1 = 153 2 = 134	1 = 4.8 2 = 4.2	CVC		
Level 8	Zz/zz/s, Xx/ks, Vv, Qqᵘ/kw	are, likes, boys, out, what, full, that	1 = −30L 2 = 10L	1 = 0.6 2 = 0.7	1 = 130 2 = 132	1 = 4.2 2 = 4.1	CVC, CCVC, CVCC		
Level 9	long ā, soft c, silent e	brother, for, hello, say, says, school, so, with, you	140L	0.9	186	5.2	VCe, CVCe (silent e), CVC		X
Level 10	long ī, soft g	jumps, funny, into, jump, look, there, zoo, this, then, friends	280L	1.5	190	5.8	CVC, CVCe, CVCC		X

(Table continues)

Scope and Sequence (continued)

Level	Focus	New sight words	Lexile	ATOS	Word count	Mean sentence length	Word patterns	Compound words	Dialog
Level 11	long ō, long ū	cast, gives, here, new, now, blue, wants	130L	0.9	209	5.2	VCe, CVC, CVCe		X
Level 12	long ē; digraphs ea, ee, ai, ay	about, all, bracelet, girls, next, yellow, by, first, was	330L	1.7	219	6.6	CV, CVC, CVvC, CVCe		X
Level 13	digraphs ie, oa, ow; compound words	after, away, help, white, throw, while, each, together, laugh	290L	1.6	226	6.6	VvC, CVv, CVvC, and compound words	rowboat, uphill, into, onto, today, boyfriend, upon, hotdog, cannot, caveman, inside	X
Level 14	final consonant blends st, nt, mp, nd	good, green, Mr., rally, walk, comes, play, plays, class	180L	1.4	226	6.3	VCC, CVCC, CCVC, CCVvC, CCVCe		
Level 15	initial consonant blends sl, br, bl, st	brow, dance, door, hi, alone, shoes, soon, when, hair	230L	1	239	5.7	VCC, CVCC, CCVC, CCVvC, CCVCe	cannot	X
Level 16	consonant blends tr, fl, sk, sp; y (long ī)	our, loves, your, today, two, their, oh, free, again	350L	1.2	214	5.6	CV, CCV, CCVC, CVCC, CCVvC		X

Level	Focus	New sight words	Lexile	ATOS	Word count	Mean sentence length	Word patterns	Compound words	Dialog
Level 17	consonant clusters scr, str	year, twelve, tonight, happy, party, other, night, were	300L	1.7	241	6.2	CCV, CCVC, CCCVC, CCVCe, CCCVCe, CCVvC, CCCVvC		X
Level 18	consonant digraphs th, sh, ch	come, both, from, more, one, done, pretty, use, breaks, push	330L	1.7	246	7	CVC, CVvC, CCCVC, CVCe, CVvr		X
Level 19	consonant digraphs wh, ph; consonant blend gr	said, text, break, only, think, should, great, fair, okay	370L	2.2	251	7	CVC, CVCe, CCV, CCVV, CCVC, CVvC, CCVVC	without	X
Level 20	consonant digraphs ng, tch; consonant blend nk	been, began, long, song, find, really	330L	2.2	272	7.2	CVC, CVCC, CCVC, CCVCC, CCCVvC	washtub	X
Level 21	r-controlled vowels er, ur, ir, or, ar	purse, buy, over, some, sure, took, mall, curve	330L	1.8	262	6.9	CVr, VrC, CVrC, CCVr, CCVrC, CVrCC, compound words	someday, driveway	X
Level 22	r-controlled vowel or; silent first letters kn, wr	floor, knew, watch, bore	410L	2.9	254	7.7	CV, CVr, CVrC, CVC, CVCC, CVCe compound word	friendship	X

(Table continues)

Scope and Sequence (continued)

Level	Focus	New sight words	Lexile	ATOS	Word count	Mean sentence length	Word patterns	Compound words	Dialog
Level 23	dipthongs oi, oy, aw, au, o	cause, derby, down, loud, who, whoa, noise	380L	2.5	288	7.6	CV, CVC, CCV, CVvC, VVC, CVrC, CCCV	soapbox, inside	X
Level 24	digraphs long o͞o, ew; ing	ball, people, fence, tight, using	400L	2.7	269	7.1	CV, CVC, CCV, CVCC, CCCV, CCVC, CVrC, CVC+ing, CCV+ing, VvC+ing, CVvC+ing, CCVCC+ing		X
Level 25	dipthongs ow, ou; y (long ē)	cook, hour, tall, hear	450L	2.3	310	7.4	VC, VCV, VCCV, VCCCV, VCCVCe, CV, CVC, CVCe, CCVC, CVCC, CVCV, CVCCV, CCVCC, CCVCCV, CVrCCV, CVCC+ing, compound words	outside, hotdogs	X
Level 26	digraph short oo; past tense marker ed	give, old, read (pronounced red), wanted	490L	2.6	329	8.4	CVC, CVCC, CCVC, CCVCC, CVCCC, CCVrC, compound word	cookbook	X

The ERSB Scope and Sequence describes the focus of each level—the sequence of graphemes, phonemes, and phonics rules learned in each level. The table also lists the sight words and word patterns covered in each level. The level of text difficulty is referenced using Lexile and ATOS measures, word count, and mean sentence length of connected text. Lexile levels estimate the difficulty level of the text based on the semantic and syntactic elements of the text. Typical first-grade text ranges from 230L to 420L (MetaMetrics, 2014). The ATOS level (Renaissance Learning, 2014) is a measure of text complexity (e.g., sentence length, word length, and word difficulty) and is based on a grade-level scale commonly associated with reading standards.

As this scope and sequence shows, ERSB was developed to follow an easy-to-hard sequence. In contrast, it also was developed to be a streamlined, efficient approach to teaching reading to students who may need many more trials to learn than readers who are nondisabled. Sometimes phonemes are introduced in larger clusters or earlier than other curricula in order to build in functional meaning for the reading passages as well as to follow this streamlined approach. In ERSB, only the most essential decoding skills are targeted and precise repetitive directions are used to simplify the overall cognitive demands on the learner.

How to Use ERSB

Welcome to **Early Reading Skills Builder (ERSB)**. This curriculum is designed for students who have acquired some early literacy skills, such as those mastered in *Early Literacy Skills Builder (ELSB)*. For example, it will be helpful if students have the following early literacy skills:

- Print concepts (knowing text goes from top to bottom and left to right), orienting a book, distinguishing between pictures and words, knowing some reading terms (letter, word, beginning, first, middle, end, last)
- Beginning stages of phonological awareness (rhyme, syllable segmentation)
- Listening comprehension (at least for literal recall)
- Some sight words

Students do not need to know letter names in order to learn to read or to begin ERSB. In general, students who have completed all seven levels of ELSB are ready for ERSB. For students who have not participated in ELSB, the list above will be helpful in determining whether students are ready to begin ERSB. This curriculum especially addresses the needs of students who are nonverbal as the software provides a voice for the phonemic awareness activities. For further recommendations of which curriculum to begin with, see the Decision Tree in Appendix A.

Planning for your students

All students should begin at Level 1, Lesson 1 and proceed through the lessons in order. Even if a student knows some of the graphemes/phonemes, decodes some words, or reads some sight words, beginning at Level 1 will help him or her develop an understanding of the learning behavior necessary to successfully complete the objectives and activities.

The lessons should be taught on a daily basis. Each lesson takes 10 to 20 minutes per student, longer for groups. Lesson length at lower levels is shorter than lessons at upper levels because the stories get longer in the upper levels. Lessons can be implemented with individual students as well as small groups. If using with a small group of students, the lessons will require more time so each student has the opportunity to participate in each activity.

Lessons can be broken into smaller time segments if necessary. For example, you might do the writing activity at a different time of the day. Lessons may also require additional practice within a level by using the print materials provided.

Although ERSB focuses on foundational reading skills, a comprehensive language arts program should address a broad range of standards for the student's grade level. Typically this would involve using interactive read-alouds to provide access to age-appropriate literature and to build language arts skills.

Getting ready to teach ERSB

To prepare for instruction, familiarize yourself with the lessons, the lesson materials, the software/app, and the instructional methods for teaching each skill. Most everything you need to teach a lesson is included in the ERSB software/app, but **it is not designed to be used without a teacher present**. Although the directions, prompts, and progress monitoring are programmed into the software/app, students will need additional instructional guidance. This guidance is suggested in each lesson plan, particularly in the section called Teaching Moment.

The instructional methods selected for these skills (i.e., time delay, least intrusive prompting, and prompt fading) are critical to student success. If not using the software/app, following the prompting procedures described in the lesson plans will help ensure these instructional procedures are as beneficial as possible, so practice the first and second lessons. Follow the 0-seconds time delay (for Lesson 1) and the 4-seconds time-delay procedures as precisely as possible. Be careful to prevent errors when possible.

The best way to promote fidelity and student success is to practice teaching these lessons before working with students.

In addition, you may need to provide physical guidance and redirection for some students to produce correct responses. The lesson plan lists what to do if the student needs help. Even though the software/app simplifies the instructional process by providing cues, timing and fading prompts, and collecting the student's performance data, your physical presence cannot be substituted.

Some students may need individualized instruction using only the print materials. ERSB includes what you need to use both or to integrate their use. Appendix B provides a quick reference to refer to when using the print materials rather than the software. Remember to use the lesson plan as your guide.

The software/app can be used individually or with small groups of students as each student creates an avatar to represent him or her. The individual whose avatar appears on screen is the student whose turn it is and whose data is being collected. Lesson planning should consider how many students will be included in the lesson, group composition, and seating arrangements. (See the User Guide for more information.)

Level/lesson formats

Lesson plans begin with an overview of the level. The level focus; the phonemic awareness, phonics, sight words, and generalization words addressed; and ATOS and Lexile measures of the connected text are listed. The objectives and the level content are also provided and will be a helpful reference if you teach a level or objectives without the software. Teaching Notes explain the focus of the level and how prompts are faded for specific objectives.

The lesson plans are organized by activities and each activity begins with images of the materials you may need. The software screen for the activity is shown and corresponding print materials are shown in the event you want to teach without using the software. The lesson plans include a teaching script so you can teach without the use of the software if you desire. This script is provided in color and is meant as a guide. It is OK to insert your own personality into the script and tailor the wording of the instruction to meet each student's preferences and needs. However, remember that the best way to promote student success is to practice using the scripts before working with students. **It is very important to review the Teaching Moment in each activity as it gives specific ideas for introducing concepts to the students.**

Lesson terminology

Some terminology is specific to reading curricula. This is how terms are defined in ERSB:

- **Phoneme**—A phoneme is a sound and the smallest unit of sound in the language. A grapheme is a letter. In ERSB, you will be pronouncing phonemes—or sounds—rather than naming graphemes. **A phoneme is represented within virgules / / and this indicates that you should say the sound a letter(s) makes, rather than saying the letter name.** The International Phonetic Alphabet (IPA) is used to transcribe phonemes using their phonetic symbols. A pronunciation guide for all phonetic symbols used in ERSB can be found in Appendix C. In addition, a brief pronunciation guide is provided in activities containing unusual symbols to help you accurately pronounce the phonemes in the activity. Note that some single phonemes are comprised of two letters (/ʃ/ is spelled sh).

- **Sight words**—These are words students are not able to decode. Many of the sight words from the Dolch list (Pressley, 2005) are used but in addition, in ERSB, words students have not yet learned to decode but are included in the connected text are also listed as sight words. In later levels, these words may become decodable. A file containing all sight words is included on the CD for printing and for providing additional practice with students.

- **Generalization words**—These are words (listed at the start of each level) that students have not specifically practiced during the lesson but with generalization of the lesson content, should be able to decode. The generalization words occur in the reading passage for the level.

- **Distractors**—Distractors are foils (incorrect responses) that give students options from which to choose. Three distractor words are provided for decoding and comprehension questions and they follow this rule: correct answer, an option starting with the same sound as the correct answer, an option ending with the same sound or containing the same middle sound as the correct answer, and one response that is not plausible.

Providing praise

To increase the likelihood that a student will make the desired response in the future, be careful to deliver praise for independent correct and prompted correct responses. Students need to know when they have performed a skill correctly. Be sure to not praise incorrect responses. Praise should be specific. For example, after a student correctly chooses the letter/sound r when you ask, "What is the first sound in /rrrɪm/?" provide specific praise, "Yes, the first sound in /rɪm/ is /r/."

Champion Readers

Each level comes with a controlled-text passage that only uses words with the graphemes/phonemes and sight words introduced in the level or earlier levels. The characters and story themes are age-appropriate for older beginning readers (e.g., preteens or teens). A reference for the character names is provided in Appendix D. The passages are provided as spiral-bound books and are also included in the software/app. Because some students may need to repeat levels in order to master the content, especially at the early levels, for Levels 1–8, a second "story" featuring the same graphemes/phonemes and sight words is provided in order to maintain interest and reduce the possibility of memorization of answers. It is recommended that all students be provided opportunities to access and interact with the software/app and the text. One idea is to use the e-book for lessons and the spiral-bound book for additional readings in other contexts or vice versa. You may also consider rotating both during instructional time if generalization is an issue.

Champion Writer

Completing the activities in the *Champion Writer* can be a challenge for some students. Here are some suggestions that may help:

- For students who have physical disabilities that may prevent them from writing their responses, use rubber stamps to stamp the letters of their responses.

- To assist students with the sentence unscramble activity, a file containing the words is included on the CD. Print the file, cut the words apart, and allow the students to rearrange them until they form the sentence. Students can then copy the sentence they formed onto the page in the *Champion Writer*.

- For students who are repeating a level, you can print individual pages of the *Champion Writer* from the CD. This file also allows you to use the lesson pages as homework assignments.

Proceeding through the lessons and monitoring progress

The first lesson of each level uses a 0-second time delay, in which you model the correct answer and ask the student to repeat your model. For each lesson thereafter, 4-seconds time delay is given before providing a model for the student to follow. If at any time, the student's accuracy for a lesson falls at 50% or less, return to 0-seconds time delay (as in Lesson 1) for one lesson. (If working with a group, this lesson needs to be conducted outside of the group.) Return to a 4-second delay for the next lesson. This can be repeated as often as necessary. The software/app collects the student's response performance as a student (or group of students) progresses through the level (see the software User Guide for more information.) Only independent, correct responses are counted toward the lesson total score (and accuracy percentage). Prompted correct responses (correct responses that occur after you have modeled the answer) should be praised, but are not counted as correct. Only data from Lessons 2–5 are collected since Lesson 1 is completely modeled and the student is not making independent responses.

Students move to the next level when they obtain 80% correct, independent responses for three consecutive lessons. If a student does not reach the 80% criteria, he or she should repeat the level, beginning at Lesson 2 using the 4-second time delay.

The software/app automates advancing students when appropriate or repeating the level when appropriate. Note that when repeating Levels 1–8, the alternate passage (Story 2) is used to avoid boredom or possible memorization of responses. If a level is repeated more than once, alternate between Story 1 and Story 2.

Although the ERSB software/app tracks correct responses and moves to the next lesson/level, once the student reaches the criteria, you should monitor correct responses to keep students moving through the curriculum. (Appendix E provides a form for collecting data manually if you desire to do manual monitoring rather than through the software.) First, it is possible to obtain the overall 80% accuracy rate to move to the next level but consistently miss items in one particular objective. If this happens, provide additional opportunities for the student to practice this skill. For example, if a student is doing well overall, but having trouble segmenting words, provide additional practice using some of the print materials provided. Provide more practice during other reading opportunities throughout the day.

Second, a student may seem to be "stuck," repeating levels without reaching the 80% criteria. Review the response patterns to determine what may be needed to keep the student progressing through the curriculum. As above, if there are certain objectives that the student is having difficulty with, provide additional opportunities to practice that skill. If the pattern fluctuates, reaching criteria one day and not the next day, the issue may be one of motivation. Providing differential reinforcement for correct responding can help. Differential reinforcement can also be useful for encouraging appropriate learning behaviors such as remaining in the seat and waiting for a turn.

Frequently asked questions

1 What comes after ERSB? Students who master ERSB will be able to read passages of text silently. They should be able to transition into a reading curriculum that builds skills through working on fluency and comprehension. They will not necessarily need the iPad to read, but may prefer using e-text. An advantage of e-text is that a student can continue to use the text-to-speech function to check understanding for specific words or lines of text they do not understand.

2 What if a student does not master a level? The levels can be repeated as many times as needed until the student achieves the mastery criterion. However, to avoid repeating a level so many times so that the student becomes bored, use some of the print materials to conduct the lesson. Or consider switching the use of the e-book and print book. You want the student to demonstrate continual progress, so review the accuracy of the individual objectives to determine whether you can provide extra practice on a specific skill in order to keep the student moving through the levels. Students may also benefit from generalization activities in which they practice their letter sounds in a variety of ways. For example, play the game "I spy…" saying, "I spy something that makes the /p/ sound." Students then find an object that begins with the sound (e.g., paper).

3 When can I begin introducing other books for the student to read? Once the students have mastered the first several levels, they may be able to use other readers with controlled vocabulary focused on the same phonemes. For example, one of our students was able to generalize to reading *Sound Out Chapter Books*. This set of books follows the same sequence of introducing letter/sounds so are a great way for students to generalize new reading skills. A print version of these books is available from High Noon Books (2005) and an e-version of the books is available from Attainment Company (2014). High Noon also offers a set of workbooks with activities for comprehension, fluency and writing.

4 How many students can be included in a small group lesson? A small group lesson will need to include students who are working on the same level/lesson. It would be too cumbersome to go back and forth between lessons for different students at the same time. Up to three or four students can be grouped together, but the number and composition of the group should depend upon the students' abilities to wait for their turn without being distracted, and how well the students can work together. You will also need to consider seating arrangements so you can reach each student easily when physical prompting is needed. Students who need more prompting should sit closest to you. You will also want students to be able to see how their peers have responded. One benefit to small groups is that students can learn from their peers. If using a small group, you need to be able to manage the program quickly to keep a steady pace. Remember to have students create an avatar in the software/app so the data will be collected accurately for each student.

5 My student seems stuck on the Segmenting II activity. What can I do? Segmenting does seem to be the most difficult skill to master. First, make sure you interrupt a student before he or she makes an error. Second, make sure you are correcting the segmentation of the entire word and not just the phoneme that was incorrect. Even if only one phoneme was incorrect, model segmenting the entire word. Also try extra practice on this skill outside of the software lesson using words from the lesson (see each level's content) and other words using the same phonemes in other settings. Using your fingers or objects (e.g., chips or blocks) to indicate and count the number of phonemes as they are spoken may also help.

6 Can a teacher assistant conduct the lessons? This depends upon the skill level of the teacher assistant. An assistant can conduct the lesson if he or she is well-trained in the prompting procedures. You will want to monitor to make sure there is good instructional fidelity. You will also want to monitor the data to make sure the student is progressing through the levels as expected. Instructional decisions regarding what to do when students are not making expected progress should be made by you.

On the way to reading!

Students may begin slowly at first in the first levels of ERSB. Remember that students are learning the format of the lessons as well as specific skills. We have found that over time, many students' pace of learning accelerates. We encourage you to persist, repeating a level or returning to 0-seconds time delay as needed, until the student begins this acceleration. One of the most exciting experiences you as a teacher can have is when your student begins to read. We hope your students will surprise you with their successes.

Development of ERSB and Research Support

The ERSB is the result of more than three years of development, evaluation, and revisions. The first step in development of the instructional strategies and scope and sequence of the skills and phonemes was a review and comparison of traditional and remedial phonics curricula such as *Early Interventions in Reading* (Mathes & Torgesen, 2005), *Reading Mastery* (Engelmann & Bruner, 2003), *Early Reading Tutor* (Gibbs, Campbell, Helf, & Cooke, 2007), and *The Phonics Primer* (Elam, 2007). The proposed scope and sequence and phoneme recordings were submitted to experts in linguistics and experts in teaching reading to students with developmental disabilities for review and comments. Several changes were made based on their recommendations. Previous research on teaching phonemic awareness and phonics to students with developmental disabilities guided the use of the direct and systematic instructional strategies described earlier (e.g., Alberto, Waugh, & Fredrick, 2010; Allor, Mathes, Roberts, Jones, & Champlin, 2010; Bradford, Shippen, Alberto, Houchins, & Flores, 2006; Browder, Ahlgrim-Delzell, Flowers, & Baker, 2012).

Iterative series of research studies were conducted over the course of three years to evaluate the scope and sequence and procedures used in the curriculum. Two teachers and two students volunteered for the first qualitative, exploratory study with the first two lessons using the GoTalk 32 Express alternative/augmentative communication (AAC) device. Each teacher-led lesson was video-recorded so both teacher and student behavior interacting with the curriculum could be monitiored. At the end of three weeks of instruction, the teachers were interviewed. Changes to the curriculum were made based on the video observations and teacher comments. After this field test, the curriculum was evaluated using a single-case research design (Ahlgrim-Delzell, Browder, & Wood, 2014). Two teachers taught the revised first three lessons of the curriculum with three students for approximately 21–23 sessions each. Fidelity of implementation of the instructional procedures was closely monitored and the teachers were interviewed about the procedures. All three students successfully demonstrated an increased ability to identify phonemes, blend phonemes to form words, and decode words. Again, teachers provided suggestions for improving the curriculum.

After the second study, the curriculum was developed to capitalize on iPad app technology. The app improved the sound quality and instructional components and procedures were programmed into the app. This reduced the amount of instructional materials required. Our second study used a randomized control trial group experiment with 32 students and 22 teachers randomly assigned to treatment and comparison conditions. Teachers assigned to the treatment condition were trained in how to use the ERSB iPad app while comparison teachers used the iPad for the same amount of time to teach sight words and conduct story-based lessons as part of their typical daily instruction. The study was conducted from October to May for nearly one school year. The students receiving ERSB instruction had significantly higher responses in identifying letter/sounds, blending phonemes to form words, and decoding words (Ahlgrim-Delzell, Browder, Wood, Preston, Kemp-Inman, in preparation).

At each step in the development of ERSB, objective data was gathered on student skill attainment, teacher and student behaviors were observed, and teachers' opinions and suggestions were solicited. The final ERSB product is a culmination of these activities translated into a blended curriculum using print and software/iPad technology.

Scripted Lessons

LEVEL 1

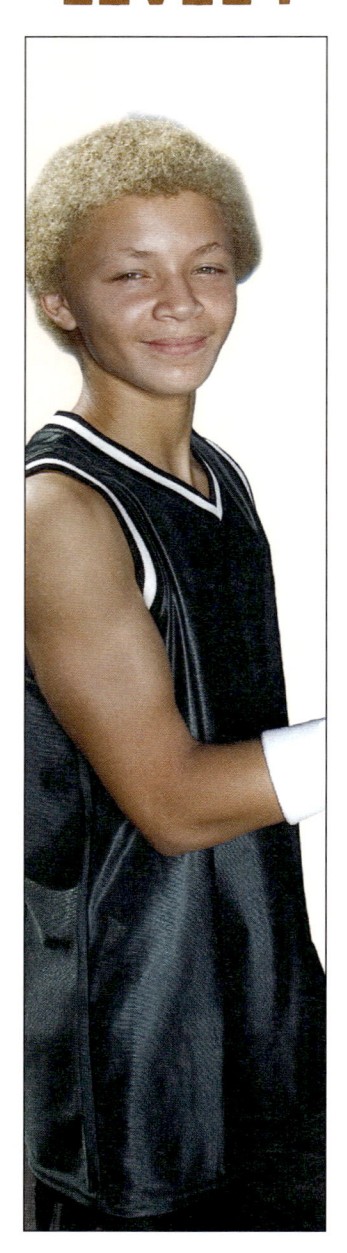

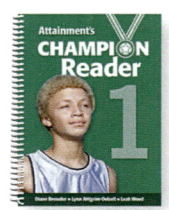

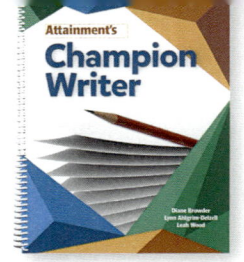

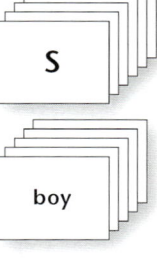

Focus
Ss, Mm, Aa (short)

Phonemic awareness
- Blend sounds for VC and CVC words
- Segment first sounds in words
- Segment sounds in VC and CVC words

Phonics
- Sounds /s/, /m/, /æ/ corresponding to graphemes Ss, Mm, Aa
- Decode VC and CVC words

Sight words
a, boy, I, is, see

Generalization words
None

Connected text
- ATOS level = Story 1: 0.2; Story 2: 0.2
- Lexile level = Story 1: −240L; Story 2: −200L

Objectives
1. Identify Ss, Mm, and Aa when given the sounds /s/, /m/, and /æ/.
2. Blend sounds to form VC and CVC words.
3. Segment the first sound in words beginning with /s/, /æ/, or /m/.
4. Segment the sounds in VC and CVC words.
5. Decode VC and CVC words and identify their meanings.
6. Read 5 new sight words.
7. Read connected text.
8. Answer comprehension questions about connected text.
9. Write responses to activities that review level objectives.

Teaching notes
This level introduces the student to the ERSB program. Level 1 introduces the letter/sounds s, m, and short a. Note to use the sound a letter makes whenever the letter appears in virgules (e.g., /s/) in the lesson plan.

For the ERSB program, Lesson 1 always demonstrates every item for the first six activities at 0-second time delay. Lessons 2–5 provide one demonstration item, and the remaining items prompt students if needed using 4-second time delay. For the comprehension questions, the least intrusive prompt is used to help students respond.

Level 1 Content

	Lesson 1	Lesson 2	Lesson 3	Lesson 4	Lesson 5
Letter/sound identification	Ss, Mm, Aa (short)				
Blending	Sam, am				
Segmenting I	Sam, man, apple, sit, mud, ant	**Demo:** mom am, soap, Monday, at, sack	**Demo:** at see, my, attic, soon, many	**Demo:** Sam moon, animal, seat, make, add	**Demo:** Sam mouse, at, sun, mess, app
Segmenting II	Sam, am				
Decoding	Sam, am				
Sight Words	a, boy, I, is, see				
Comprehension questions (correct response in **bold**)	Story 1: See Sam				
	What is Sam? (Sam, am, see, **boy**)	Who did the girl see? (man, Tim, see, **Sam**)	What is Sam? (is, big, Sam, **boy**)	Who did the girl see? (Tim, see, **Sam**, is)	What is Sam? (is, big, **boy**, toy) Who did the girl see? (sat, Tam, **Sam**, see)
	Story 2: Sam Is a Boy				
	What is the boy's name? (**Sam**, see, boy, Tam)	Who did the girl see? (man, **Sam**, see, Tim)	Who is a boy? (boy, is, big, **Sam**)	What did the girl see? (see, **boy**, dog, is)	Who did the girl see? (is, **Sam**, bat, see) Who is a boy? (**Sam**, Tam, boy, see)

Letter/sound identification

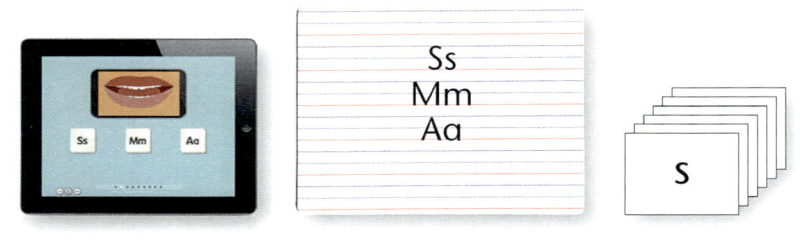

Objective 1
Identify Ss, Mm, and Aa when given the sounds /s/, /m/, and /æ/.
Pronunciation: /æ/ as in a̱m

Prompting
- Lesson 1: Time delay 0 seconds
- Lessons 2–5: Time delay 4 seconds

Activity directions
I'll say a sound, and you find the letter that makes that sound.

Teaching moment
✔ Note that the emphasis in this activity is on the sounds the letters make. Introduce the letter/sounds Ss, Mm, and Aa. Point to the tiles on the software screen or dry-erase board and say, **Let's learn the sounds /s/, /m/, and /æ/.**

✔ If the student struggles, use visual and articulatory cues that show the student how a sound is made (e.g., point to your lips to say /mmm/).

✔ If the student does not know uppercase from lowercase letters, use the flashcards to practice matching them.

✔ If the student chooses an incorrect response, give a reminder to not guess but to wait and you will help. You can also add to the directions, **If you are not sure of the answer, don't guess. Wait for me to help you.**

Cue	Student's independent response	If student needs help
What letter says /s̱/?	Finds the letter Ss to make the /s̱/ sound.	For Lesson 1, model finding the correct response, and continue pointing to it until the student finds it. If no response or an incorrect response, physically guide the student to find the letter and say, **This is /s̱/.** For Lessons 2–5, if no response after 4 seconds or an incorrect response, model finding the letter, and continue pointing to it until the student finds it. If needed, physically guide the student to find the letter and say, **This is /s̱/. You touch it.**

Repeat with Mm and Aa.

ERSB Teacher's Guide ■ Level 1

Blending

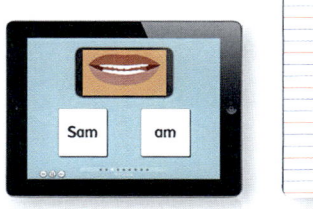

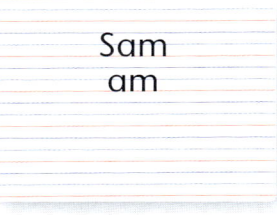

Objective 2
Blend sounds to form VC and CVC words.
Pronunciation: /æ/ as in am

Prompting
- Lesson 1: Time delay 0 seconds
- Lessons 2–5: Time delay 4 seconds

Activity directions
I'll say some sounds. You blend the sounds together and find the word they make.

Teaching moment

✔ It is easier to blend a final consonant onto a CV string (e.g., Sa—m) than to blend an initial consonant onto a VC string (e.g., S—am); therefore, the first two levels in ERSB focus on blending the final consonant onto a CV or V string.

✔ To make it easier for the student, prolong the sounds in the CV or V string followed by a pause before adding the final consonant.

✔ If needed, use the dry-erase board to demonstrate blending using fewer words as distractors.

✔ If the student chooses an incorrect response, give a reminder to not guess but to wait and you will help. You can also add to the directions, **If you are not sure of the answer, don't guess. Wait for me to help you.**

Cue	Student's independent response	If student needs help
/sæ/ /m/. Which word am I saying?	Finds the word Sam.	For Lesson 1, model finding the correct response, and continue pointing to it until the student finds it. If no response or an incorrect response, physically guide the student to find the word. For Lessons 2–5, if no response after 4 seconds or an incorrect response, model finding the word and say, **This is Sam. You touch it.** Continue pointing to it until the student finds it. If needed, physically guide the student to find the word.

Repeat with the content for each lesson; see **Level 1 Content** on p. 27.

Segmenting I

Objective 3
Segment the first sound in words beginning with /s/, /æ/, or /m/.
Pronunciation: /æ/ as in <u>a</u>m

Prompting
- Lesson 1: Time delay 0 seconds
- Lessons 2–5: Time delay 4 seconds

Activity directions
I'll say a word. You show me the first sound you hear in the word.

Teaching moment
✔ In learning to segment sounds in words, it is easier to segment the initial sound than the middle or ending sound; so for this level, this activity focuses on segmenting the initial sound in words.

✔ Pause for one second between the direction ("What is the first sound in") and the target word to prepare the student for the target word.

✔ This activity helps the student segment sounds by emphasizing or slightly prolonging the first sound in the word when possible.

✔ If the student chooses an incorrect response, give a reminder to not guess but to wait and you will help. You can also add to the directions, **If you are not sure of the answer, don't guess. Wait for me to help you.**

Cue	Student's independent response	If student needs help
What is the first sound in (1 sec. pause) **Sam?**	Finds <u>s</u> to say /s/.	For Lesson 1, if no response or an incorrect response, physically guide the student to touch <u>s</u>. Say, **The first sound is /s/.**
		For Lessons 2–5, if no response after 4 seconds or an incorrect response, model finding the sound and say, **The first sound is /s/. You touch it.** If needed, physically guide the student to find /s/.

Repeat with the <u>content</u> for each lesson; see **Level 1 Content** on p. 27.

Segmenting II

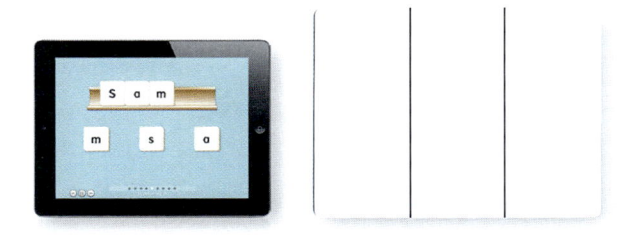

Objective 4
Segment the sounds in VC and CVC words.
Pronunciation: /æ/ as in am

Prompting
- Lesson 1: Time delay 0 seconds
- Lessons 2–5: Time delay 4 seconds

Activity directions
Use the sounds you learned to sound out some words. I'll say a word, and you sound it out.

Teaching moment
✔ To help the student segment all of the sounds in the word, hold up a finger for each sound the student needs to find.

✔ Or divide the dry-erase board into sections to indicate how many sounds are in a word.

✔ If the student chooses an incorrect response, give a reminder to not guess but to wait and you will help. You can also add to the directions, **If you are not sure of the answer, don't guess. Wait for me to help you.**

✔ If the student makes an error on even one sound, have the student listen as you segment **all** the sounds in the word in the correct sequence. Then restate to touch the sounds in the word.

Cue	Student's independent response	If student needs help
Sound out the word Sam.	Finds s, a, and m for the sounds /s/, /æ/, and /m/.	For Lesson 1, if no response or an incorrect response, physically guide the student to touch s, a, and m to segment the word. Then say the blended word.
		For Lessons 2–5, if no response after 4 seconds or an incorrect response, say, **Listen, /s/ /æ/ /m/. Touch the sounds in Sam.**
		If still no response or an incorrect response, model segmenting the word by touching and saying each sound. Then say, **Touch the sounds in Sam.**
		If still no response or an incorrect response, say, **Let's touch the sounds in Sam.** Then physically guide the student to touch each sound while you say it.

Repeat with the content for each lesson; see **Level 1 Content** on p. 27.

ERSB Teacher's Guide ■ Level 1

Decoding

Objective 5
Decode VC and CVC words and identify their meanings.
Pronunciation: /æ/ as in am

Prompting
- Lesson 1: Time delay 0 seconds
- Lessons 2–5: Time delay 4 seconds

Activity directions
Now, use the sounds and letters you learned to read a word and find its picture.

Teaching moment

✓ Be certain the student knows the name of each picture.

✓ In this level, demonstrate sounding out the word to be decoded by first pointing to each letter in the word while saying its sound, then blending the sounds together to say the word, and then touching the picture of the word. Prolong the sounds to stretch out the word.

✓ If the student chooses an incorrect response, give a reminder to not guess but to wait and you will help. You can also add to the directions, **If you are not sure of the answer, don't guess. Wait for me to help you.**

Cue	Student's independent response	If student needs help
First, let's hear each picture's name.	Listens as each picture is named.	
For Lesson 1 and demonstration items, touch each letter as you stretch out the sounds in the word, **/sss/ /æ/ /mmm/**. Then touch the picture and say, **Here is Sam**. Point to the picture of Sam until the student finds it.	Finds the picture of Sam.	For Lesson 1, if no response or an incorrect response, physically guide the student to touch the picture of Sam.
For Lessons 2–5, model decoding by touching each letter and saying its sound. Then touch the picture. Say, **Your turn. Read this word /s/ /æ/ /m/ and find the picture**. Point to the picture of Sam until the student finds it.		For Lessons 2–5, if no response or an incorrect response, model sounding out the word while you point to each letter and find the picture. Say, **This is /s/ /æ/ /m/. Here is the picture of Sam. Now you read Sam and find the picture**. Physically guide the student's hand if needed.

Repeat for all with the content for each lesson; see **Level 1 Content** on p. 27.

Sight words

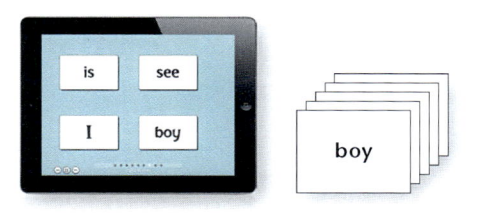

Objective 6
Read 5 new sight words.

Prompting
- Lesson 1: Time delay 0 seconds
- Lessons 2–5: Time delay 4 seconds

Activity directions
Sight words are tricky because you can't sound them out. You have to remember what they look like. Find the word.

Teaching moment
✔ The pace between presentation of words is purposely rapid to keep the student motivated.

✔ Use the sight word flashcards to provide extra practice of sight word reading. Provide up to 4 response options for students to choose from.

✔ If the student chooses an incorrect response, give a reminder to not guess but to wait and you will help. You can also add to the directions, **If you are not sure of the answer, don't guess. Wait for me to help you.**

✔ Create a word wall with sight words from this level.

Cue	Student's independent response	If student needs help
Find the word boy.	Finds the word boy.	For Lesson 1, if no response or an incorrect response, physically guide the student to find boy. Say, **This is boy.** For Lessons 2–5, if no response after 4 seconds or an incorrect response, model finding the word and say, **This is boy. You touch it.** Physically guide the student to find the word if needed.

Repeat with the new sight words and review sight words, words required for reading the story for this level; see **Level 1 Content** on p. 27.

Reading text / Comprehension questions

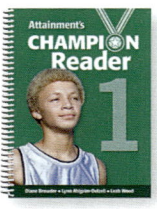

Sam
am
see
boy

Objective 7 / Objective 8
Read connected text. / Answer comprehension questions about connected text.

Prompting
Least intrusive prompt

Activity directions
Now that you know how to read words, you can read a page from the story. Today you will read about a boy named Sam.

> **Teaching moment**
>
> ✓ In this level in the software, the text is read to the student when he or she touches the word. Point to the words to indicate to the student to read each word.
>
> ✓ One page of the story is read during each lesson, followed by comprehension questions. If repeating this level, Story 2 will be used in the software.
>
> ✓ Use **Champion Reader 1** to show the title of the story and to point out the characters. It can also be used to give students additional reading practice. The comprehension questions that could be asked if not using the software and possible response options are listed in the **Level 1 Content** on p. 27. Write response options on the dry-erase board for students to read.

Cue	Student's independent response	If student needs help
For Lessons 1–5, point to each word on the page and model reading it. Say, **Your turn.** In Lesson 5, give the student the opportunity to read sentence-by-sentence after the model is given.	Touches each word in the sentence to read it.	If no response, model touching each word while you say, **Read the sentence. Touch Sam, touch is, touch a, and touch boy**. Point to each word until the student touches it. If the student touches the wrong word, point to the correct word and say, **Here is Sam**. If the student does not respond or stops responding, physically guide the student to touch each word. Say, **Here is Sam. Here is is. Here is a. Here is boy**.

(Table continues)

ERSB Teacher's Guide ■ Level 1

Cue	Student's independent response	If student needs help
After the student reads the sentence(s) on the page, say, **Let's answer some questions about the story. What is Sam?**	Chooses the word boy.	If no response or an incorrect response, read the sentence again, and ask, **What is Sam?** If still no response or an incorrect response, read the sentence, **Sam is a boy**, then physically guide the student to find boy, and say, **Boy. Sam is a boy**.

Repeat with the content for each lesson; see **Level 1 Content** on p. 27.

Closing /Writing activity

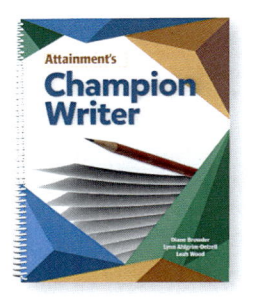

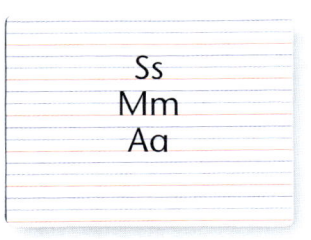

Objective 9
Write responses to activities that review level objectives.

Activity directions
Your lesson is over. GREAT reading today! Let's complete a page in your Champion Writer.

Teaching moment

✔ In order to keep the lesson from becoming too long, consider completing the writing activity at another time of the day.

✔ Some students may need adaptations to complete the writing page in **Champion Writer**; see p. 20 for ideas.

✔ Use the dry-erase board and an erasable marker to give the student practice in writing/forming the letter/sounds of this level.

LEVEL 2

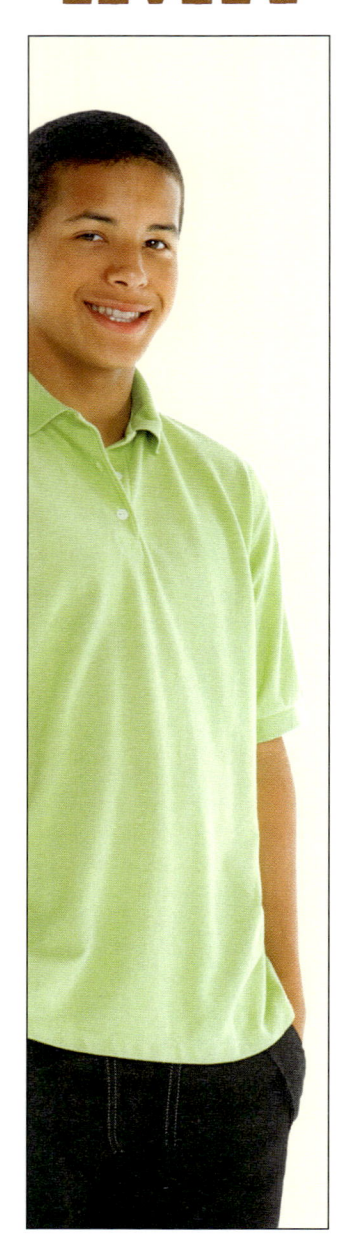

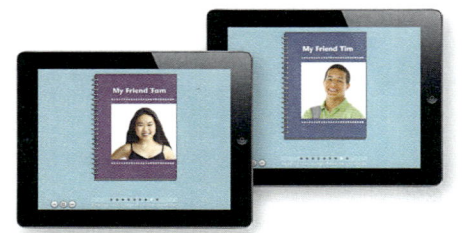

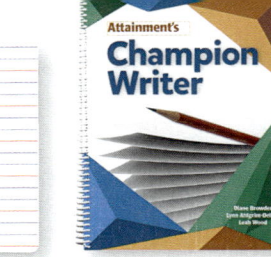

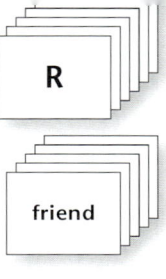

Focus
Rr, Tt, Ii (short)

Phonemic awareness
- Blend sounds for CVC words
- Segment first sounds in words
- Segment sounds in CVC words

Phonics
- Sounds /r/, /t/, /ɪ/, and /s/ corresponding to graphemes Rr, Tt/tt, Ii, and ss
- Decode CVC words

Sight words
friend, girl, my, on, the

Generalization word
sat

Connected text
- ATOS level = Story 1: 1.6; Story 2: .6
- Lexile level = Story 1: 100L; Story 2: 0L

Objectives
1. Identify Rr, Tt/tt, Ii, and ss when given the sounds /r/, /t/, /ɪ/, and /s/.
2. Blend sounds to form CVC words.
3. Segment the first sound in words beginning with /r/, /t/, or /ɪ/.
4. Segment the sounds in CVC words.
5. Decode CVC words and identify their meanings.
6. Read 5 new sight words.
7. Read connected text.
8. Answer comprehension questions about connected text.
9. Write responses to activities that review level objectives.

Teaching notes
Level 2 introduces the letter/sounds Rr, Tt, and short Ii and reviews Level 1 Content. In addition, double ss is added to the Ss tile. Note to use the sound a letter makes whenever the letter appears in virgules (e.g., /t/) in the lesson plan.

For the ERSB program, Lesson 1 always demonstrates every item for the first six activities at 0-second time delay. Lessons 2–5 provide one demonstration item, and the remaining items prompt students if needed using 4-second time delay. For the comprehension questions, the least intrusive prompt is used to help students respond.

Level 2 Content

	Lesson 1	**Lesson 2**	**Lesson 3**	**Lesson 4**	**Lesson 5**
Letter/sound identification	**New:** Rr, Tt, Ii (short) (ss added to Ss tile; tt added to Tt tile) **Review:** Ss, Mm, Aa (short)				
Blending	mat, miss, ram, sit, Sam, rim	**Demo:** ram mat, rat, Tam, Mim, rim	**Demo:** rat rim, mitt, sit, mat, ram	**Demo:** Tam Sam, mat, ram, Mim, mitt	**Demo:** Tam Sam, sit, ram, Mim, mitt
Segmenting I	rat, tub, ick, rain, time, is	**Demo:** Tam in, roar, ten, it, writ	**Demo:** it rake, to, inch, right, turn	**Demo:** ram tip, itch, reach, tell, inside	**Demo:** rat tap, top, run, ick, in
Segmenting II	Tam, Sam, rim, ram, Mim, mitt	**Demo:** mat mitt, Tam, sit, Sam, rim	**Demo:** ram miss, sat, Tam, Mim, rim	**Demo:** rat rim, miss, sit, mat, Tam	**Demo:** ram Mim, mat, sit, rat, Sam
Decoding	ram, sit, rim, Tam, mat, rat	**Demo:** Sam rim, ram, sit, Tam, mat, rat	**Demo:** Sam miss, mat, Tam, rim, Tim, Mim	**Demo:** Sam miss, rim, Tam, sit, am, Tim	**Demo:** Sam rat, rim, ram, sit, Tam, mat
Sight Words	**New:** friend, girl, my, on, the **Review:** a, boy, I, is, see				
Comprehension questions (correct response in **bold**)	\multicolumn{5}{}				

Story 1: My Friend Tim

	Lesson 1	Lesson 2	Lesson 3	Lesson 4	Lesson 5
	What is Tam? (boy, mat, bat, **girl**)	Who sat on a mat? (Sam, **Tam**, Mat, Sit)	What did the rat sit on? (rat, **mat**, on, sit)	What does Tam see? (a, see, **rat**, boy)	Who is the girl? (Sam, rat, girl, **Tam**)
	Who is Sam's friend? (Tim, Mat, **Tam**, Sat)	Who do you see? (**Tam**, Sat, Sam, See)	What is on the mat? (mat, sat, **rat**, on)	Who is Sam's friend? (**rat**, mat, on, sat)	Who is a friend? (Tim, mat, **Tam**, boy)

Story 2: Sam Is a Boy

	Lesson 1	Lesson 2	Lesson 3	Lesson 4	Lesson 5
	Who is the boy? (Tam, bat, girl, **Tim**)	Who is Sam's friend? (Sam, mat, on, **Tim**)	Who is on the mat? (**girl**, see, mat, boy)	What is Tim on? (Sam, rat, **mat**, sit)	Who is Sam's friend? (Sam, mat, on, **Tim**)
	What is Tim? (rat, **friend**, mat, girl)	What is Tim on? (rat, sat, **mat**, girl)	Who is the girl? (Sam, **Tam**, sat, Tim)	Who does Tam see? (Tam, the, **Tim**, see)	What is Tim on? (rat, sat, **mat**, girl)

Letter/sound identification

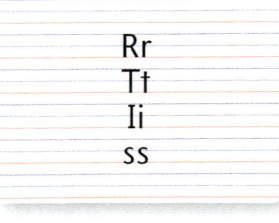

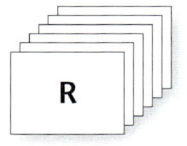

Objective 1
Identify Rr, Tt/tt, Ii, and ss when given the sounds /r/, /t/, /ɪ/, and /s/.
Pronunciation: /ɪ/ as in rim

Prompting
- Lesson 1: Time delay 0 seconds
- Lessons 2–5: Time delay 4 seconds

Activity directions
I'll say a sound, and you find the letter that makes that sound.

Teaching moment

✔ Note that the emphasis in this activity is on the sounds the letters make. Introduce the letter/sounds Rr, Tt, and Ii to the student. Point to the tiles on the software screen or write and point to them on the dry-erase board and say, **Let's learn the sounds /r/, /t/, and /ɪ/.** Point out the tt and ss on the Tt and Ss tiles. **These letters together also say /s/. Notice the tt on the Tt tile. These letters together also say /t/.**

✔ If the student struggles, use visual and articulatory cues that show the student how a sound is made (e.g., point to your mouth to say /t/).

✔ If the student does not know uppercase from lowercase letters, use the flashcards to practice matching them.

✔ If the student chooses an incorrect response, give a reminder to not guess but to wait and you will help. You can also add to the directions, **If you are not sure of the answer, don't guess. Wait for me to help you.**

Cue	Student's independent response	If student needs help
What letter says /r/?	Finds the letter Rr to make the /r/ sound.	For Lesson 1, model finding the correct response, and continue pointing to it until the student finds it. If no response or an incorrect response, physically guide the student to find the letter and say, **This is /r/.** For Lessons 2–5, if no response after 4 seconds or an incorrect response, model finding the letter, and continue pointing to it until the student finds it. If needed, physically guide the student to find the letter and say, **This is /r/. You touch it.**

Repeat with Tt and Ii, and Level 1 review: Ss, Aa, and Mm.

Blending

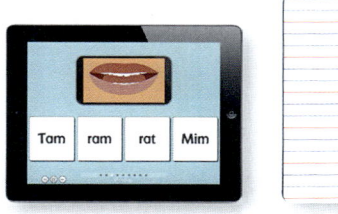

Objective 2
Blend sounds to form CVC words.
Pronunciation: /æ/ as in m<u>a</u>t

Prompting
- Lesson 1: Time delay 0 seconds
- Lessons 2–5: Time delay 4 seconds

Activity directions
I'll say some sounds. You blend the sounds together and find the word they make.

Teaching moment
✔ It is easier to blend a final consonant onto a CV string (e.g., ma—t) than to blend an initial consonant onto a VC string (e.g., m—at); therefore, this level continues to focus on blending the final consonant onto a CV or V string.

✔ To make it easier for the student, the sounds in the CV or V string are prolonged and followed by a pause before adding the final consonant.

✔ If needed, use the dry-erase board to demonstrate blending using fewer words as distractors.

✔ If the student chooses an incorrect response, give a reminder to not guess but to wait and you will help. You can also add to the directions, **If you are not sure of the answer, don't guess. Wait for me to help you.**

Cue	Student's independent response	If student needs help
/m<u>æ</u>/ /<u>t</u>/. Which word am I saying?	Finds the word <u>mat</u>.	For Lesson 1, model finding the correct response, and continue pointing to it until the student finds it. If no response or an incorrect response, physically guide the student to find the word.
		For Lessons 2–5, if no response after 4 seconds or an incorrect response, model finding the word and say, **This is <u>mat</u>. You touch it.** Continue pointing to it until the student finds it. If needed, physically guide the student to find the word.

Repeat with the <u>content</u> for each lesson; see **Level 2 Content** on p. 37.

Segmenting I

Objective 3
Segment the first sound in words beginning with /r/, /t/, or /ɪ/.
Pronunciation: /r/ as in <u>r</u>am

Prompting
- Lesson 1: Time delay 0 seconds
- Lessons 2–5: Time delay 4 seconds

Activity directions
I'll say a word. You show me the first sound you hear in the word.

Teaching moment
✔ In learning to segment sounds in words, it is easier to segment the initial sound than the middle or ending sound; so for this level, this activity focuses on segmenting the initial sound in words.

✔ Pause for one second between the direction ("What is the first sound in") and the target word to prepare the student for the target word.

✔ This activity helps the student segment sounds by emphasizing or slightly prolonging the first sound in the word when possible. Point to your mouth as you produce the initial sound if needed.

✔ If the student chooses an incorrect response, give a reminder to not guess but to wait and you will help. You can also add to the directions, **If you are not sure of the answer, don't guess. Wait for me to help you.**

Cue	Student's independent response	If student needs help
What is the first sound in (1 sec. pause) **rrrat?**	Finds <u>r</u> to say /<u>r</u>/.	For Lesson 1, if no response or an incorrect response, physically guide the student to touch <u>r</u>. Say, **The first sound is /<u>r</u>/.**
		For Lessons 2–5, if no response after 4 seconds or an incorrect response, model finding the sound and say, **The first sound is /<u>r</u>/. You touch it.** If needed, physically guide the student to find /<u>r</u>/.

Repeat with the <u>content</u> for each lesson; see **Level 2 Content** on p. 37.

Segmenting II

Objective 4
Segment the sounds in CVC words.
Pronunciation: /æ/ as in r<u>a</u>m

Prompting
- Lesson 1: Time delay 0 seconds
- Lessons 2–5: Time delay 4 seconds

Activity directions
Use the sounds you learned to sound out some words. I'll say a word, and you sound it out.

Teaching moment
✔ To help the student segment all of the sounds in the word, hold up a finger for each sound the student needs to find. Remember to hold up fingers for sounds, not letters (e.g., the word *mitt* has 3 sounds but 4 letters; the word *miss* has 3 sounds but 4 letters).

✔ Or divide the dry-erase board into sections to indicate how many sounds are in a word.

✔ If the student chooses an incorrect response, give a reminder to not guess but to wait and you will help. You can also add to the directions, **If you are not sure of the answer, don't guess. Wait for me to help you.**

✔ If the student makes an error on even one sound, have the student listen as you segment **all** the sounds in the word in the correct sequence. Then restate to touch the sounds in the word.

Cue	Student's independent response	If student needs help
Sound out the word <u>Tam</u>.	Touches <u>t</u>, <u>a</u>, and <u>m</u> for the sounds /t/, /æ/, and /m/.	For Lesson 1, if no response or an incorrect response, physically guide the student to touch <u>t</u>, <u>a</u>, and <u>m</u> to blend the sounds together. For Lessons 2–5, if no response after 4 seconds or an incorrect response, say, **Listen, /<u>t</u>/ /<u>æ</u>/ /<u>m</u>/. Touch the sounds in <u>Tam</u>.** If still no response or an incorrect response, model segmenting the word by touching and saying each sound. Then say, **Your turn. Touch the sounds in <u>Tam</u>.** If still no response or an incorrect response, say, **Let's touch the sounds in <u>Tam</u>.** Then physically guide the student to touch each sound while you say it.

Repeat with the <u>content</u> for each lesson; see **Level 2 Content** on p. 37.

Decoding

Objective 5
Decode CVC words and identify their meanings.
Pronunciation: /æ/ as in r<u>a</u>m

Prompting
- Lesson 1: Time delay 0 seconds
- Lessons 2–5: Time delay 4 seconds

Activity directions
Now, use the sounds and letters you learned to read a word and find its picture.

Teaching moment
✓ Be certain the student knows the name of each picture.

✓ In this level, for Lessons 2–5, sound out the word to be decoded by pointing to each letter in the word while saying its sound. Prolong the sounds to stretch out the word. However, fade out pointing to the picture response. Tell the student to point to the picture of the word they read.

✓ If the student chooses an incorrect response, give a reminder to not guess but to wait and you will help. You can also add to the directions, **If you are not sure of the answer, don't guess. Wait for me to help you.**

Cue	Student's independent response	If student needs help
First, let's hear each picture's name.	Listens as each picture is named.	
For Lesson 1 and demonstration items, touch each letter as you stretch out the sounds in the word, <u>/rrr/</u> <u>/æ/</u> <u>/mmm/</u>. Then touch the picture and say, **Here is ram.** Point to the picture of <u>ram</u> until the student finds it.	Finds the picture of <u>ram</u>.	For Lesson 1, if no response or an incorrect response, physically guide the student to touch the picture of <u>ram</u>.
For Lessons 2–5, model decoding by touching each letter and saying its sound. Then say, **Find the picture of the word you read.**	Finds the picture of <u>rat</u>.	For Lessons 2–5, if no response or an incorrect response, model sounding out the word while you point to each letter and find the picture. Say, **This is /r/ /æ/ /t/. Here is the picture of <u>rat</u>. Now you read <u>rat</u> and find the picture.** Physically guide the student's hand if needed.

Repeat with the <u>content</u> for each lesson; see **Level 2 Content** on p. 37.

Sight words

Objective 6
Read 5 new sight words.

Prompting
- Lesson 1: Time delay 0 seconds
- Lessons 2–5: Time delay 4 seconds

Activity directions
Sight words are tricky because you can't sound them out. You have to remember what they look like. Find the word.

Teaching moment
✔ The pace between presentation of words is purposely rapid to keep the student motivated.

✔ Use the sight word flashcards to provide extra practice of sight word reading. Provide up to 4 response options for students to choose from.

✔ If the student chooses an incorrect response, give a reminder to not guess but to wait and you will help. You can also add to the directions, **If you are not sure of the answer, don't guess. Wait for me to help you.**

✔ Create a word wall with sight words from this level.

Cue	Student's independent response	If student needs help
Find the word girl.	Finds the word girl.	For Lesson 1, if no response or an incorrect response, physically guide the student to find girl. Say, **This is girl.** For Lessons 2–5, if no response after 4 seconds or an incorrect response, model finding the word and say, **This is girl. You touch it.** Physically guide the student to find the word if needed.

Repeat with the new sight words and review sight words, words required for reading the story for this level; see **Level 2 Content** on p. 37.

ERSB Teacher's Guide ■ Level 2

Reading text / Comprehension questions

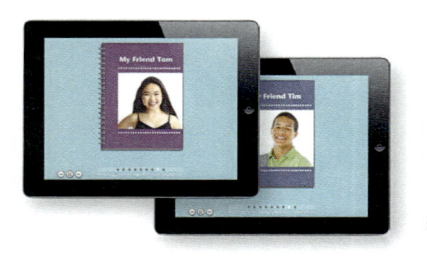

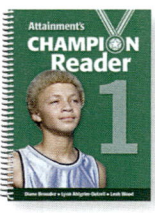

boy
mat
bat
girl

Objective 7 / Objective 8
Read connected text. / Answer comprehension questions about connected text.

Prompting
Least intrusive prompt

Activity directions
Now that you know how to read words, you can read a page from the story. This story is about Sam and his friends.

Teaching moment
✓ In this level in the software, the text is read to the student when he or she touches the word. Point to the words to indicate to the student to read each word.

✓ One page of the story is read during each lesson, followed by comprehension questions. If repeating this level, Story 2 will be used in the software.

✓ Use **Champion Reader 1** to show the title of the story and to point out the characters. It can also be used to give students additional reading practice. The comprehension questions that could be asked if not using the software and possible response options are listed in the **Level 2 Content** on p. 37. Write response options on the dry-erase board for students to read.

Cue	Student's independent response	If student needs help
Say, **You start. Touch each word to read.** Point to each word in each sentence to indicate to the student to read the words. Read the words as the student touches them.	Touches each word in the sentence(s) to read it.	If no response, point to each word and say, **Touch each word to read the sentence.** If the student still does not respond or stops responding, model touching each word and say, **You touch the words.** If the student still does not respond, physically guide the student to touch each word. If the student touches the wrong word, point to the correct word and say, **Here is Tam.**

(Table continues)

ERSB Teacher's Guide ■ Level 2

Cue	Student's independent response	If student needs help
After the student reads the sentence(s) on the page, say, **Let's answer some questions about the story. What is Tam?**	Chooses the word girl.	If no response or an incorrect response, read the sentence again, while pointing to each word. Then ask the question again. If still no response or an incorrect response, read the sentence with the answer, **Tam is a girl**, then physically guide the student to find girl, and say, **Girl. Tam is a girl**.

Repeat with the content for each lesson; see **Level 2 Content** on p. 37.

Closing /Writing activity

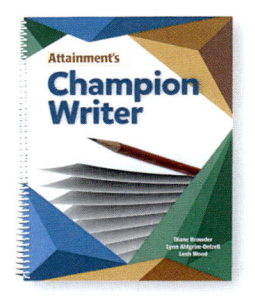

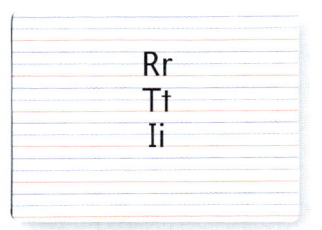

Objective 9
Write responses to activities that review level objectives.

Activity directions
Your lesson is over. GREAT reading today! Let's complete a page in your Champion Writer.

Teaching moment

✔ In order to keep the lesson from becoming too long, consider completing the writing activity at another time of the day.

✔ Some students may need adaptations to complete the writing page in **Champion Writer;** see p. 20 for ideas.

✔ Use the dry-erase board and an erasable marker to give the student practice in writing/forming the letter/sounds of this level.

LEVEL 3

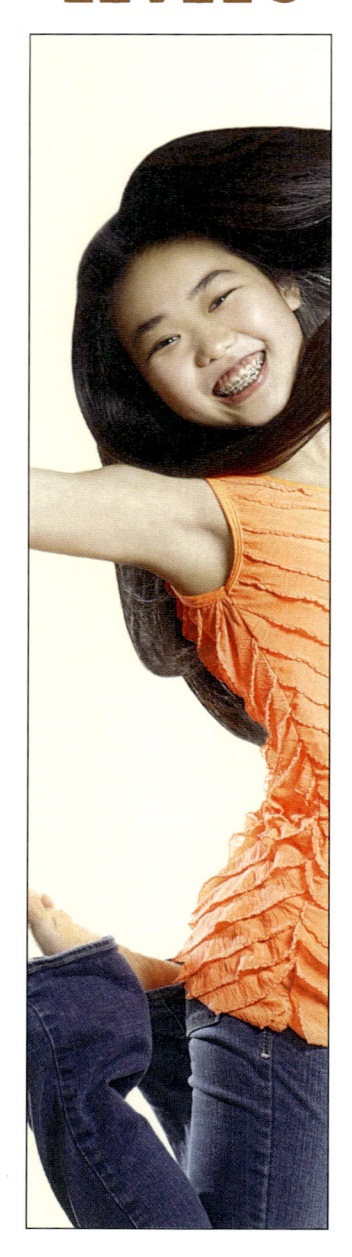

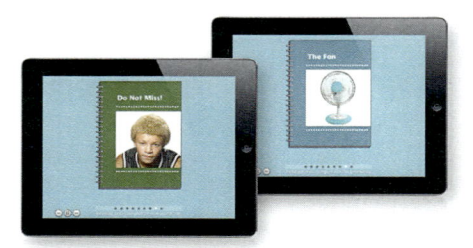

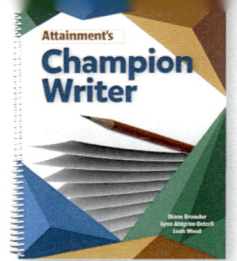

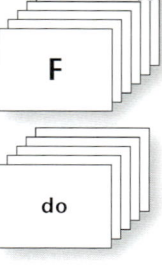

Focus
Ff, Nn, Oo (short)

Phonemic awareness
- Blend sounds for CVC words
- Segment first sounds in words
- Segment sounds in CVC words

Phonics
- Sounds /f/, /n/, and /a/ (short o) corresponding to graphemes Ff, Nn, and Oo
- Decode VC and CVC words

Sight words
do, me, no, yes

Generalization words
in, man, Tom

Connected text
- ATOS level = Story 1: .6; Story 2: .3
- Lexile level = Story 1: –80L; Story 2: –110L

Objectives
1. Identify Ff, Nn, and Oo when given the sounds /f/, /n/, and /a/ (short o).
2. Blend sounds to form CVC words.
3. Segment the first sound in words beginning with /f/, /n/, or /a/.
4. Segment the sounds in CVC words.
5. Decode VC and CVC words and identify their meanings.
6. Read 4 new sight words.
7. Read connected text.
8. Answer comprehension questions about connected text.
9. Write responses to activities that review level objectives.

Teaching notes
Level 3 introduces the letter/sounds Ff, Nn, and short Oo. Note to use the sound a letter makes whenever the letter appears in virgules (e.g., /f/) in the lesson plan. Also in this level, prompts for sounding out words to be decoded are faded to whispering the sounds. Whisper reading is also used for Reading Text to get students started in silent reading.

As in the previous two levels, Lesson 1 demonstrates the activities at 0-second time delay and Lessons 2–5 prompt students (if needed) using 4-second time delay. For the comprehension questions, the least intrusive prompt is used to help students respond.

Level 3 Content

	Lesson 1	Lesson 2	Lesson 3	Lesson 4	Lesson 5
Letter/sound identification	**New:** Ff, Nn, Oo (short) **Review:** Rr, Tt, Ii (short)				
Blending	Ron, tin, fat, fit, tot, rot	**Demo:** fan ran, Ron, riff, not, fin	**Demo:** fit rot, tot, tan, Ron, tin	**Demo:** not fin, Tom, mom, fan, ran	**Demo:** tot tin, Ron, mom, fat, tan
Segmenting I	fit, new, on, fig, now, octopus	**Demo:** not on, for, next, odd, food	**Demo:** on fall, nice, otter, fin, name	**Demo:** fan near, on, far, night, October	**Demo:** fan nest, fun, food, night, October
Segmenting II	not, fin, top, mom, fan, ran	**Demo:** Ron tin, fat, mom, tot, not	**Demo:** fan ran, Ron, riff, not, fin	**Demo:** fit rot, tot, tan, Ron, tin	**Demo:** fit rot, tot, tan, Ron, tin
Decoding	fan, mom, Ron, fin, rim, miss	**Demo:** rat fit, tan, tot, rot, fin, on	**Demo:** rat not, tin, rot, mom, tan, fat	**Demo:** rat Ron, fin, miss, tan, rim, tot	**Demo:** rat rot, fat, tan, fin, Ron, tot
Sight Words	**New:** do, me, no, yes **Review:** friend, see, the, my				
Comprehension questions (correct response in **bold**)	\multicolumn{5}{c}{Story 1: Do Not Miss!}				
	Who is fit? (Tim, **Sam**, mat, see) Who should not miss? (sit, rim, Tom, **Sam**)	Who is fit? (Ron, boy, tin, **Tom**) What is the boy's name? (in, boy, rim, **Ron**)	Who does Sam see? (Ron, **Tam**, my, tot) Who missed the ball? (Sam, **Tam**, rot, the)	Who is Ron's friend? (on, **Tam**, Ron, a) Did Tam put it in? (no, **yes**, see, the)	What did Sam do? (rim, **sit**, ran, yes) Is Tom a man? (**yes**, see, I, Sam)
	\multicolumn{5}{c}{Story 2: The Fan}				
	Who is Sam's friend? (not, **Ron**, me, on) Who is sitting? (**Sam**, see, Tim, fin)	Who is Ron's friend? (**Tim**, fit, Tam, my) Tim is not fat. What is he? (tot, no, **fit**, fin)	What did Tim do at the fan? (fit, fin, the, **sit**) What is on the mat? (Tim, **fan**, mat, friend)	What is Mim? (man, **tot**, fan, tan) Who did Ron say no to? (Ron, mom, not, **Mim**)	Who is the tot? (**Mim**, sit, man, Sam) What did Mim do? (yes, **sit**, me, see)

Letter/sound identification

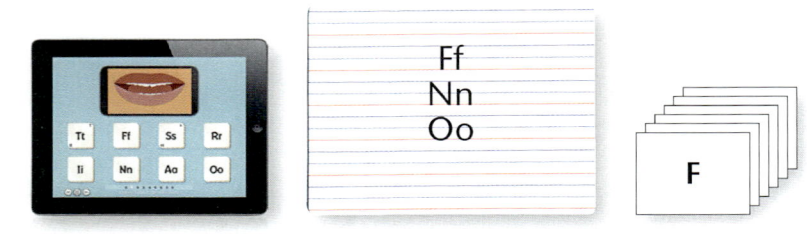

Objective 1
Identify Ff, Nn, Oo when given the sounds /f/, /n/, and /a/.
Pronunciation: /a/ as in t<u>o</u>t

Prompting
- Lesson 1: Time delay 0 seconds
- Lessons 2–5: Time delay 4 seconds

Activity directions
I'll say a sound, and you find the letter that makes that sound.

Teaching moment
✔ Note that the emphasis in this activity is on the sounds the letters make. Introduce the letter/sounds Ff, Nn, and Oo to the student. Point to the tiles on the software screen or write and point to them on the dry-erase board and say, **Let's learn the sounds /f/, /n/, and /a/.**

✔ If the student struggles, use visual and articulatory cues that show the student how a sound is made (e.g., point to your mouth to say /fff/).

✔ If the student does not know uppercase from lowercase letters, use the flashcards to practice matching them.

✔ If the student chooses an incorrect response, give a reminder to not guess but to wait and you will help. You can also add to the directions, **If you are not sure of the answer, don't guess. Wait for me to help you.**

Cue	Student's independent response	If student needs help
What letter says /f/?	Finds the letter <u>F</u>f to make the /<u>f</u>/ sound.	For Lesson 1, model finding the correct response, and continue pointing to it until the student finds it. If no response or an incorrect response, physically guide the student to find the letter and say, **This is /<u>f</u>/.** For Lessons 2–5, if no response after 4 seconds or an incorrect response, model finding the letter, and continue pointing to it until the student finds it. If needed, physically guide the student to find the letter and say, **This is /<u>f</u>/. You touch it.**

Repeat with Nn and Oo, and Level 2 review: Rr, Tt, and Ii.

Blending

Objective 2
Blend sounds to form CVC words.
Pronunciation: /a/ as in t<u>o</u>t

Prompting
- Lesson 1: Time delay 0 seconds
- Lessons 2–5: Time delay 4 seconds

Activity directions
I'll say some sounds. You blend the sounds together and find the word they make.

Teaching moment
✔ The next (more difficult) step in blending is to blend final consonants onto a VC or V string (e.g., m—att). This level presents blending that is a bit more difficult.

✔ If needed, use the dry-erase board to demonstrate blending using fewer words as distractors.

✔ If the student chooses an incorrect response, give a reminder to not guess but to wait and you will help. You can also add to the directions, **If you are not sure of the answer, don't guess. Wait for me to help you.**

Cue	Student's independent response	If student needs help
/r/ /<u>an</u>/. Which word am I saying?	Finds the word <u>Ron</u>.	For Lesson 1, model finding the correct response, and continue pointing to it until the student finds it. If no response or an incorrect response, physically guide the student to find the word. For Lessons 2–5, if no response after 4 seconds or an incorrect response, model finding the word and say, **This is <u>Ron</u>. You touch it.** Continue pointing to it until the student finds it. If needed, physically guide the student to find the word.

Repeat with the <u>content</u> for each lesson; see **Level 3 Content** on p. 47.

Segmenting I

Objective 3
Segment the first sound in words beginning with /f/, /n/, or /a/.
Pronunciation: /a/ as in t*o*t

Prompting
- Lesson 1: Time delay 0 seconds
- Lessons 2–5: Time delay 4 seconds

Activity directions
I'll say a word. You show me the first sound you hear in the word.

Teaching moment
✔ In learning to segment sounds in words, it is easier to segment the initial sound than the middle or ending sound; therefore, this activity focuses on segmenting the initial sound in words.

✔ Pause for one second between the direction ("What is the first sound in") and the target word to prepare the student for the target word.

✔ This activity helps the student segment sounds by emphasizing or slightly prolonging the first sound in the word when possible. Point to your mouth as you produce the initial sound if needed.

✔ If the student chooses an incorrect response, give a reminder to not guess but to wait and you will help. You can also add to the directions, **If you are not sure of the answer, don't guess. Wait for me to help you.**

Cue	Student's independent response	If student needs help
What is the first sound in (1 sec. pause) **fffit?**	Finds f to say /f/.	For Lesson 1, if no response or an incorrect response, physically guide the student to touch f. Say, **The first sound is /f/.** For Lessons 2–5, if no response after 4 seconds or an incorrect response, model finding the sound and say, **The first sound is /f/. You touch it.** If needed, physically guide the student to find /f/.

Repeat with the content for each lesson; see **Level 3 Content** on p. 47.

Segmenting II

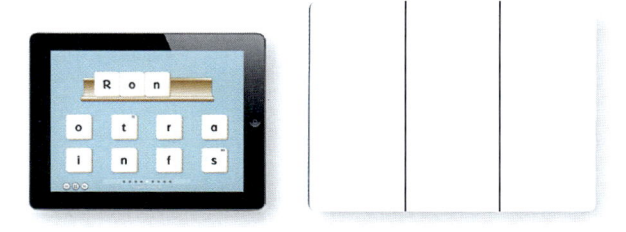

Objective 4
Segment the sounds in CVC words.
Pronunciation: /a/ as in t<u>o</u>t

Prompting
- Lesson 1: Time delay 0 seconds
- Lessons 2–5: Time delay 4 seconds

Activity directions
Use the sounds you learned to sound out some words. I'll say a word, and you sound it out.

Teaching moment
✔ To help the student segment all of the sounds in the word, hold up a finger for each sound the student needs to find.

✔ Or divide the dry-erase board into sections to indicate how many sounds are in a word.

✔ If the student chooses an incorrect response, give a reminder to not guess but to wait and you will help. You can also add to the directions, **If you are not sure of the answer, don't guess. Wait for me to help you.**

✔ If the student makes an error on even one sound, have the student listen as you segment **all** the sounds in the word in the correct sequence. Then restate to touch the sounds in the word.

Cue	Student's independent response	If student needs help
Sound out the word <u>not</u>.	Touches <u>n</u>, <u>o</u>, and <u>t</u> for the sounds /n/, /a/ and /t/.	For Lesson 1, if no response after 4 seconds or an incorrect response, physically guide the student to touch <u>n</u>, <u>o</u>, and <u>t</u> to blend the sounds together.
		For Lessons 2–5, if no response after 4 seconds or an incorrect response, say, **Listen, /n/ /a/ /t/. Touch the sounds in <u>not</u>.**
		If still no response or an incorrect response, model segmenting the word by touching and saying each sound. Then say, **Your turn. Touch the sounds in <u>not</u>.**
		If still no response or an incorrect response, say, **Let's touch the sounds in <u>not</u>.** Then physically guide the student to touch each sound while you say it.

Repeat with the <u>content</u> for each lesson; see **Level 3 Content** on p. 47.

Decoding

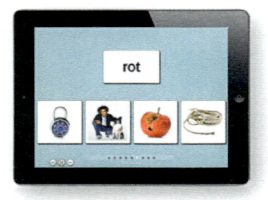

Objective 5
Decode VC and CVC words and identify their meanings.
Pronunciation: /æ/ as in f<u>a</u>n

Prompting
- Lesson 1: Time delay 0 seconds
- Lessons 2–5: Time delay 4 seconds

Teaching moment
✔ Be certain the student knows the name of each picture.

✔ In this level begin to fade modeling how to sound out the word to be decoded as indicated below.

✔ If the student chooses an incorrect response, give a reminder to not guess but to wait and you will help. You can also add to the directions, **If you are not sure of the answer, don't guess. Wait for me to help you.**

Activity directions
Now, use the sounds and letters you learned to read a word and find its picture.

Cue	Student's independent response	If student needs help
First, let's hear each picture's name.	Listens as each picture is named.	
For Lesson 1, touch each letter as you stretch out the sounds in the word, **/fff/ /æ/ /nnn/. Fan.** Touch the picture and say, **Here is <u>fan</u>.** Point to the picture of <u>fan</u> until the student finds it.	Finds the picture of <u>fan</u>.	For Lesson 1, if no response or an incorrect response, physically guide the student to touch the picture of <u>fan</u>.
For Lessons 2–5, point to each letter in the word and whisper its sound. Don't say the whole word. Say, **Read the word. Then point to the picture of the word you read.**	Finds the picture of <u>fit</u>.	For Lessons 2–5, if no response, touch each letter as you whisper the sounds in the word. Touch the picture. Say, **Here is <u>fit</u>. Now you read <u>fit</u> and find the picture.** Physically guide the student's hand if needed.
		If an incorrect response, point to the letters in the word and say, **This says <u>fan</u>.** Touch the picture. **Here is <u>fan</u>.** Remove your hand and say, **Now you read <u>fan</u> and find the picture.** Physically guide the student's hand if needed.

Repeat with the <u>content</u> for each lesson; see **Level 3 Content** on p. 47.

Sight words

Objective 6
Read 4 new sight words.

Prompting
- Lesson 1: Time delay 0 seconds
- Lessons 2–5: Time delay 4 seconds

Activity directions
Sight words are tricky because you can't sound them out. You have to remember what they look like. **Find the word.**

Teaching moment
✔ The pace between presentation of words is purposely rapid to keep the student motivated.

✔ Use the sight word flashcards to provide extra practice of sight word reading. Provide up to 4 response options for students to choose from.

✔ If the student chooses an incorrect response, give a reminder to not guess but to wait and you will help. You can also add to the directions, **If you are not sure of the answer, don't guess. Wait for me to help you.**

✔ Create a word wall with sight words from this level.

Cue	Student's independent response	If student needs help
Find the word no.	Finds the word no.	For Lesson 1, if no response or an incorrect response, physically guide the student to find no. Say, **This is no.**
		For Lessons 2–5, if no response after 4 seconds or an incorrect response, model finding the word and say, **This is no. You touch it.** Physically guide the student to find the word if needed.

Repeat with the new sight words and review sight words, words required for reading the story for this level; see **Level 3 Content** on p. 47.

Reading text / Comprehension questions

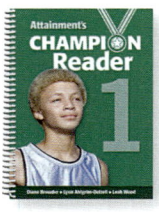

Tim
Sam
mat
see

Teaching moment

✔ In this level, the student is told to read the text silently. The prompt from previous levels of reading the text for the student is now faded to whisper reading of the text.

✔ One page of the story is read during each lesson, followed by comprehension questions. If repeating this level, Story 2 will be used in the software.

✔ Use **Champion Reader 1** to show the title of the story and to point out the characters. It can also be used to give students additional reading practice. The comprehension questions that could be asked if not using the software and possible response options are listed in the **Level 3 Content** on p. 47. Write response options on the dry-erase board for students to read.

Objective 7 / Objective 8
Read connected text. / Answer comprehension questions about connected text.

Prompting
Least intrusive prompt

Activity directions
Now that you know how to read words, you can read a page from the story. Today you will read the story in your head. The story is about Sam and his friends and basketball.

Cue	Student's independent response	If student needs help
Say, **You start. Touch each word to read.** Point to each word in each sentence to indicate to the student to touch to read them. Whisper the words as the student touches them to help the student read silently.	Touches each word to hear it whisper read.	If no response, say, **Read the sentences.** Point to each word until the student touches it. If the student touches the wrong word, point to the correct word and say, **Here is <u>see</u>.** If the student still does not respond or stops responding, physically guide the student to touch each word. Say, **Here is <u>see</u>. Here is <u>Sam</u>.**

(Table continues)

ERSB Teacher's Guide ■ Level 3

Cue	Student's independent response	If student needs help
After the student reads the sentences on the page, say, **Let's answer some questions about the story. Who is fit?**	Chooses the word <u>Sam</u>.	If no response or an incorrect response, read the sentence again, while pointing to each word. Then ask the question again. If still no response or an incorrect response, read the sentence with the answer, <u>Sam is fit</u>, then physically guide the student to find <u>Sam</u>, and say, <u>Sam</u>. <u>Sam is fit</u>.

Repeat with the <u>content</u> for each lesson; see **Level 3 Content** on p. 47.

Closing /Writing activity

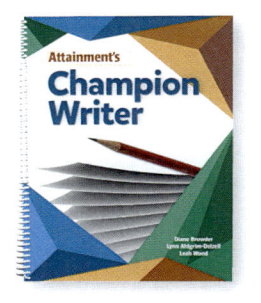

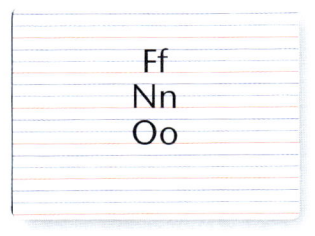

Objective 9
Write responses to activities that review level objectives.

Activity directions
Your lesson is over. GREAT reading today! Let's complete a page in your Champion Writer.

Teaching moment

✔ In order to keep the lesson from becoming too long, consider completing the writing activity at another time of the day.

✔ Some students may need adaptations to complete the writing page in **Champion Writer**; see p. 20 for ideas.

✔ Use the dry-erase board and an erasable marker to give the student practice in writing/forming the letter/sounds of this level.

ERSB Teacher's Guide ■ Level 3

LEVEL 4

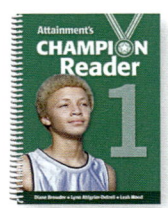

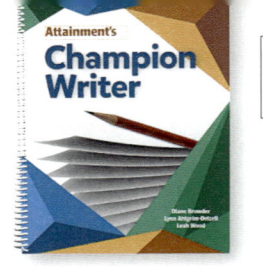

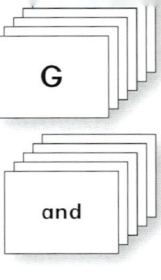

Focus
Gg, Dd, Uu (short)

Phonemic awareness
- Blend sounds for CVC words
- Segment first sounds in words
- Segment sounds in CVC words

Phonics
- Sounds /g/, /d/, and /ʌ/ corresponding to graphemes Gf, Dd, and Uu
- Decode CVC words

Sight words
and, dog, has, he, they, where

Generalization words
got, fun, sad

Connected text
- ATOS level = Story 1: .2; Story 2: .3
- Lexile level = Story 1: –90L; Story 2: –120L

Objectives
1 Identify Gg, Dd, and Uu when given the sounds /g/, /d/, and /ʌ/.

2 Blend sounds to form CVC words.

3 Segment the first sound in words beginning with /g/, /d/, and /ʌ/.

4 Segment the sounds in CVC words.

5 Decode CVC words and identify their meanings.

6 Read 6 new sight words.

7 Read connected text.

8 Answer comprehension questions about connected text.

9 Write responses to activities that review level objectives.

Teaching notes
Level 4 introduces the letter/sounds Gg (hard g), Dd, and Uu. This level assumes the students now know how to complete each activity, so the demonstration item for Lessons 2–5 is optional, except for decoding, which may still require demonstration. If students are confused about how to complete an activity, they can click the demo button. The whisper technique for demonstrating how to sound out a word during decoding is faded in this level.

In this level, the student begins to read the connected text silently. The prompt from previous levels of reading the text for the student is now faded to whisper reading of the text only if the student requires it.

Level 4 Content

	Lesson 1	Lesson 2	Lesson 3	Lesson 4	Lesson 5
Letter/sound identification	**New:** Gg, Dd, Uu (short) **Review:** Ff, Nn, Oo (short)				
Blending	rag, nod, mud, sag, gum, rod	**Optional demo:** gum dug, fig, run, dim, sod, tag	**Optional demo:** gum mad, rid, tug, nag, Don, did	**Optional demo:** gum Dad, gig, rug, dot, mug, did	**Optional demo:** gum mud, gig, Dad, nag, Don, did
Segmenting I	Gus, duck, up, good, do, us	**Optional demo:** good Dad, ugly, goat, dot, until, go	**Optional demo:** good ugh, gum, did, up, get, down	**Optional demo:** good dug, go, under, gate, day, umbrella	**Optional demo:** good game, go, dip, ugh, day, ump
Segmenting II	Dad, gig, rug, dot, nod, did	**Optional demo:** gig rag, nod, mud, sag, gum, rod	**Optional demo:** gig dug, fig, run, dim, sod, tag	**Optional demo:** gig mad, rid, tug, nag, Don, did	**Optional demo:** gig mad, rid, tug, nag, Don, dim
Decoding	dug, gum, run, rod, mud, tag	**Optional demo:** fan mad, fig, tug, tag, rag, rod	**Optional demo:** fan Dad, tag, rug, gum, mad, fig	**Optional demo:** fan rag, sod, mud, dot, dug, gum	**Optional demo:** fan dug, rod, mud, gum, mad, dot
Sight Words	**New:** and, dog, has, he, they, where **Review:** I, no, see, the, yes				
Comprehension questions (correct response in **bold**)	Story 1: Gus the Dog				
	Who is sad? (**Sam**, Tim, sit, go) What did Sam get? (do, go, **dog**, tug)	What did Gus do? (bun, **run**, red, Sam) What did Gus do with the rag? (too, fig, **tug**, has)	Who was lost? (**Gus**, go, bus, the) Where did Gus dig? (Mom, dim, **mud**, he)	Who is mad? (**Sam**, yam, so, bee) Who dug in the mud? (**Gus**, pop, yes, tug) What did Gus dig in? (**mud**, dot, me, Pat)	What did Gus do on the rug? (**sit**, rat, day, sod) Who is Gus? (mud, **dog**, the, mat) Who is not mad? (sit, **Sam**, Tam, like)
	Story 2: Mim and Gus				
	Who is the tot? (**Mim**, mud, Tam, see) What did Tim see? (gum, in, **Gus**, yes)	Who got the mitt? (Mim, **dog**, want, do) What does Gus have? (Mim, but, **mitt**, tug)	Who ran? (man, Tam, Gus, **Mim**) Who is missing (tip, **Gus**, yes, go)	Where is Mim? (**mud**, she, mop, did) What did Gus do? (**dug**, mitt, Gus, tug) Who else is in the mud? (go, **Gus**, Mim, bus)	Who ran? (dog, **Dad**, Tam, bug) Who has the mitt? (mat, Gus, **Mim**, fun) Who got the mitt from Mim? (**Gus**, Rat, Ron, Bun)

Letter/sound identification

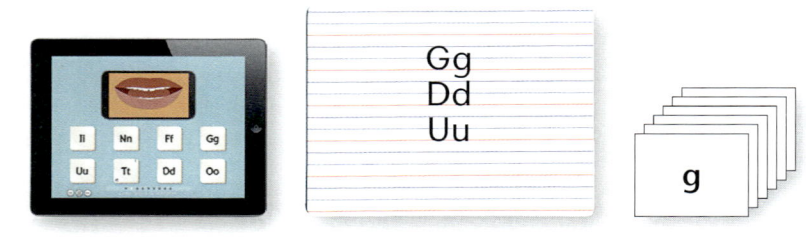

Objective 1
Identify Gg, Dd, and Uu when given the sounds /g/, /d/, and /ʌ/.
Pronunciation: /ʌ/ as in g<u>u</u>m

Prompting
- Lesson 1: Time delay 0 seconds
- Lessons 2–5: Time delay 4 seconds

Activity directions
I'll say a sound, and you find the letter that makes that sound.

Teaching moment
✔ Note that the emphasis in this activity is on the sounds the letters make. Introduce the letter/sounds Gg, Dd, and Uu to the student. Point to the tiles on the software screen or write and point to them on the dry-erase board, **Let's learn the sounds /g/, /d/, and /ʌ/.**

✔ If the student struggles, use visual and articulatory cues that show the student how a sound is made (e.g., point to your lips to say /d/).

✔ If the student does not know uppercase from lowercase letters, use the flashcards to practice matching them.

✔ If the student chooses an incorrect response, give a reminder to not guess but to wait and you will help. You can also add to the directions, **If you are not sure of the answer, don't guess. Wait for me to help you.**

Cue	Student's independent response	If student needs help
What letter says /g/?	Finds the letter <u>G</u>g to make the /g/ sound.	For Lesson 1, model finding the correct response, and continue pointing to it until the student finds it. If no response or an incorrect response, physically guide the student to find the letter and say, **This is /g/.** For Lessons 2–5, if no response after 4 seconds or an incorrect response, model finding the letter, and continue pointing to it until the student finds it. If needed, physically guide the student to find the letter and say, **This is /g/. You touch it.**

Repeat with Dd and Uu, and Level 3 review: Ff, Nn, and Oo.

Blending

Objective 2
Blend sounds to form CVC words.
Pronunciation: /æ/ as in rag

Prompting
- Lesson 1: Time delay 0 seconds
- Lessons 2–5: Time delay 4 seconds

Activity directions
I'll say some sounds. You blend the sounds together and find the word they make.

Teaching moment
✔ The next (more difficult) step in blending is to blend final consonants onto a VC or V string (e.g., r—ag). This level presents blending that is a bit more difficult.

✔ If needed, use the dry-erase board to demonstrate blending using fewer words as distractors.

✔ If the student chooses an incorrect response, give a reminder to not guess but to wait and you will help. You can also add to the directions, **If you are not sure of the answer, don't guess. Wait for me to help you.**

Cue	Student's independent response	If student needs help
/r/ /æg/. Which word am I saying?	Finds the word rag.	For Lesson 1, model finding the correct response, and continue pointing to it until the student finds it. If no response or an incorrect response, physically guide the student to find the word. For Lessons 2–5, if no response after 4 seconds or an incorrect response, model finding the word and say, **This is rag. You touch it.** Continue pointing to it until the student finds it. If needed, physically guide the student to find the word.

Repeat with the content for each lesson; see **Level 4 Content** on p. 57.

Segmenting I

Objective 3
Segment the first sound in words beginning with /g/, /d/, and /ʌ/.
Pronunciation: /ʌ/ as in g<u>u</u>m

Prompting
- Lesson 1: Time delay 0 seconds
- Lessons 2–5: Time delay 4 seconds

Activity directions
I'll say a word. You show me the first sound you hear in the word.

Teaching moment
✔ In learning to segment sounds in words, it is easier to segment the initial sound than the middle or ending sound; therefore, this activity focuses on segmenting the initial sound in words.

✔ Pause for one second between the direction ("What is the first sound in") and the target word to prepare the student for the target word.

✔ This activity helps the student segment sounds by emphasizing or slightly prolonging the first sound in the word (when possible). Point to your mouth as you produce the initial sound if needed.

✔ If the student chooses an incorrect response, give a reminder to not guess but to wait and you will help. You can also add to the directions, **If you are not sure of the answer, don't guess. Wait for me to help you.**

Cue	Student's independent response	If student needs help
What is the first sound in (1 sec. pause) G<u>u</u>s?	Finds g to say /g/.	For Lesson 1, if no response or an incorrect response, physically guide the student to touch g. Say, **The first sound is /g/.**
		For Lessons 2–5, if no response after 4 seconds or an incorrect response, model finding the sound and say, **The first sound is /g/. You touch it.** If needed, physically guide the student to find /g/.

Repeat with the content for each lesson; see **Level 4 Content** on p. 57.

Segmenting II

Objective 4
Segment the sounds in CVC words.
Pronunciation: /æ/ as in r<u>a</u>g

Prompting
- Lesson 1: Time delay 0 seconds
- Lessons 2–5: Time delay 4 seconds

Activity directions
Use the sounds you learned to sound out some words. I'll say a word, and you sound it out.

Teaching moment
✔ To help the student segment all of the sounds in the word, hold up a finger for each sound the student needs to find.

✔ Or divide the dry-erase board into sections to indicate how many sounds are in a word.

✔ If the student chooses an incorrect response, give a reminder to not guess but to wait and you will help. You can also add to the directions, **If you are not sure of the answer, don't guess. Wait for me to help you.**

✔ If the student makes an error on even one sound, have the student listen as you segment **all** the sounds in the word in the correct sequence. Then restate to touch the sounds in the word.

Cue	Student's independent response	If student needs help
Sound out the word <u>Dad</u>.	Touches <u>d</u>, <u>a,</u> and <u>d</u> for the sounds /<u>d</u>/, /æ/, and /<u>d</u>/.	For Lesson 1, if no response or an incorrect response, physically guide the student to touch <u>d</u>, <u>a</u>, and <u>d</u> to segment the sounds in the word.
		For Lessons 2–5, if no response after 4 seconds or an incorrect response, say, **Listen, /<u>d</u>/ /æ/ /<u>d</u>/. Touch the sounds in <u>dad</u>.**
		If still no response or an incorrect response, model segmenting the word by touching and saying each sound. Then say, **Your turn. Touch the sounds in <u>dad</u>.**
		If still no response or an incorrect response, say, **Let's touch the sounds in <u>dad</u>.** Then physically guide the student to touch each sound while you say it.

Repeat with the <u>content</u> for each lesson; see **Level 4 Content** on p. 57.

ERSB Teacher's Guide ■ Level 4

Decoding

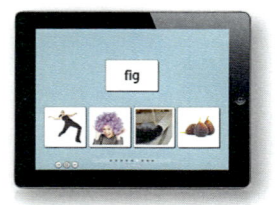

Objective 5
Decode CVC words and identify their meanings.
Pronunciation: /ʌ/ as in g<u>u</u>m, /æ/ as in f<u>a</u>n

Prompting
- Lesson 1: Time delay 0 seconds
- Lessons 2–5: Time delay 4 seconds

Activity directions
Now, use the sounds and letters you learned to read a word and find its picture.

Teaching moment
✔ Be certain the student knows the name of each picture.

✔ In this level, the demonstration prompt to sound out/decode the word is further faded and silent reading of the word to be decoded is emphasized. For demonstration items, point to each letter in the word being decoded (do not whisper it or make the sound). Then point to the picture of the word. For the remaining items in Lessons 2, point to each letter in the word to be decoded and have the student find the picture representing the word. For Lessons 3–5, simply point to the word and have the student find the picture.

✔ If the student chooses an incorrect response, give a reminder to not guess but to wait and you will help. You can also add to the directions, **If you are not sure of the answer, don't guess. Wait for me to help you.**

Cue	Student's independent response	If student needs help
First, let's hear each picture's name.	Listens as each picture is named.	
For Lesson 1, point to the word, then touch each letter silently. Point next to the picture of dug and say, **Read the word and find the picture.**	Finds the picture of <u>dug</u>.	For Lesson 1, if no response or incorrect, whisper the sounds in the word, /<u>d</u>/ /<u>ʌ</u>/ /<u>g</u>/. Touch the picture and say, **Here is <u>dug</u>.**
For Lessons 2–5, only point to the word and say, **Read the word and find the picture.**	Finds the picture of <u>Dad</u>.	For Lessons 2–5, if no response after 4 seconds, point to the sounds in the word and whisper, /d/ /æ/ /d/. Then touch the picture and say, **Here is <u>Dad</u>. Now you read <u>Dad</u> and find the picture.** Physically guide the student's hand if needed. If an incorrect response, point to the letters in the word as you say, **This says <u>dug</u>.** Touch the picture and say, **Here is the picture of <u>dug</u>.** Remove your finger and say, **Now you read <u>dug</u> and find the picture.** Physically guide the student's hand if needed.

Repeat with the <u>content</u> for each lesson; see **Level 4 Content** on p. 57.

Sight words

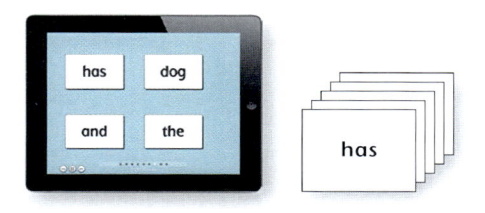

Objective 6
Read 6 new sight words.

Prompting
- Lesson 1: Time delay 0 seconds
- Lessons 2–5: Time delay 4 seconds

Activity directions
Sight words are tricky because you can't sound them out. You have to remember what they look like. Find the word.

Teaching moment
✔ Note that the word *dog* is included as a sight word because the vowel o is not truly a short o sound; rather it is /ɔ/.

✔ The pace between presentation of words is purposely rapid to keep the student motivated.

✔ Use the sight word flashcards to provide extra practice of sight word reading. Provide up to 4 response options for students to choose from.

✔ If the student chooses an incorrect response, give a reminder to not guess but to wait and you will help. You can also add to the directions, **If you are not sure of the answer, don't guess. Wait for me to help you.**

✔ Create a word wall with sight words from this level.

Cue	Student's independent response	If student needs help
Find the word has.	Finds the word has.	For Lesson 1, if no response or an incorrect response, physically guide the student to find has. Say, **This is has.** For Lessons 2–5, if no response after 4 seconds or an incorrect response, model finding the word and say, **This is has. You touch it.** Physically guide the student to find the word if needed.

Repeat with the new sight words and review sight words, words required for reading the story for this level; see **Level 4 Content** on p. 57.

ERSB Teacher's Guide ■ Level 4

Reading text / Comprehension questions

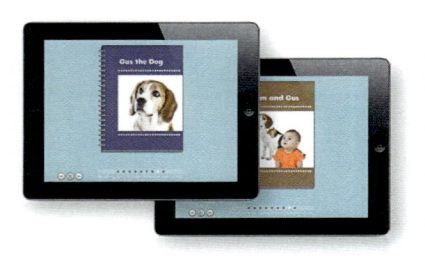

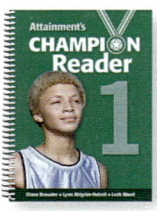

Sam
Tim
sit
go

Objective 7 / Objective 8
Read connected text. / Answer comprehension questions about connected text.

Prompting
Least intrusive prompt

Activity directions
Now you can read a page from the story. You will read about a dog named Gus. You will read the story in your head.

Teaching moment
✔ In this level, the student is told to read the text silently. The prompt from previous levels of reading the text for the student is now faded. The student can still touch the word to hear it whisper read.

✔ One page of the story is read during each lesson, followed by comprehension questions. If repeating this level, Story 2 will be used in the software.

✔ Use **Champion Reader 1** to show the title of the story and to point out the characters. It can also be used to give students additional reading practice. The comprehension questions that could be asked if not using the software and possible response options are listed in the **Level 4 Content** on p. 57. Write response options on the dry-erase board for students to read.

Cue	Student's independent response	If student needs help
Say, **Read this story silently in your head.** For Lesson 1, point to each word in the sentences but do not read the word. For Lessons 2–5, do not read to the student or point to the words.	Reads the sentences silently.	

(Table continues)

Cue	Student's independent response	If student needs help
After the student reads the sentences on the page, say, **Let's answer some questions about the story. Who is sad?**	Chooses the word Sam.	If no response or an incorrect response, say, **Read this sentence again**. Point to each word in the sentence that has the answer, then ask the question again.
		If still no response or an incorrect response, read the sentence with the answer to the student, **Sam is sad**. Then ask, **Who is sad?**
		If still no response or an incorrect response, physically guide the student to find Sam, and say, **Sam**. **Sam is sad**.

Repeat with the content for each lesson; see **Level 4 Content** on p. 57.

Closing /Writing activity

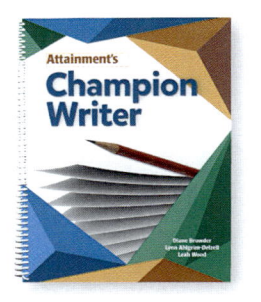

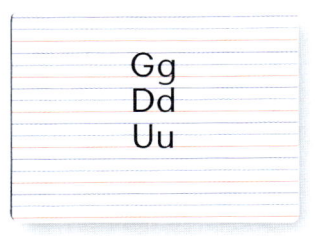

Objective 9
Write responses to activities that review level objectives.

Activity directions
Your lesson is over. GREAT reading today! Let's complete a page in your Champion Writer.

Teaching moment

✔ In order to keep the lesson from becoming too long, consider completing the writing activity at another time of the day.

✔ Some students may need adaptations to complete the writing page in **Champion Writer**; see p. 20 for ideas.

✔ Use the dry-erase board and an erasable marker to give the student practice in writing/forming the letter/sounds of this level.

ERSB Teacher's Guide ■ **Level 4**

LEVEL 5

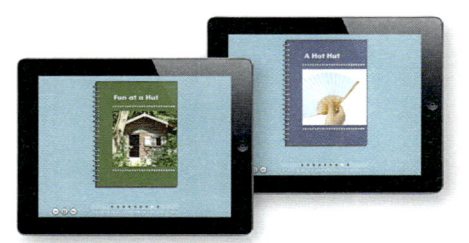

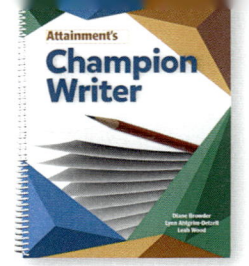

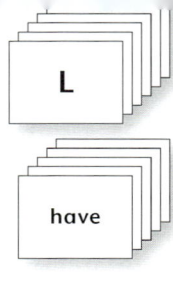

Focus
Ll, Hh, Kk (hard c and ck)

Phonemic awareness
- Blend sounds for CVC words
- Segment first sounds in words
- Segment sounds in CVC words

Phonics
- Sounds /l/, /h/, and /k/ corresponding to graphemes Ll/ll, Hh, and Kk/c/ck
- Decode CVC words

Sight words
have, log, she, to, we

Generalization words
can, cat, cut, hiss, kit, luck

Connected text
- ATOS level = Story 1: .6; Story 2: 1.4
- Lexile level = Story 1: 0L; Story 2: 0L

Objectives
1 Identify Ll/ll, Hh, and Kk/c/ck when given the sounds /l/, /h/, and /k/.
2 Blend sounds to form CVC words.
3 Segment the first sound in words beginning with /l/, /h/, and /k/.
4 Segment the sounds in CVC words.
5 Decode CVC words and identify their meanings.
6 Read 5 new sight words.
7 Read connected text.
8 Answer comprehension questions about connected text.
9 Write responses to activities that review level objectives.

Teaching notes
The letter/sounds Ll, Hh, and Cc (hard c) are introduced in Level 5. The c and ck are added to the Kk tile to indicate that c/ck make the sound /k/ like Kk. The tile for Ll also has ll added to it to indicate that the double ll says /l/.

In Level 5, for blending, students are now given 3 individual sounds to blend together; they blend the sounds and identify the word the sounds make. Students begin to decode words without a model of how to sound out the word. The demonstration prompt to sound out/decode the word is completely faded and silent reading of the word to be decoded is emphasized. The student also reads the connected text silently.

Level 5 Content

	Lesson 1	Lesson 2	Lesson 3	Lesson 4	Lesson 5
Letter/sound identification	**New:** Ll, Hh, Kk/c/ck, **Review:** Gg, Dd, Uu (short)				
Blending	cot, kick, hot, sack, hug, lug	**Optional demo:** hug cot, had, hut, tack, hum, lick	**Optional demo:** hug Kim, lot, ham, lock, kid, him	**Optional demo:** hug hit, lid, lit, sock, rack, dot	**Optional demo:** hug lit, hit, lock, sack, rack, dot
Segmenting I	Kim, him, lock, kid, ham, lot	**Optional demo:** him hill, lid, cold, hard, lit, keep	**Optional demo:** him lot, car, help, like, kick, hotdog	**Optional demo:** him cot, had, little, cold, hut, lake	**Optional demo:** him ham, hill, lock, like, hut, hold
Segmenting II	hit, lid, lit, sock, rack, dot	**Optional demo:** hit lock, kick, hot, sack, hug, lug	**Optional demo:** hit cot, had, hut, tack, hum, lick	**Optional demo:** hit Kim, lot, ham, lock, kid, him	**Optional demo:** hit rack, lit, hot, luck, sack, hum
Decoding	cot, hot, hut, tack, hum, lick	**Demo:** luck Kim, lid, ham, lock, kid, hat	**Demo:** luck hid, lid, lit, sock, rack, dock	**Demo:** luck lot, kick, hot, sack, hug, duck	**Demo:** luck ham, kick, hat, duck, hug, sock
Sight Words	**New:** have, log, she, to, we **Review:** and, my, they, where				
Comprehension questions (correct response in **bold**)	\multicolumn{5}{c}{Story 1: Fun at a Hut}				

| Comprehension questions (correct response in **bold**) | Who is Kim's friend? (**Tam,** cat, Tim, eat)
Where is the hut? like, hug, **hill,** friend) | What is fun? (has, **hut,** bat, boy)
What did they get? (**log,** go, lit, can) | What did they see? (**cat,** ham, can, see)
What did Kim get? (cat, full, what, **cut**) | Where is Kim? (**cot,** log, they, kick)
Who is a ham? (**Tam,** Tlm, hut, fun) | Where was the fun? (**hut,** have, log, cut)
What was lit? (lit, **log,** dog, we)
What did Kim get? (can, get, gum, **cut**) |

Story 2: A Hot Hut

	Lesson 1	Lesson 2	Lesson 3	Lesson 4	Lesson 5
	What do Kim and Tam have? (**hut,** cut, he, girl) What is wrong with the hut? (cut, hill, **hot,** does)	What can Kim do? (**fan,** and, fun, no) How did Tam feel? (**hot,** bat, hill, Gus)	What did they see? (dug, Ron, **dock,** cat) Where did Kim and Tam run to? (**dock,** hill, dig, luck)	What is Kim? (Tam, hill, **ham,** they) Who is not hot? (Ron, Gus, **Tam,** bug)	Who has a hut? (Gus, **Kim,** Tim, like) Where is the hut? (fun, **hill,** luck, log) What did they see? (**dock,** bed, luck, dot)

Letter/sound identification

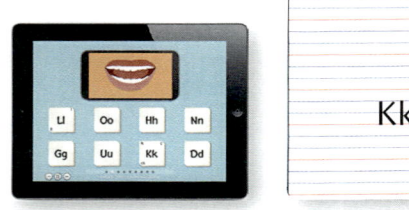

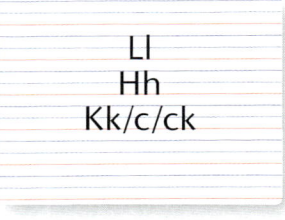

Objective 1
Identify Ll/ll, Hh, and Kk/c/ck when given the sounds /l/, /h/, and /k/.
Pronunciation: /k/ as in lo<u>ck</u>, <u>c</u>old, and <u>k</u>ind

Prompting
- Lesson 1: Time delay 0 seconds
- Lessons 2–5: Time delay 4 seconds

Activity directions
I'll say a sound, and you find the letter that makes that sound.

Teaching moment

✔ Note that the emphasis in this activity is on the sounds the letters make. Introduce the letter/sounds Ll, Hh, and c/ck Point to the tiles on the software screen or write and point to them on the dry-erase board, **Let's learn the sounds /l/, /h/, and /k/.** Also point out the ll on the Ll tile and c and ck on the Kk tile. **Notice the ll on this tile. The two ls together also say /l/. On this tile, k, ck, and c all say /k/.**

✔ If the student struggles, use visual and articulatory cues that show the student how a sound is made, (e.g., point to your mouth to say /l/).

✔ If the student does not know uppercase from lowercase letters, use the flashcards to practice matching them.

✔ If the student chooses an incorrect response, give a reminder to not guess but to wait and you will help. You can also add to the directions, **If you are not sure of the answer, don't guess. Wait for me to help you.**

Cue	Student's independent response	If student needs help
What letter says /<u>l</u>/?	Finds the letter L<u>l</u> to make the /<u>l</u>/ sound.	For Lesson 1, model finding the correct response, and continue pointing to it until the student finds it. If no response or an incorrect response, physically guide the student to find the letter and say, **This is /<u>l</u>/.** For Lessons 2–5, if no response after 4 seconds or an incorrect response, model finding the letter, and continue pointing to it until the student finds it. If needed, physically guide the student to find the letter and say, **This is /<u>l</u>/. You touch it.**

Repeat with Hh, and Kk/c/ck, and Level 4 review: Gg, Dd, and Uu.

Blending

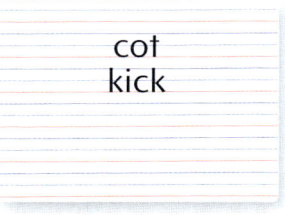

Objective 2
Blend sounds to form CVC words.
Pronunciation: /a/ as in c<u>o</u>t, /ʌ/ as in c<u>u</u>t

Prompting
- Lesson 1: Time delay 0 seconds
- Lessons 2–5: Time delay 4 seconds

Activity directions
I'll say some sounds. You blend the sounds together and find the word they make.

Teaching moment
✔ The next (most difficult) step in blending is to blend all sounds in a word when the word is presented in a segmented form. This level presents blending of three sounds for CVC words.

✔ To make it easier for the student, the sounds may be prolonged or followed by a pause between sounds to help the student process each sound.

✔ Use the dry-erase board to demonstrate blending using fewer words as distractors.

✔ Note that when you segment the sounds in words, do not add additional sounds (e.g., *cot* is correctly segmented as /k/ /a/ /t/, not /k/ /ʌ/ /tʌ/).

Cue	Student's independent response	If student needs help
/k/ /a/ /t/. Which word am I saying?	Finds the word <u>cot</u>.	For Lesson 1, model finding the correct response, and continue pointing to it until the student finds it. If no response or an incorrect response, physically guide the student to find the word. For Lessons 2–5, if no response after 4 seconds or an incorrect response, model finding the word and say, **This is <u>cot</u>. You touch it.** Continue pointing to it until the student finds it. If needed, physically guide the student to find the word.

Repeat with the <u>content</u> for each lesson; see **Level 5 Content** on p. 67.

Segmenting I

Objective 3
Segment the first sound in words beginning with /l/, /h/, and /k/.
Pronunciation: /k/ as in lo<u>ck</u>, <u>c</u>old, and <u>k</u>ind

Prompting
- Lesson 1: Time delay 0 seconds
- Lessons 2–5: Time delay 4 seconds

Activity directions
I'll say a word. You show me the first sound you hear in the word.

Teaching moment
✔ In learning to segment sounds in words, it is easier to segment the initial sound than the middle or ending sound; therefore, this activity focuses on segmenting the initial sound in words.

✔ Pause for one second between the direction ("What is the first sound in") and the target word to prepare the student for the target word.

✔ This activity helps the student segment sounds by emphasizing or slightly prolonging the first sound in the word (when possible). Point to your mouth as you produce the initial sound if needed.

✔ If the student chooses an incorrect response, give a reminder to not guess but to wait and you will help. You can also add to the directions, **If you are not sure of the answer, don't guess. Wait for me to help you.**

Cue	Student's independent response	If student needs help
What is the first sound in (1 sec. pause) **Kim?**	Finds <u>k</u> to say /<u>k</u>/.	For Lesson 1, if no response or an incorrect response, physically guide the student to touch <u>k</u>. Say, **The first sound is /<u>k</u>/.**
		For Lessons 2–5, if no response after 4 seconds or an incorrect response, model finding the sound and say, **The first sound is /<u>k</u>/. You touch it.** If needed, physically guide the student to find /<u>k</u>/.

Repeat with the <u>content</u> for each lesson; see **Level 5 Content** on p. 67.

Segmenting II

Objective 4
Segment the sounds in CVC words.
Pronunciation: /ɪ/ as in h<u>i</u>t

Prompting
- Lesson 1: Time delay 0 seconds
- Lessons 2–5: Time delay 4 seconds

Activity directions
Use the sounds you learned to sound out some words. I'll say a word, and you sound it out.

Teaching moment

✔ To help the student segment all of the sounds in the word, hold up a finger for each sound the student needs to find. Remember to hold up fingers for sounds, not letters (e.g., the word *rack* has 3 sounds but 4 letters).

✔ Or divide the dry-erase board into sections to indicate how many sounds are in a word.

✔ If the student chooses an incorrect response, give a reminder to not guess but to wait and you will help. Add to the directions, **If you are not sure of the answer, don't guess. Wait for me to help you.**

✔ If the student makes an error on even one sound, have the student listen as you segment **all** the sounds in the word in the correct sequence. Then restate to touch the sounds in the word.

Cue	Student's independent response	If student needs help
Sound out the word <u>hit</u>.	Touches <u>h</u>, <u>i</u>, and <u>t</u> for the sounds /<u>h</u>/, /<u>ɪ</u>/, and /<u>t</u>/.	For Lesson 1, if no response or an incorrect response, physically guide the student to touch <u>h</u>, <u>i</u>, and <u>t</u> to segment the sounds in the word. For Lessons 2–5, if no response after 4 seconds or an incorrect response, say, **Listen, /hhh/ /ɪ/ /t/. Touch the sounds in <u>hit</u>.** If still no response or an incorrect response, model segmenting the word by touching and saying each sound. Then say, **Your turn. Touch the sounds in <u>hit</u>.** If still no response or an incorrect response, say, **Let's touch the sounds in <u>hit</u>.** Then physically guide the student to touch each sound while you say it.

Repeat with the <u>content</u> for each lesson; see **Level 5 Content** on p. 67.

ERSB Teacher's Guide ■ Level 5

Decoding

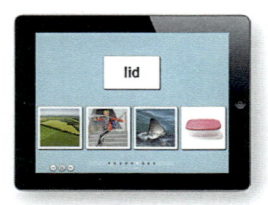

Objective 5
Decode CVC words and identify their meanings.
Pronunciation: /ɪ/ as in K<u>i</u>m

Prompting
- Lesson 1: Time delay 0 seconds
- Lessons 2–5: Time delay 4 seconds

Activity directions
Now, use the sounds and letters you learned to read a word and find its picture.

Teaching moment

✓ Be certain the student knows the name of each picture.

✓ In this level, the demonstration prompt to sound out/decode the word is completely faded and silent reading of the word to be decoded is emphasized. For Lesson 1 and demonstration items, point to the word being decoded (do not whisper it or make the letter sounds). Then point to the picture of the word. For the remaining items in Lessons 2–5, give the direction to read the word and find the picture of the word read.

✓ If the student chooses an incorrect response, give a reminder to not guess but to wait and you will help. You can also add to the directions, **If you are not sure of the answer, don't guess. Wait for me to help you.**

Cue	Student's independent response	If student needs help
First, let's hear each picture's name.	Listens as each picture is named.	
For Lesson 1, point to the word then touch the picture and say, **Here is cot. Your turn. Read the word and find the picture.**	Finds the picture of <u>cot</u>.	For Lesson 1, if no response or an incorrect response, physically guide the student to touch the picture of <u>cot</u>.
For Lessons 2–5, say, **Read the word and find the picture.**	Finds the picture of <u>Kim</u>.	For Lessons 2–5, if no response after 4 seconds, point to the word and say, **This is /k/ /ɪ/ /m/.** Then touch the picture and say, **Here is Kim. Now you read Kim and find the picture.** Physically guide the student's hand if needed.
		For Lessons 2–5, if an incorrect response, point to the letters in the word as you say, **This says Kim.** Touch the picture and say, **Here is the picture of Kim.** Remove your finger and say, **Now you read Kim and find the picture.** Physically guide the student's hand if needed.

Repeat with the <u>content</u> for each lesson; see **Level 5 Content** on p. 67.

Sight words

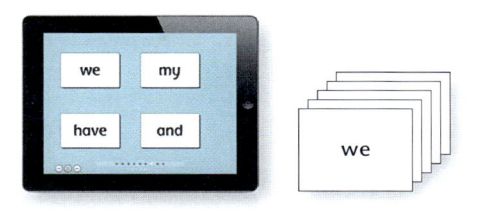

Objective 6
Read 5 new sight words.

Prompting
- Lesson 1: Time delay 0 seconds
- Lessons 2–5: Time delay 4 seconds

Activity directions
Sight words are tricky because you can't sound them out. You have to remember what they look like. Find the word.

Teaching moment

✔ The pace between presentation of words is purposely rapid to keep the student motivated.

✔ Use the sight word flashcards to provide extra practice of sight word reading. Provide up to 4 response options for students to choose from.

✔ Create a word wall with sight words from this level.

✔ If the student chooses an incorrect response, give a reminder to not guess but to wait and you will help. You can also add to the directions, **If you are not sure of the answer, don't guess. Wait for me to help you.**

Cue	Student's independent response	If student needs help
Find the word we.	Finds the word we.	For Lesson 1, if no response or an incorrect response, physically guide the student to find we. Say, **This is we.** For Lessons 2–5, if no response after 4 seconds or an incorrect response, model finding the word and say, **This is we. You touch it.** Physically guide the student to find the word if needed.

Repeat with the new sight words and review sight words, words required for reading the story for this level; see **Level 5 Content** on p. 67.

Reading text / Comprehension questions

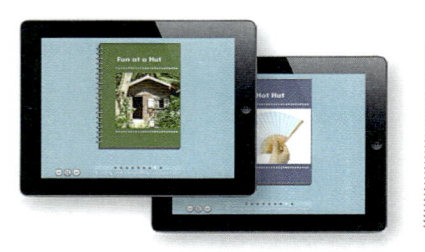

Tam
cat
Tim
eat

Teaching moment
✔ In this level, the student is told to read the text silently in his or her head.

✔ One page of the story is read during each lesson, followed by comprehension questions. If repeating this level, Story 2 will be used in the software.

✔ Use **Champion Reader 2** to show the title of the story and to point out the characters. It can also be used to give students additional reading practice. The comprehension questions that could be asked if not using the software and possible response options are listed in the **Level 5 Content** on p. 67. Write response options on the dry-erase board for students to read.

Objective 7 / Objective 8
Read connected text. / Answer comprehension questions about connected text.

Prompting
Least intrusive prompt

Activity directions
Now that you know how to read words, you can read a page from the story. Today you will read about Kim and Tam.

Cue	Student's independent response	If student needs help
Say, **Read this story silently in your head.** Do not read to the student or point to the words.	Reads the sentences silently.	
After the student reads the sentences on the page, say, **Let's answer some questions about the story. Who is Kim's friend?**	Chooses the word <u>Tam</u>.	If no response or an incorrect response, say, **Read this sentence again.** Point to each word in the sentence that has the answer, then ask the question again. If still no response or an incorrect response, read the sentence with the answer to the student, <u>Tam is Kim's friend</u>. Then ask, **Who is Kim's friend?** If still no response or an incorrect response, physically guide the student to find <u>Tam</u>, and say, <u>Tam</u>. <u>Tam is Kim's friend</u>.

Repeat with the <u>content</u> for each lesson; see **Level 5 Content** on p. 67.

Closing /Writing activity

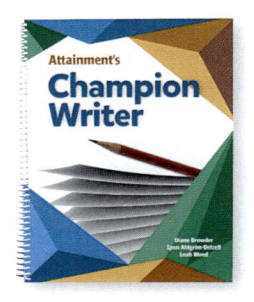

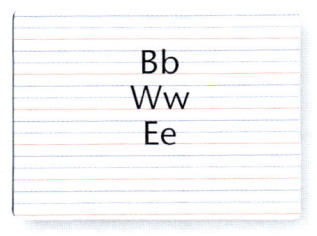

Objective 9
Write responses to activities that review level objectives.

Activity directions
Your lesson is over. GREAT reading today! Let's complete a page in your Champion Writer.

Teaching moment
- ✔ In order to keep the lesson from becoming too long, consider completing the writing activity at another time of the day.
- ✔ Some students may need adaptations to complete the writing page in **Champion Writer**; see p. 20 for ideas.
- ✔ Use the dry-erase board and an erasable marker to give the student practice in writing/forming the letter/sounds of this level.

LEVEL 6

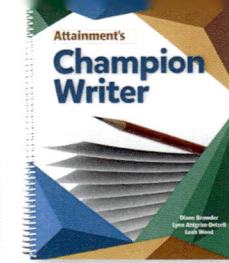

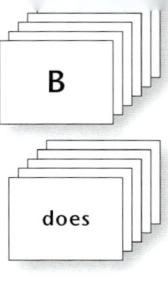

Focus
Bb, Ww, and Ee (short)

Phonemic awareness
- Blend sounds for CVC words
- Segment first sounds in words
- Segment sounds in CVC words

Phonics
- Sounds /b/, /w/, and /ɛ/ corresponding to graphemes Bb, Ww, and Ee
- Decode CVC words

Sight words
does, go, his, like, too

Generalization words
Ben, bit, but, get, let, will

Connected text
- ATOS level = Story 1: .3; Story 2: .3
- Lexile level = Story 1: –50L; Story 2: 10L

Objectives
1 Identify Bb, Ww, and Ee when given the sounds /b/, /w/, and /ɛ/.
2 Blend sounds to form CVC words.
3 Segment the first sound in words beginning with /b/, /w/, and /ɛ/.
4 Segment the sounds in CVC words.
5 Decode CVC words and identify their meanings.
6 Read 5 new sight words.
7 Read connected text.
8 Answer comprehension questions about connected text.
9 Write responses to activities that review level objectives.

Teaching notes
The letter/sounds Bb, Ww, and Ee (short e) are introduced in Level 6. As in Level 5, for blending, students are given 3 individual sounds; they blend the sounds together and identify the word the sounds make. For decoding, students begin to decode the word independently. The model of sounding the word out for is faded except for demonstration. For Reading Text, students read the text silently in their heads. Two stories are still provided to give students extra practice in reading connected text using these beginning reading skills.

Level 6 Content

	Lesson 1	Lesson 2	Lesson 3	Lesson 4	Lesson 5
Letter/sound identification	**New**: Bb, Ww, Ee (short) **Review**: Ll, Hh, Kk, c/ck				
Blending	bug, wet, bus, bet, lab, wig	Optional demo: Sam bat, wit, bed, cab, bam, bud	Optional demo: Sam wet, led, red, back, web, ban	Optional demo: Sam bat, beg, web, bad, bus, led	Optional demo: Sam led, beg, web, wet, bus, bat
Segmenting I	wet, ball, end, want, ever, bed	Optional demo: bet bat, wet, egg, bus, we, enter	Optional demo: bet elephant, boy, web, echo, boat, Wednesday	Optional demo: bet bug, winter, enter, web, week, elevator	Optional demo: bet bus. win, egg, bat, week, enter
Segmenting II	bus, beg, web, bat, bob, led	Optional demo: bam bug, deck, bus, bad, lab, wig	Optional demo: bad beg, wet, bed, cab, bam, bud	Optional demo: bam wet, Ben, red, back, web, ban	Optional demo: bam wet, bat, bug, back, lab, bob
Decoding	bus, wag, bed, cab, bag, bud	Optional demo: hug wet, bam, red, back, ten, web	Optional demo: hug bat (pic 1), beg, web, bud, big, fed	Optional demo: hug bug, lab, bus, bob, win, wig	Optional demo: hug bag, lab, ten, bat (pic 2), win, wag
Sight Words	**New**: does, go, his, like, too **Review**: and, have, no, she				
Comprehension questions (correct response in **bold**)	\<colspan Story 1: Bag a Bug\>				
	Who sees a bug? (Tim, big, **Kim**, bug) What does Kim use to catch a bug? (big, web, **bag**, are)	Who is on Kim's bus? (Sam, **Ben**, like, off) Does Ben like bugs? (Ben, **no**, off, yes)	What does Kim see? (get, **web**, dock, wet) What is the bug's bed? (bug, we, boy, **web**)	What will get the bug? (bug, **bat**, red, no) What will the bat like? (**bug**, bat, friend, see) Who bit a red bug? (wet, Kim, **bat**, a)	Does Kim have a bug on her bus? (yes, **no**, bus, Kim) What did Kim get off of? (**bus**, yes, big, the) What color was her bag? (**red**, bed, bug, bag) What did Kim catch in the bag? (**bug**, I, boy, web)
	\<Story 2: Ben at Bat\>				
	What does Ben have? (bed, web, **bat**, he) Who is at bat? (**Ben**, Bat, Run, Yes)	Who might catch the ball? (Sam, go, too, **Tim**) Did Tim get the ball? (**no**, yes, on, the)	What color team is at bat? (Web, Too, Rack, **Red**) Who can hit the ball? (Tim, boy, bus, **Kim**) Did Kim hit the ball? (the, yes, **no**, big)	What score does Red have? (on, **ten**, me, too) Who was at bat? (**Tim**, Sam, Bat, Red) Who has the ball it his mitt? (Tim, Big, **Ben**, Red)	Who got a hit? (Bug, Tam, **Ben**, Sam) Who else got a hit? (**Kim**, Sam, Big, Hit) Did Tim have a mitt? (hit, **yes**, no, mitt) What color team won? (Wet, **Red**, Lot, Run)

Letter/sound identification

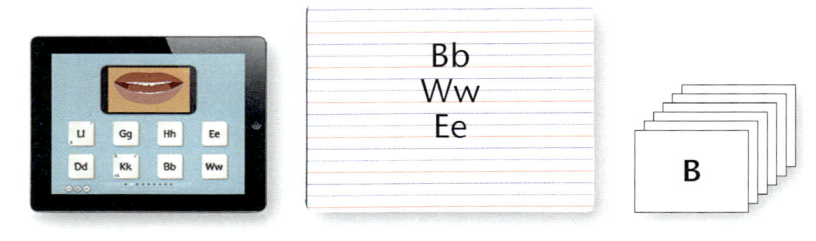

Objective 1
Identify Bb, Ww, and Ee when given the sounds /b/, /w/, and /ɛ/.
Pronunciation: /ɛ/ as in b<u>e</u>t

Prompting
- Lesson 1: Time delay 0 seconds
- Lessons 2–5: Time delay 4 seconds

Activity directions
I'll say a sound, and you find the letter that makes that sound.

Teaching moment
✔ Introduce Bb, Ww, and Ee to the student, **Let's learn the sounds /b/, /w/, and /ɛ/.** Point to the tiles on the software screen or write and point to them on the dry-erase board.

✔ If the student struggles, use visual and articulatory cues that show the student how a sound is made, (e.g., point to your mouth to say /b/).

✔ If the student does not know uppercase from lowercase letters, use the flashcards to practice matching them.

✔ If the student chooses an incorrect response, give a reminder to not guess but to wait and you will help. You can also add to the directions, **If you are not sure of the answer, don't guess. Wait for me to help you.**

Cue	Student's independent response	If student needs help
What letter says /<u>b</u>/?	Finds the letter <u>B</u>b to make the /<u>b</u>/ sound.	For Lesson 1, model finding the correct response, and continue pointing to it until the student finds it. If no response or an incorrect response, physically guide the student to find the letter and say, **This is /<u>b</u>/.** For Lessons 2–5, if no response after 4 seconds or an incorrect response, model finding the letter, and continue pointing to it until the student finds it. If needed, physically guide the student to find the letter and say, **This is /<u>b</u>/. You touch it.**

Repeat with Ww and Ee and Level 5 review: Ll, Hh, and Kk/c/ck

Blending

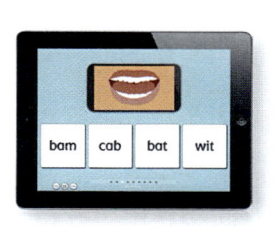

bug
bus

Objective 2
Blend sounds to form CVC words.
Pronunciation: /ʌ/ as in b<u>u</u>g

Prompting
- Lesson 1: Time delay 0 seconds
- Lessons 2–5: Time delay 4 seconds

Activity directions
I'll say some sounds. You blend the sounds together and find the word they make.

Teaching moment
✔ The blending task in this level is to blend all sounds in a word when the word is presented in a segmented form. This level presents blending of three sounds for CVC words.

✔ To make it easier for the student, the sounds may be prolonged or followed by a pause between sounds to help the student process each sound.

✔ Use the dry-erase board to demonstrate blending using fewer words as distractors.

✔ Note that when you segment the sounds in words, do not add additional sounds (e.g., *bug* is correctly segmented as /b/ /ʌ/ /g/, not /bʌ/ /ʌ/ /gʌ/.

Cue	Student's independent response	If student needs help
/<u>b</u>/ /<u>ʌ</u>/ /<u>g</u>/. Which word am I saying?	Finds the word <u>bug</u>.	For Lesson 1, model finding the correct response, and continue pointing to it until the student finds it. If no response or an incorrect response, physically guide the student to find the word. For Lessons 2–5, if no response after 4 seconds or an incorrect response, model finding the word and say, **This is <u>bug</u>. You touch it.** Continue pointing to it until the student finds it. If needed, physically guide the student to find the word.

Repeat with the <u>content</u> for each lesson; see **Level 6 Content** on p. 77.

ERSB Teacher's Guide ■ Level 6

Segmenting I

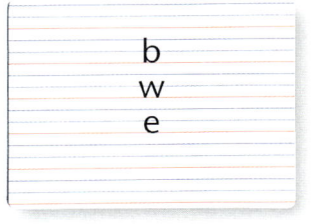

Objective 3
Segment the first sound in words beginning with /b/, /w/, and /ɛ/.
Pronunciation: /ɛ/ as in b<u>e</u>t

Prompting
- Lesson 1: Time delay 0 seconds
- Lessons 2–5: Time delay 4 seconds

Activity directions
I'll say a word. You show me the first sound you hear in the word.

Teaching moment
✔ In learning to segment sounds in words, it is easier to segment the initial sound than the middle or ending sound; therefore, this activity focuses on segmenting the initial sound in words.

✔ Pause for one second between the direction ("What is the first sound in") and the target word to prepare the student for the target word.

✔ This activity helps the student segment sounds by emphasizing or slightly prolonging the first sound in the word (when possible). Point to your mouth as you produce the initial sound if needed.

✔ If the student chooses an incorrect response, give a reminder to not guess but to wait and you will help. You can also add to the directions, **If you are not sure of the answer, don't guess. Wait for me to help you.**

Cue	Student's independent response	If student needs help
What is the first sound in (1 sec. pause) **wet?**	Finds <u>w</u> to say /w/.	For Lesson 1, if no response or an incorrect response, physically guide the student to touch <u>w</u>. Say, **The first sound is /w/.**
		For Lessons 2–5, if no response after 4 seconds or an incorrect response, model finding the sound and say, **The first sound is /w/. You touch it.** If needed, physically guide the student to find /w/.

Repeat with the <u>content</u> for each lesson; see **Level 6 Content** on p. 77.

Segmenting II

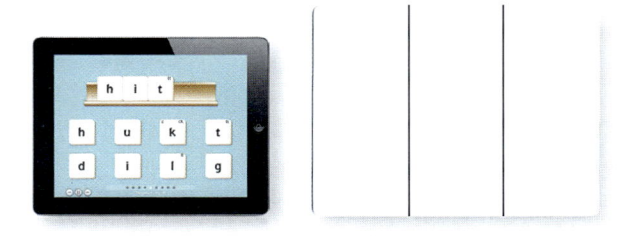

Objective 4
Segment the sounds in CVC words.
Pronunciation: ɛ/ as in b<u>e</u>t, /ʌ/ as in b<u>u</u>s

Prompting
- Lesson 1: Time delay 0 seconds
- Lessons 2–5: Time delay 4 seconds

Activity directions
Use the sounds you learned to sound out some words. I'll say a word, and you sound it out.

Teaching moment
✔ To help the student segment all of the sounds in the word, hold up a finger for each sound the student needs to find.

✔ Or use the dry-erase board to indicate how many sounds are in a word.

✔ If the student chooses an incorrect response, give a reminder to not guess but to wait and you will help. Add to the directions, **If you are not sure of the answer, don't guess. Wait for me to help you.**

✔ If the student makes an error on even one sound, have the student listen as you segment **all** the sounds in the word in the correct sequence. Then restate to touch the sounds in the word.

Cue	Student's independent response	If student needs help
Sound out the word <u>bus</u>.	Touches <u>b</u>, <u>u,</u> and <u>s</u> for the sounds /b/ /ʌ/ /s/.	For Lesson 1, if no response or an incorrect response, physically guide the student to touch <u>b</u>, <u>u</u>, and <u>s</u> to segment the sounds in the word.
		For Lessons 2–5, if no response after 4 seconds or an incorrect response, say, **Listen, /b/ /ʌ/ /sss/. Touch the sounds in <u>bus</u>**.
		If still no response or an incorrect response, model segmenting the word by touching and saying each sound. Then say, **Your turn. Touch the sounds in <u>bus</u>.**
		If still no response or an incorrect response, say, **Let's touch the sounds in <u>bus</u>.** Then physically guide the student to touch each sound while you say it.

Repeat with the <u>content</u> for each lesson; see **Level 6 Content** on p. 77.

Decoding

Objective 5
Decode CVC words and identify their meanings.
Pronunciation: /ɛ/ as in b<u>e</u>t

Prompting
- Lesson 1: Time delay 0 seconds
- Lessons 2–5: Time delay 4 seconds

Activity directions
Now, use the sounds and letters you learned to read a word and find its picture.

Teaching moment
✔ Be certain the student knows the name of each picture.

✔ In this level, the demonstration prompt to sound out/decode the word is completely faded. For Lesson 1 and demonstration items, do not point to the word being decoded, just point next to the picture of the word. For the remaining items in Lessons 2–5, give the direction to read the word and find the picture of the word read.

✔ If the student does not respond, point to the word but do not say it. Prolong or emphasize the sounds (when possible) as you model sounding the word out.

Cue	Student's independent response	If student needs help
First, let's hear each picture's name.	Listens as each picture is named.	
For Lesson 1, do not point to the word. Point next to the picture of the word and say, **Here is bus. Your turn. Read the word and find the picture.**	Finds the picture of <u>bus</u>.	For Lesson 1, if no response or an incorrect response, physically guide the student to touch the picture of <u>bus</u>.
For Lessons 2–5, say, **Read the word and find the picture.**	Finds the picture of <u>wet</u>.	For Lessons 2–5, if no response after 4 seconds, point to the word and say, **This is /w/ /ɛ/ /t/.** Then touch the picture and say, **Here is wet. Now you read wet and find the picture.** Physically guide the student's hand if needed.
		For Lessons 2–5, if an incorrect response, point to the letters in the word as you say, **This says wet.** Touch the picture and say, **Here is the picture of wet.** Remove your finger and say, **Now you read wet and find the picture.** Physically guide the student's hand if needed.

Repeat with the <u>content</u> for each lesson; see **Level 6 Content** on p. 77.

Sight words

Objective 6
Read 5 new sight words.

Prompting
- Lesson 1: Time delay 0 seconds
- Lessons 2–5: Time delay 4 seconds

Activity directions
Sight words are tricky because you can't sound them out. You have to remember what they look like. Find the word.

Teaching moment
✔ The pace between presentation of words should be rapid to keep the student motivated.

✔ Use the sight word flashcards to provide extra practice of sight word reading. Provide up to 4 response options for students to choose from.

✔ Create a word wall with sight words from this level.

✔ If the student chooses an incorrect response, give a reminder to not guess but to wait and you will help. You can also add to the directions, **If you are not sure of the answer, don't guess. Wait for me to help you.**

Cue	Student's independent response	If student needs help
Find the word like.	Finds the word like.	For Lesson 1, if no response or an incorrect response, physically guide the student to find like. Say, **This is like.** For Lessons 2–5, if no response after 4 seconds or an incorrect response, model finding the word and say, **This is like. You touch it.** Physically guide the student to find the word if needed.

Repeat with the <u>new sight words</u> and <u>review sight words</u>, words required for reading the story for this level; see **Level 6 Content** on p. 77.

Reading text / Comprehension questions

Tim
big
Kim
bug

Teaching moment

✔ In this level, the student reads the text silently. One page of the story is read during each lesson, followed by comprehension questions. If repeating this level, Story 2 will be used in the software.

✔ Use **Champion Reader 2** to show the title of the story and to point out the characters. It can also be used to give students additional reading practice. The comprehension questions that could be asked if not using the software and possible response options are listed in the **Level 6 Content** on p. 77. Write response options on the dry-erase board for students to read.

Objective 7 / Objective 8
Read connected text. / Answer comprehension questions about connected text.

Prompting
Least intrusive prompt

Activity directions
Now that you know how to read words, you can read a page from the story. Today you will read about Kim and Ben.

Cue	Student's independent response	If student needs help
Say, **Read this story silently in your head.** Do not read to the student or point to the words.	Reads the sentences silently.	
After the student reads the sentences on the page, say, **Let's answer some questions about the story. What does Ben have?**	Chooses the word <u>bat</u>.	If no response or an incorrect response, say, **Read this sentence again**. Point to each word in the sentence that has the answer, then ask the question again. If still no response or an incorrect response, read the sentence with the answer to the student, **He has a big bat**. Then ask, **What does Ben have?** If still no response or an incorrect response, physically guide the student to find <u>bat</u> and say, **bat. Ben has a bat**.

Repeat with the <u>content</u> for each lesson; see **Level 6 Content** on p. 77.

Closing / Writing activity

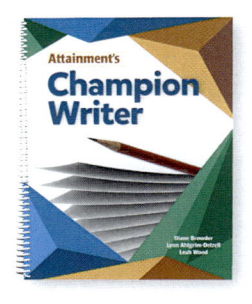

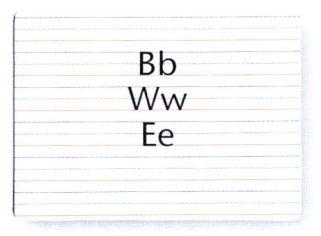

Objective 9
Write responses to activities that review level objectives.

Activity directions
Your lesson is over. GREAT reading today! Let's complete a page in your Champion Writer.

Teaching moment
✔ In order to keep the lesson from becoming too long, consider completing the writing activity at another time of the day.

✔ Some students may need adaptations to complete the writing page in **Champion Writer**; see p. 20 for ideas.

✔ Use the dry-erase board and an erasable marker to give the student practice in writing/forming the letter/sounds of this level.

LEVEL 7

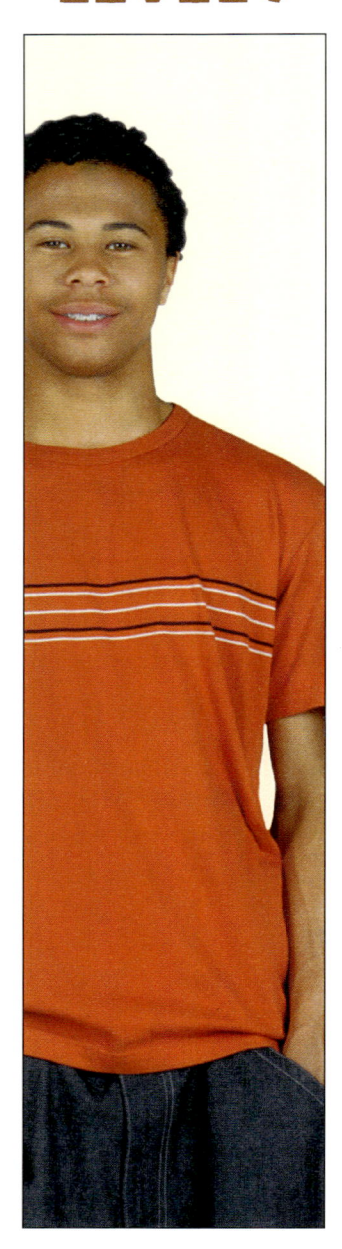

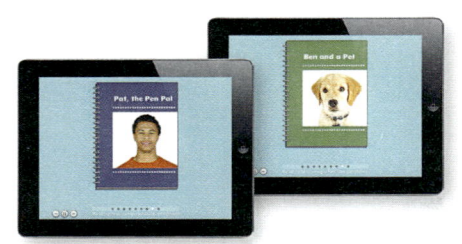

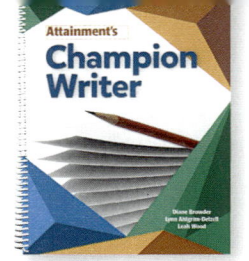

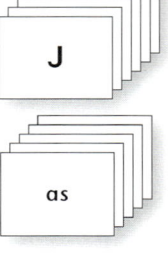

Focus
Jj, Pp, Yy

Phonemic awareness
- Blend sounds for CVC words
- Segment first sounds in words
- Segment sounds in CVC words

Phonics
- Sounds /ʤ/, /p/, and /j/ corresponding to graphemes Jj, Pp, and Yy
- Decode CVC words

Sight words
as, be, bee, eat, of, want

Generalization words
jam, Jed, job, map, pal, Pat, pick, pig, yap, yell, yet, yip, yuck, up

Connected text
- ATOS level = Story 1: .5; Story 2: .3
- Lexile level = Story 1: 90L; Story 2: 40L

Objectives
1. Identify Jj, Pp, and Yy when given the sounds /ʤ/, /p/, and /j/.
2. Blend sounds to form CVC words.
3. Segment the first sound in words beginning with /ʤ/, /p/, and /j/.
4. Segment the sounds in CVC words.
5. Decode CVC words and identify their meanings.
6. Read 6 new sight words.
7. Read connected text.
8. Answer comprehension questions about connected text.
9. Write responses to activities that review level objectives.

Teaching notes
The letter/sounds Jj, Pp, and Yy are introduced in Level 7. Two stories are still provided to give students extra practice in reading using these beginning skills.

In this level, for Blending, students continue to blend three sounds to identify CVC words. For decoding, emphasis is on decoding a word and identifying its meaning independently. The model of sounding the word out for is faded except for demonstration and when the student requires support. For Reading Text, students read the text silently in their heads. Two stories are still provided to give students extra practice in reading connected text using these beginning reading skills.

Level 7 Content

	Lesson 1	Lesson 2	Lesson 3	Lesson 4	Lesson 5
Letter/sound identification	**New:** Jj, Pp, Yy **Review:** Bb, Ww, Ee (short)				
Blending	Yum, jig, hop, peg, pot, tip	**Optional demo:** tip jet, pack, pup, lip, pan, mop	**Optional demo:** tip jug, lap, pet, pad, yak, pop	**Optional demo:** tip pen, yes, yam, jab, tab, pop	**Optional demo:** tip hop, jig, pup, pad, pot, pop
Segmenting I	jug, pay, yell, jump, pan, your	**Optional demo:** your pen, yes, just, pop, you, jab	**Optional demo:** your Yum, jig, peg, yes, jar, pot	**Optional demo:** your jet, pet, yarn, Jan, pack, year	**Optional demo:** your jug, pants, yarn, Jan, pack, yard
Segmenting II	pen, yes, yam, jab, tap, pop	**Optional demo:** jab yum, jig, hop, peg, pot, tip	**Optional demo:** jab jet, pack, pup, lip, pan, mop	**Optional demo:** jab jug, lap, pet, pad, yak, pin	**Optional demo:** jab jet, lap, hop, pad, Yum, peg
Decoding	jet, pack, pup, lip, pop, mop	**Optional demo:** bug pet, lap, pen (pic 1), pad, peg, peck	**Optional demo:** bug pen (pic 2), pop, yam, pack, lip, yes	**Optional demo:** bug yum, pan, hop, peg, pot, mop	**Optional demo:** bug pup, lip, hop, lap, pit, mom
Sight Words	**New:** as, be, bee, eat, of, want **Review:** like, my, see, we				
Comprehension questions (correct response in **bold**)			Story 1: Ben and a Pet		
	What can Ron do in a hat? (**jam**, pat, jar, in) Where did Ron meet Pat? (man, jam, **jet**, Pat)	What is the pig's name? (Yip, Tim, **Yum**, dig) What will the pig eat? (**yam**, pig, eat, Pat) What will Yum dig up? (**bug**, jam, bag, hat)	What does Ron have? (pan, lip, wet, **pet**) What is the pet's name? (**Jed**, Yum, Pat, jet) Where does Ron put Jed? (**pen**, pig, hat, cab)	Who has a job? (**Pat**, jam, jug, pig) What kind of job does Pat have? (Pat, **wet**, jam, we) What does Pat have? (hug, jam, have, **jug**)	What does Ron get? (pan, man, bus, **map**) Does Ron want to see Pat? (get, no, **yes**, she) What did Ron get in first? (**cab**, jet, pig, cat) What did Ron get in last? (cab, jet, **bus**, big)
			Story 2: Pat, the Pen Pal		
	What does Ben want? (pan, **pet**, hot, have) What does Ben see? (pig, jam, **bug**, bus) Does Ben want a bug as a pet? (**no**, yes, hot, it)	What does Ben see? (**cat**, bug, hot, pan) What did Ben hop on? (**bus**, bed, pet, yes) Does Ben have a pet yet? (yes, eat, yam, **no**)	What does Ben eat? (**jam**, jet, got, man) What is in the jam? (pig, **bee**, pet, hat) Is a bee a pet? (yes, **no**, hop, net)	What is in the pen? (**pig**, pat, bug, hot) What can the pig do? (**eat**, hut, yum, pig) What does the pig eat? (jam, eat, **yam**, jet)	Where is the pup? (**pen**, jet, bus, bug) What did Ben do to the pup? (**pet**, jet, pan, bin) What did the pup do? (**lick**, jam, bee, lip)

Letter/sound identification

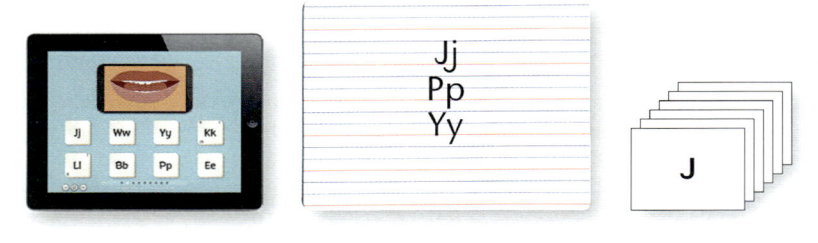

Objective 1
Identify Jj, Pp, and Yy when given the sounds /dʒ/, /p/, and /j/.
Pronunciation: /dʒ/ as in jam, /j/ as in yum

Prompting
- Lesson 1: Time delay 0 seconds
- Lessons 2–5: Time delay 4 seconds

Activity directions
I'll say a sound, and you find the letter that makes that sound.

Teaching moment
✔ Introduce Jj, Pp, and Yy to the student, **Let's learn the sounds /dʒ/, /p/, and /j/.** Point to the tiles on the software screen or write and point to them on the dry-erase board.

✔ If the student struggles, use visual and articulatory cues that show the student how a sound is made, (e.g., point to your mouth to say /dʒ/).

✔ If the student does not know uppercase from lowercase letters, use the flashcards to practice matching them.

✔ If the student chooses an incorrect response, give a reminder to not guess but to wait and you will help. You can also add to the directions, **If you are not sure of the answer, don't guess. Wait for me to help you.**

Cue	Student's independent response	If student needs help
What letter says /dʒ/?	Finds the letter Jj to make the /dʒ/ sound.	For Lesson 1, model finding the correct response, and continue pointing to it until the student finds it. If no response or an incorrect response, physically guide the student to find the letter and say, **This is /dʒ/.** For Lessons 2–5, if no response after 4 seconds or an incorrect response, model finding the letter, and continue pointing to it until the student finds it. If needed, physically guide the student to find the letter and say, **This is /dʒ/. You touch it.**

Repeat with Pp and Yy, and Level 6 review: Bb, Ww, and Ee (short).

Blending

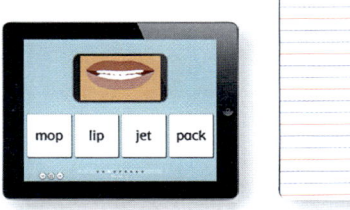

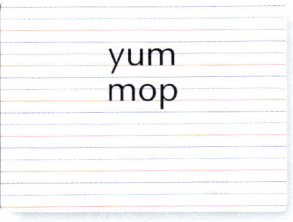

Objective 2
Blend sounds to form CVC words.
Pronunciation: /dʒ/ as in jam, /j/ as in yum, /ʌ/ as in yum

Prompting
- Lesson 1: Time delay 0 seconds
- Lessons 2–5: Time delay 4 seconds

Activity directions
I'll say some sounds. You blend the sounds together and find the word they make.

Teaching moment
✔ The blending task in this level is to blend all sounds in a word when the word is presented in a segmented form. This level presents blending of three sounds for CVC words.

✔ To make it easier for the student, the sounds may be prolonged or followed by a pause between sounds to help the student process each sound.

✔ Use the dry-erase board to demonstrate blending using fewer word distractors.

✔ Note that when you segment the sounds in words, do not add additional sounds (e.g., jug is correctly segmented as /dʒ/ /ʌ/ /g/, not /dʒ/ /ʌ/ /gʌ/).

Cue	Student's independent response	If student needs help
/j/ /ʌ/ /m/. Which word am I saying?	Finds the word yum.	For Lesson 1, model finding the correct response, and continue pointing to it until the student finds it. If no response or an incorrect response, physically guide the student to find the word. For Lessons 2–5, if no response after 4 seconds or an incorrect response, model finding the word and say, **This is yum. You touch it.** Continue pointing to it until the student finds it. If needed, physically guide the student to find the word.

Repeat with the content for each lesson; see **Level 7 Content** on p. 87.

Segmenting I

Objective 3
Segment the first sound in words beginning with /dʒ/, /p/, and /j/.
Pronunciation: /j/ as in yum, /dʒ/ as in jug

Prompting
- Lesson 1: Time delay 0 seconds
- Lessons 2–5: Time delay 4 seconds

Activity directions
I'll say a word. You show me the first sound you hear in the word.

Teaching moment
✔ In learning to segment sounds in words, it is easier to segment the initial sound than the middle or ending sound; therefore, this activity focuses on segmenting individual sounds in words.

✔ Pause for one second between the direction ("What is the first sound in") and the target word to prepare the student for the target word.

✔ This activity helps the student segment sounds by emphasizing or slightly prolonging the first sound in the word when possible.

✔ If the student chooses an incorrect response, give a reminder to not guess but to wait and you will help. You can also add to the directions, **If you are not sure of the answer, don't guess. Wait for me to help you.**

Cue	Student's independent response	If student needs help
What is the first sound in (1 sec. pause) **jug?**	Finds j to say /dʒ/.	For Lesson 1, if no response or an incorrect response, physically guide the student to touch j. Say, **The first sound is /dʒ/.**
		For Lessons 2–5, if no response after 4 seconds or an incorrect response, model finding the sound and say, **The first sound is /dʒ/. You touch it.** If needed, physically guide the student to find /dʒ/.

Repeat with the content for each lesson; see **Level 7 Content** on p. 87.

Segmenting II

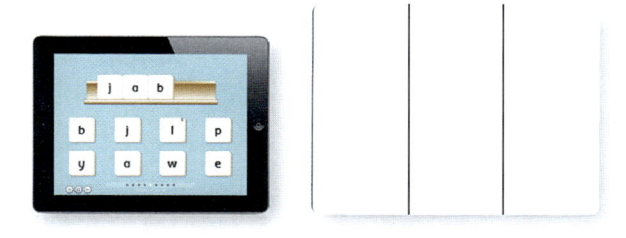

Objective 4
Segment the sounds in CVC words.
Pronunciation: /ɛ/ as in p<u>e</u>n

Prompting
- Lesson 1: Time delay 0 seconds
- Lessons 2–5: Time delay 4 seconds

Activity directions
Use the sounds you learned to sound out some words. I'll say a word, and you sound it out.

Teaching moment
✔ To help the student segment all of the sounds in the word, hold up a finger for each sound the student needs to find. Remember to hold up fingers for sounds, not letters (e.g., the word *yell* has 3 sounds but 4 letters).

✔ Or use the dry-erase board to indicate how many sounds are in a word.

✔ If the student chooses an incorrect response, give a reminder to not guess but to wait and you will help. Add to the directions, **If you are not sure of the answer, don't guess. Wait for me to help you.**

✔ If the student makes an error on even one sound, have the student listen as you segment **all** the sounds in the word in the correct sequence. Then restate to touch the sounds in the word.

Cue	Student's independent response	If student needs help
Sound out the word <u>pen</u>.	Touches <u>p</u>, <u>e</u>, and <u>n</u> for the sounds /p/, /ɛ/, and /n/.	For Lesson 1, if no response or an incorrect response, physically guide the student to touch <u>p</u>, <u>e</u>, and <u>n</u> to segment the sounds in the word. For Lessons 2–5, if no response after 4 seconds or an incorrect response, say, **Listen, /p/ /ɛ/ /nnn/. Touch the sounds in <u>pen</u>.** If still no response or an incorrect response, model segmenting the word by touching each letter and saying each sound. Then say, **Your turn. Touch the sounds in <u>pen</u>.** If still no response or an incorrect response, say, **Let's touch the sounds in <u>pen</u>.** Then physically guide the student to touch each sound while you say it.

Repeat with the <u>content</u> for each lesson; see **Level 7 Content** on p. 87.

Decoding

Objective 5
Decode CVC words and identify their meanings.
Pronunciation: /ɛ/ as in p<u>e</u>n

Prompting
- Lesson 1: Time delay 0 seconds
- Lessons 2–5: Time delay 4 seconds

Activity directions
Now, use the sounds and letters you learned to read a word and find its picture.

Teaching moment

✔ Be certain the student knows the name of each picture.

✔ Students may need you to continue to demonstrate how to sound out/decode the word. Point to the word, sound it out and prolong (if possible) each letter sound as you say it. Then say the word and find the picture representing it. Be sure to follow this demonstration with independent responding by the student.

✔ If the student chooses an incorrect response, give a reminder to not guess but to wait and you will help. You can also add to the directions, **If you are not sure of the answer, don't guess. Wait for me to help you.**

Cue	Student's independent response	If student needs help
First, let's hear each picture's name.	Listens as each picture is named.	
For Lesson 1, point to the word then touch the picture and say, **Here is jet. Your turn. Read the word and find the picture.**	Finds the picture of <u>jet</u>.	For Lesson 1, if no response or an incorrect response, physically guide the student to touch the picture of <u>jet</u>.
For Lessons 2–5, say, **Read the word and find the picture.**	Finds the picture of <u>pet</u>.	For Lessons 2–5, if no response after 4 seconds, point to the word and say, **This is /p/ /ɛ/ /t/.** Then touch the picture and say, **Here is pet. Now you read <u>pet</u> and find the picture.** Physically guide the student's hand if needed.
		For Lessons 2–5, if an incorrect response, point to the letters in the word as you say, **This says <u>pet</u>.** Touch the picture and say, **Here is the picture of <u>pet</u>.** Remove your finger and say, **Now you read <u>pet</u> and find the picture.** Physically guide the student's hand if needed.

Repeat with the <u>content</u> for each lesson; see **Level 7 Content** on p. 87.

Sight words

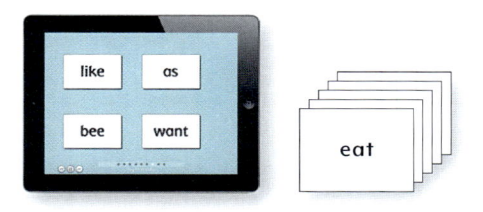

Objective 6
Read 6 new sight words.

Prompting
- Lesson 1: Time delay 0 seconds
- Lessons 2–5: Time delay 4 seconds

Activity directions
Sight words are tricky because you can't sound them out. You have to remember what they look like. Find the word.

Teaching moment
✔ The pace between presentation of words should be rapid to keep the student motivated.

✔ Use the sight word flashcards to provide extra practice of sight word reading. Provide up to 4 response options for students to choose from.

✔ If the student chooses an incorrect response, give a reminder to not guess but to wait and you will help. You can also add to the directions, **If you are not sure of the answer, don't guess. Wait for me to help you.**

Cue	Student's independent response	If student needs help
Find the word <u>eat</u>.	Finds the word <u>eat</u>.	For Lesson 1, if no response or an incorrect response, physically guide the student to find <u>eat</u>. Say, **This is <u>eat</u>.** For Lessons 2–5, if no response after 4 seconds or an incorrect response, model finding the word and say, **This is <u>eat</u>. You touch it.** Physically guide the student to find the word if needed.

Repeat with the <u>new sight words</u> and <u>review sight words</u>, words required for reading the story for this level; see **Level 7 Content** on p. 87.

Reading text / Comprehension questions

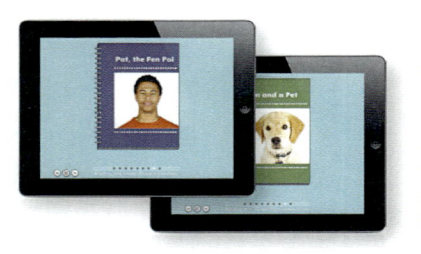

jam
pat
jar
in

Objective 7 / Objective 8
Read connected text. / Answer comprehension questions about connected text.

Prompting
Least intrusive prompt

Activity directions
Now that you know how to read words, you can read a page from the story. Today you will read about Pat (or Ben).

Teaching moment

✓ In this level, the student is told to read the text silently in his or her head.

✓ One page of the story is read during each lesson, followed by comprehension questions. If repeating this level, Story 2 will be used in the software.

✓ Use **Champion Reader 2** to show the title of the story and to point out the characters. It can also be used to give students additional reading practice. The comprehension questions that could be asked if not using the software and possible response options are listed in the **Level 7 Content** on p. 87. Write response options on the dry-erase board for students to read.

Cue	Student's independent response	If student needs help
Say, **Read this story silently in your head.** Do not read to the student or point to the words.	Reads the sentences silently.	
After the student reads the sentences on the page, say, **Let's answer some questions about the story. What can Ron do in a hat?**	Chooses the word <u>jam</u>.	If no response or an incorrect response, say, **Read this sentence again**. Point to each word in the sentence that has the answer, then ask the question again. If still no response or an incorrect response, read the sentence with the answer to the student, <u>**I can jam in a hat**</u>. Then ask, <u>**What can Ron do in a hat?**</u> If still no response or an incorrect response, physically guide the student to find <u>jam</u>, and say, <u>jam</u>. <u>**Ron can jam in a hat**</u>.

Repeat with the <u>content</u> for each lesson; see **Level 7 Content** on p. 87.

Closing /Writing activity

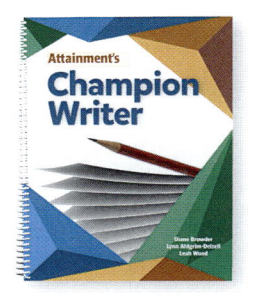

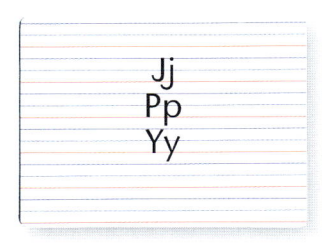

Objective 9
Write responses to activities that review level objectives.

Activity directions
Your lesson is over. GREAT reading today! Let's complete a page in your Champion Writer.

Teaching moment

✔ In order to keep the lesson from becoming too long, consider completing the writing activity at another time of the day.

✔ Some students may need adaptations to complete the writing page in **Champion Writer**; see p. 20 for ideas.

✔ Use the dry-erase board an erasable marker to give the student practice in writing/forming the letter/sounds of this level.

LEVEL 8

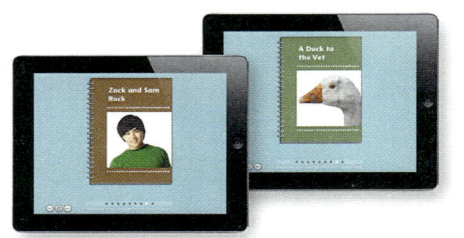

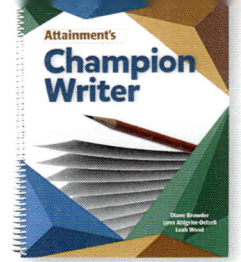

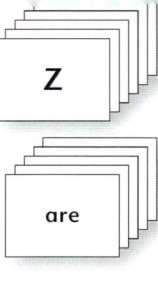

Focus
Zz, Xx, Vv, Qq^u

Phonemic awareness
- Blend sounds for CVC, CCVC, and CVCC words
- Segment first sounds in words
- Segment sounds in CVC and CCVC words

Phonics
- Sounds /z/, /ks/, /v/, and /kw/ corresponding to graphemes Zz/zz/s, Xx/ks, Vv, and Qq^u/kw
- Decode CVC and CCVC words

Sight words
are, boys, full, likes, out, that, what

Generalization words
gets, picks, quick, quit, zips, zag, zags, zig, zigs, wiz

Connected text
- ATOS level = Story 1: .6; Story 2: .7
- Lexile level = Story 1: –30L; Story 2: 10L

Objectives
1. Identify Zz/zz/s, Xx/ks, Vv, and Qq^u/kw when given the sounds /z/, /ks/, /v/, and /kw/.
2. Blend sounds to form CVC, CCVC, and CVCC words.
3. Segment the first sound(s) in words.
4. Segment the sounds in CVC and CCVC words.
5. Decode CVC and CCVC words and identify their meanings.
6. Read 7 new sight words.
7. Read connected text.
8. Answer comprehension questions about connected text.
9. Write responses to activities that review level objectives.

Teaching notes
The letter/sounds Zz, Xx, Vv, and Qq are introduced in Level 8. Note that Xx actually says two sounds /ks/ so students will see ks in the corner of the Xx tile. In addition, Qq always includes u and together they say two sounds /kw/. Students will see the kw in the corner of the Qq^u tile. Students will also see the s letter in the corner of the Zz tile because sometimes the letter s says /z/.

Because X and Qq^u consonants are produced with two sounds, the Segmenting I activity asks students to listen for the first two sounds (when appropriate).

Level 8 Content

	Lesson 1	Lesson 2	Lesson 3	Lesson 4	Lesson 5
Letter/sound identification	New: Xx/ks, Vv, Zz/zz/s, Qq^u/kw Review: Jj, Pp, Yy				
Blending	van, Zeb, quill, fuzz, vac, hugs	Optional demo: hugs Zack, pigs, box, quiz, wiz, vat	Optional demo: hugs zip, vex, digs, jazz, quip, tugs	Optional demo: hugs quack, rigs, vet, Max, zap, biz	Optional demo: hugs quack, rigs, vet, Max, zap, biz
Segmenting I	zip*, queen**, very*, zoo*, quiet**, vent*	Optional demo: zip* quack**, vat*, zap*, quiz**, vac*, Zeb*	Optional demo: zip* van*, zipper*, quake**, voice*, zebra*, quail**	Optional demo: zip* Zack*, quest**, visit*, zero*, quarter**, vest*	Optional demo: zip* very*, queen**, vat*, zero*, zebra*, violet*
Segmenting II	quack, rigs, vet, Max, zap, biz	Optional demo: zip van, vex, quill, fuzz, vac, hugs	Optional demo: zip Zack, pigs, box, quiz, wiz, vat	Optional demo: box zip, vex, has, jazz, quip, mugs	Optional demo: box zip, vex, has, jazz, quip, mugs
Decoding	Zack, pigs, box, quiz, vet, tubs	Optional demo: jet zip, cabs, digs, rubs, quill, vac	Optional demo: jet quack, legs, vet, wigs, Zack, dads	Optional demo: jet van, beds, quill, fuzz, box, hugs	Optional demo: jet van, beds, quill, fuzz, box, hugs
Sight Words	New: are, boys, full, likes, out, that, what Review: does, go, has, he, is, see, the, they, too				
Comprehension questions (correct response in **bold**)	\<colspan: Story 1: Zack and Sam Rock\>				
	What does Zack like to do? (what, **rock**, not, run) Does Sam quit? (yes, can, **no**, tub)	What is full? (fuzz, **van**, vet, ran) Who likes to rock? (huts, van, **boys**, beds) What do the friends do? (**rock**, run, Zack, van)	What did the boys get stuck in? (pigs, **mud**, my, had) What do the boys dig in? (Zack, had, mom, **mud**) Are the boys happy? (Yam, **no**, yes, out)	Who does not quit? (Mom, did, **Dad**, zip) What got out of the mud? (full, vet, pan, **van**) What did the boys hear? (**quack**, quit, pigs, Zack) What did the boys see? (does, quack, legs, **duck**)	How did Sam feel? (**sick**, zip, are, see) Who did Dad get? (**doc**, like, dug, friend) Who gets well? (**Sam**, man, not, sun) What did Sam and Zack do? (bin, **rock**, says, Ron)
	\<colspan: Story 2: A Duck to the Vet\>				
	What did Zack and Sam do? (**sit**, see, pat, bug) Where do they sit? (**deck**, mud, yuck, duck) What do they pick up? (**rock**, pig, ran, Zack)	What can Zack do? (pop, zoo, sad, **zip**) Who is quick? (**Zack**, Tam, zig, log) What is Sam? (vet, **wiz**, wet, we)	What do they see? (back, get, **duck**, see) Who is sick? (back, log, cat, **duck**) What do they drive? (**van**, bus, vet, ran) Where do they go? (**vet**, Sam, hop, box)	Who is mad? (**duck**, cat, luck, does) Who is quick? (bet, **vet**, and, van) Where is the duck? (box, pat, man, **pen**) Why did the duck stay at the vet? (luck, **sick**, see, hop)	Who has the duck? (mat, **vet**, Sam, van) Who is sad? (Tim, **Sam**, Zack, box) Who is back? (dog, **duck**, yuck, and) What can the duck do? (**quack**, mud, quill, duck)

* first sound   **first two sounds

ERSB Teacher's Guide ■ Level 8

Letter/sound identification

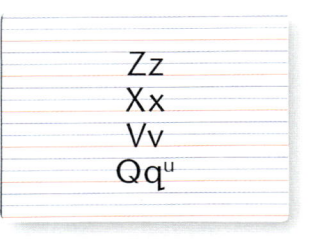

Objective 1
Identify Zz/zz/s, Xx/ks, Vv, and Qqᵘ/kw when given the sounds /z/, /ks/, /v/, and /kw/.
Pronunciation: /z/ as in zip, hugs; /ks/ as in Max; /kw/ as in quill

Prompting
- Lesson 1: Time delay 0 seconds
- Lessons 2–5: Time delay 4 seconds

Activity directions
I'll say a sound, and you find the letter that makes that sound.

Teaching moment

✔ Introduce the Zz tile. Z is made like s except Zz uses voice made in your throat. Point out zz in the corner of the Zz tile. Say, **The zz makes a /z/ sound too, just like one z.** Point out the letter s on the tile. Say, **Sometimes s makes the /z/ sound, especially when it is added to words to make a plural, like boys and toys.**

✔ Introduce the Xx tile. Tell students, **Xx makes two sounds, /k/ and /s/ together, /ks/.**

✔ Introduce the Vv sound. Say, **Vv is made just like Ff (teeth to lips) except Vv uses voice made in the throat.**

✔ Finally, introduce the Qqᵘ. Say, **Qqᵘ makes two sounds, /k/ and /w/ together /kw/, and that is why kw is in the corner of the Qqᵘ tile.**

✔ If the student chooses an incorrect response, give a reminder to not guess but to wait and you will help. You can also add to the directions, **If you are not sure of the answer, don't guess. Wait for me to help you.**

Cue	Student's independent response	If student needs help
What letter says /z/?	Finds the letter tile Zz to make the /z/ sound.	For Lesson 1, model finding the correct response, and continue pointing to it until the student finds it. If no response or an incorrect response, physically guide the student to find the letter and say, **This is /z/**. For Lessons 2–5, if no response after 4 seconds or an incorrect response, model finding the letter, and continue pointing to it until the student finds it. If needed, physically guide the student to find the letter and say, **This is /z/. You touch it.**

Repeat with Zz/zz/s, Xx/ks, Vv, and Qqᵘ/kw, and Level 7 review: Jj, Pp, and Yy.

Blending

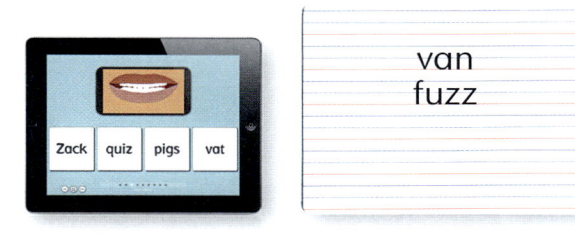

Objective 2
Blend sounds to form CVC, CCVC, and CVCC words.
Pronunciation: /æ/ as in b<u>a</u>t, /ʌ/ as in h<u>u</u>g

Prompting
- Lesson 1: Time delay 0 seconds
- Lessons 2–5: Time delay 4 seconds

Activity directions
I'll say some sounds. You blend the sounds together and find the word they make.

Teaching moment
✔ The blending task in this level is to blend all sounds in a word when the word is presented in a segmented form. This level presents blending of three sounds for CVC words and 4 sounds for CCVC and CVCC words.

✔ To make it easier for the student, the sounds may be prolonged or followed by a pause between sounds to help the student process each sound.

✔ Use the dry-erase board to demonstrate blending using fewer distractors.

✔ Note that when you segment the sounds in words, do not add additional sounds (e.g., *hugs* is correctly segmented as /h/ /ʌ/ /g/ /z/, not /h/ /ʌ/ /g ʌ/ /z/).

Cue	Student's independent response	If student needs help
/v/ /æ/ /n/. **Which word am I saying?**	Finds the word <u>van</u>.	For Lesson 1, model finding the correct response, and continue pointing to it until the student finds it. If no response or an incorrect response, physically guide the student to find the word. For Lessons 2–5, if no response after 4 seconds or an incorrect response, model finding the word and say, **This is <u>van</u>. You touch it.** Continue pointing to it until the student finds it. If needed, physically guide the student to find the word.

Repeat with the <u>content</u> for each lesson; see **Level 8 Content** on p. 97.

Segmenting I

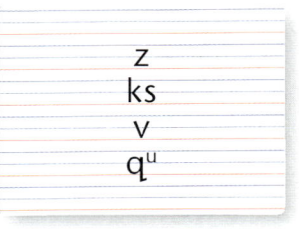

Objective 3
Segment the first sound(s) in words.
Pronunciation: /kw/ as in quill

Prompting
- Lesson 1: Time delay 0 seconds
- Lessons 2–5: Time delay 4 seconds

Activity directions
I'll say a word. You show me the first sound or first two sounds you hear in the word.

Teaching moment
✔ In learning to segment sounds in words, it is easier to segment the initial sound than the middle or ending sound; therefore, this activity focuses on segmenting individual sounds in words. Note however, that Xx and Qq^u, say two sounds and therefore students are given the direction to listen for the first two sounds in words containing x or q.

✔ Pause for one second between the direction ("What is the first sound in/What are the first two sounds in") and the target word to prepare the student for the target word.

✔ This activity helps the student segment sounds by emphasizing or slightly prolonging the first sound in the word when possible.

✔ If the student chooses an incorrect response, give a reminder to not guess but to wait and you will help. You can also add to the directions, **If you are not sure of the answer, don't guess. Wait for me to help you.**

Cue	Student's independent response	If student needs help
What is the first sound in (1 sec. pause) **zip?**	Finds Zz to say /z/.	For Lesson 1, if no response or an incorrect response, physically guide the student to touch z. Say, **The first sound is /z/.**
What are the first two sounds in (1 sec. pause) **queen?**	Finds Qq^u to say /kw/.	For Lessons 2–5, if no response after 4 seconds or an incorrect response, model finding the sound and say, **The first sound is /z/. You touch it.** If needed, physically guide the student to find /z/.

Repeat with the content for each lesson; see **Level 8 Content** on p. 97.

Segmenting II

Objective 4
Segment the sounds in CVC and CCVC words.
Pronunciation: /kw/ as in quill, /æ/ as in van

Prompting
- Lesson 1: Time delay 0 seconds
- Lessons 2–5: Time delay 4 seconds

Activity directions
Use the sounds you learned to sound out some words. I'll say a word, and you sound it out.

Teaching moment
✓ If the student chooses an incorrect response, give a reminder to not guess but to wait and you will help. Add to the directions, **If you are not sure of the answer, don't guess. Wait for me to help you.**

✓ If the student makes an error on even one sound, have the student listen as you segment **all** the sounds in the word in the correct sequence. Then restate to touch the sounds in the word.

Cue	Student's independent response	If student needs help
Sound out the word quack.	Touches qu, a, and ck for the sounds /kw/, /æ/, and /k/.	For Lesson 1, if no response or an incorrect response, physically guide the student to touch p, e, and n to segment the sounds in the word. For Lessons 2–5, if no response after 4 seconds or an incorrect response, say, **Listen, /kw/ /æ/ /k/. Touch the sounds in quack.** If still no response or an incorrect response, model segmenting the word by touching each letter and saying each sound. Then say, **Your turn. Touch the sounds in quack.** If still no response or an incorrect response, say, **Let's touch the sounds in quack.** Then physically guide the student to touch each sound while you say it.

Repeat with the content for each lesson; see **Level 8 Content** on p. 97.

Decoding

Objective 5
Decode CVC and CCVC words and identify their meanings.
Pronunciation: /ɪ/ as in zip

Prompting
- Lesson 1: Time delay 0 seconds
- Lessons 2–5: Time delay 4 seconds

Teaching moment
✓ Be certain the student knows the name of each picture.

✓ Students may need you to continue to demonstrate how to sound out/decode the word. Point to the word, sound it out and prolong (if possible) each letter sound as you say it. Then say the word and find the picture representing it. Be sure to follow this demonstration with independent responding by the student.

✓ If the student chooses an incorrect response, give a reminder to not guess but to wait and you will help. You can also add to the directions, **If you are not sure of the answer, don't guess. Wait for me to help you.**

Activity directions
Now, use the sounds and letters you learned to read a word and find its picture.

Cue	Student's independent response	If student needs help
First, let's hear each picture's name.	Listens as each picture is named.	
For Lesson 1, point to the word then touch the picture and say, **Here is jet. Your turn. Read the word and find the picture.**	Finds the picture of Zack.	For Lesson 1, if no response or an incorrect response, physically guide the student to touch the picture of Zack.
For Lessons 2–5, say, **Read the word and find the picture.**	Finds the picture of zip.	For Lessons 2–5, if no response after 4 seconds, point to the word and say, **This is /zzz/ /ɪ/ /p/.** Then touch the picture and say, **Here is zip. Now you read zip and find the picture.** Physically guide the student's hand if needed.
		For Lessons 2–5, if an incorrect response, point to the letters in the word as you say, **This says zip.** Touch the picture and say, **Here is the picture of zip.** Remove your finger and say, **Now you read zip and find the picture.** Physically guide the student's hand if needed.

Repeat with the content for each lesson; see **Level 8 Content** on p. 97.

Sight words

Objective 6
Read 7 new sight words.

Prompting
- Lesson 1: Time delay 0 seconds
- Lessons 2–5: Time delay 4 seconds

Activity directions
Sight words are tricky because you can't sound them out. You have to remember what they look like. Find the word.

Teaching moment
- ✔ The pace between presentation of words should be rapid to keep the student motivated.
- ✔ Use the sight word flashcards to provide extra practice of sight word reading. Provide up to 4 response options for students to choose from.
- ✔ If the student chooses an incorrect response, give a reminder to not guess but to wait and you will help. You can also add to the directions, **If you are not sure of the answer, don't guess. Wait for me to help you.**

Cue	Student's independent response	If student needs help
Find the word are.	Finds the word are.	For Lesson 1, if no response or an incorrect response, physically guide the student to find are. Say, **This is are.** For Lessons 2–5, if no response after 4 seconds or an incorrect response, model finding the word and say, **This is are. You touch it.** Physically guide the student to find the word if needed.

Repeat with the <u>new sight words</u> and <u>review sight words</u>, words required for reading the story for this level; see **Level 8 Content** on p. 97.

ERSB Teacher's Guide ■ Level 8

103

Reading text / Comprehension questions

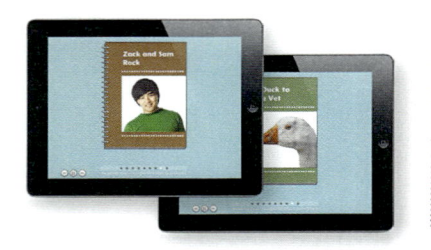

what
rock
not
run

Teaching moment

✔ In this level, the student is told to read the text silently in his or her head.

✔ One page of the story is read during each lesson, followed by comprehension questions. If repeating this level, Story 2 will be used in the software.

✔ Use **Champion Reader 2** to show the title of the story and to point out the characters. It can also be used to give students additional reading practice. The comprehension questions that could be asked if not using the software and possible response options are listed in the **Level 8 Content** on p. 97. Write response options on the dry-erase board for students to read.

Objective 7 / Objective 8
Read connected text. / Answer comprehension questions about connected text.

Prompting
Least intrusive prompt

Activity directions
Now that you know how to read words, you can read a page from the story. Today you will read about Zack and Sam.

Cue	Student's independent response	If student needs help
Say, **Read this story silently in your head.** Do not read to the student or point to the words.	Reads the sentences silently.	Reads the sentences silently.
After the student silently reads the sentences on the page, say, **Let's answer some questions about the story. What does Zack like to do?**	Chooses the word rock.	If no response or an incorrect response, say, **Read this sentence again**. Point to each word in the sentence that has the answer, then ask the question again. If still no response or an incorrect response, read the sentence with the answer to the student, **Zack likes to rock**. Then ask, **What does Zack like to do?** If still no response or an incorrect response, physically guide the student to find rock, and say, **rock. Zack likes to rock**.

Repeat with the content for each lesson; see **Level 8 Content** on p. 97.

Closing/Writing activity

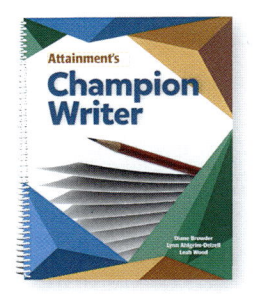

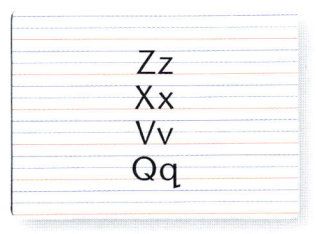

Objective 9
Write responses to activities that review level objectives.

Activity directions
Your lesson is over. GREAT reading today! Let's complete a page in your Champion Writer.

Teaching moment
✔ Some students may need adaptations to complete the writing page; see p. 20 for ideas.

✔ Use the dry-erase board (lined side) and a water-based marker to give the student additional practice in writing/forming the uppercase and lowercase letters.

LEVEL 9

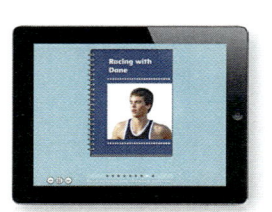

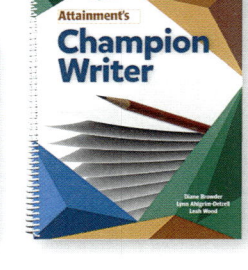

Focus
Long ā, soft c, silent e

Phonemic awareness
- Blend sounds for VCe and CVCe words
- Segment first sounds in words
- Segment sounds in CVC and CVCe words

Phonics
- Sounds /eɪ/ and /s/ corresponding to graphemes ā and c (soft c)
- Decode VCe, CVC, and CVCe words

Sight words
brother, for, hello, say, says, school, so, with, you

Generalization words
gaze, hate, Lane, sake, same

Connected text
- ATOS level = .9
- Lexile level = 140L

Objectives

1 Identify ā and c (soft c) when given the sounds /eɪ/ and /s/.

2 Blend sounds to form VCe and CVCe words.

3 Segment the first and middle sounds in words.

4 Segment the sounds in CVC and CVCe words.

5 Decode VCe, CVC, and CVCe words and identify their meanings.

6 Read 9 new sight words.

7 Read connected text.

8 Answer comprehension questions about connected text.

9 Write responses to activities that review level objectives.

Teaching notes
This level introduces students to the concept of vowels and that long vowels say their name. The level begins with long a; long ā is marked with a line above it. Silent e is introduced in this level as a letter that is not spoken but makes the vowel in the word long. Finally, soft c is introduced. Soft c says /s/ so it is placed in the corner of the s tile.

In Segmenting I, students now begin to listen for middle sounds, a more difficult skill. Uppercase letters no longer appear on the letter tiles in the software.

Note: From this level forward, for the first six activities, the cue and the prompts in the lesson plans represent those used for time delay at 4 seconds. Refer to the software (or to earlier levels) for demonstrations and prompts using time delay of 0 seconds for Lesson 1.

Level 9 Content

	Lesson 1	Lesson 2	Lesson 3	Lesson 4	Lesson 5
Letter/sound identification	**New:** long ā, soft c (added to the s tile) **Review:** Xx/ks, Vv, Zz/zz/s, Qqᵘ/kw				
Blending	face, race, fate, kale, cape, pack	**Optional demo:** face Jane, Sam, ace, dame, Dane	**Optional demo:** face take, cap, sock, cape, lace	**Optional demo:** face made, Jane, Jan, race, wave	**Optional demo:** made dame, ace, take, kale, face
Segmenting I	Listen for the *middle* sound in each word. race, sit, Dane, ram, tape, icy	Listen for the *middle* sound in each word. **Optional demo:** race wave, mat, Jake, pace, pit	Listen for the *first* sound in each word. **Optional demo:** ace angel, city, van, zip, ick	Listen for the *first* sound in each word. **Optional demo:** ace cereal, acorn, zip, center, vest	Listen for the *middle* sound in each word. **Optional demo:** race wave, rack, Dane, icy, ram
Segmenting II	face, cake, Dane, mace, tape, mack	**Optional demo:** face cape, race, jack, rock, lace	**Optional demo:** face wave, race, pack, Jane, win	**Optional demo:** face cape, Dane, cap, pick, mace	**Optional demo:** face rock, cape, pick, lock, wave
Decoding	cane, ape, rake, face, Jake, wave	**Optional demo:** cane race, gate, tape, Dane, van	**Optional demo:** cane wave, Jane, lace, Jake, lock	**Optional demo:** cane Dane, face, cake, cape, cap	**Optional demo:** cane tape, rake, cap, wave, cape
Sight Words	**New:** brother, for, hello, say, says, school, so, with, you **Review:** as, go, I, to				
Comprehension questions (correct response in **bold**)	What does Dane like to do? (**race**, gaze, icy, rack) What does Dane hit? (cape, **tape**, tin, six)	Who does Mom want Dane to take? (Tim, **Jake**, Jane, Eat) How old is Jake? (out, ten, sun, **six**)	Who did Mom say can race with Dane? (**Jake**, Dane, Rake, Kim) What name does Mom yell? (**Dane**, Jon, Jim, Tim)	What does Jake have on? (**cape**, pat, cap, that) Who is Dane's friend? (Pat, Jim, **Jane**, Kim) What does Jane like? (cane, mad, **cape**, pig)	Who said, "Let me see you race"? (**Jane**, Dane, Jake, Boat) Who is with Jake? (Kim, **Jane**, Dane, Jon) What does Dane do? (face, eat, **race**, school) Who waved at Jake and Jane? (Tim, **Dane**, Jon, Jane)

Letter/sound identification

ā
c

Objective 1
Identify ā and c (soft c) when given the sounds /eɪ/ and /s/.
Pronunciation: /eɪ/ as in ape, /æ/ as in am

Prompting
- Lesson 1: Time delay 0 seconds
- Lessons 2–5: Time delay 4 seconds

Activity directions
I'll say a sound, and you find the letter that makes that sound.

Teaching moment

✓ Introduce the concept of vowels. Say, **The letters a, e, i, o, and u are called vowels. Vowels can make different sounds. You already learned that a says /æ/. Today, you will see ā with a line above it.** Point to the tile on the software screen showing ā or write and point to it on the dry-erase board. **The line means a says its name, /eɪ/. That's called a long vowel. Long vowels say their name.**

✓ Also introduce the soft c. Point to the tile on the software screen showing c on the corner of the s tile or write and point to it on the dry-erase board. Say, **Notice the c on the s tile. Sometimes c says /s/ like s. You already know the /s/ sound.**

✓ If the student chooses an incorrect response, give a reminder to not guess but to wait and you will help. You can also add to the directions, **If you are not sure of the answer, don't guess. Wait for me to help you.**

✓ Note: From this level forward, for the first six activities, the cue and the prompts in the lesson plans represent those used for time delay at 4 seconds. Refer to the software (or to earlier levels) for demonstrations and prompts using time delay of 0 seconds for Lesson 1.

Cue	Student's independent response	If student needs help
What letter says /eɪ/?	Finds the letter ā to make the /eɪ/ sound.	If no response after 4 seconds or an incorrect response, model finding the letter/sound, and continue pointing to it until the student finds it. If needed, physically guide the student to find the letter and say, **This is /eɪ/. You touch it.**

Repeat with soft c, and Level 8 review: Zz/z/zz/s, Xx/x/ks, Vv/v, and Qqᵘ/kw.

Blending

Objective 2
Blend sounds to form VCe and CVCe words.
Pronunciation: /eɪ/ as in ape, /ʌ/ as in up

Prompting
- Lesson 1: Time delay 0 seconds
- Lessons 2–5: Time delay 4 seconds

Activity directions
I'll say some sounds. You blend the sounds together and find the word they make.

Teaching moment

✔ Introduce silent e. Point to the word *face* on the software screen or write and point to it on the dry-erase board. Say, **Notice this word has an e at the end. You don't say the e; it is silent. Silent e makes the vowel a say its name: /eɪ/. This word says face.**

✔ Prolong or emphasize the sounds at the beginning, middle, or end to help the student identify the word. Note that when you segment the sounds in words, do not add additional sounds to consonants (e.g., for d, say, /d/ not /dʌ/.

✔ Provide a one-second pause between the sounds to help students process them.

✔ **Note:** From this level forward, for the first six activities, the cue and the prompts in the lesson plans represent those used for time delay at 4 seconds. Refer to the software (or to earlier levels) for demonstrations and prompts using time delay of 0 seconds for Lesson 1.

Cue	Student's independent response	If student needs help
/f/ /eɪ/ /s/. **Which word am I saying?**	Finds the word face.	If no response after 4 seconds or an incorrect response, model finding the word and say, **This is face. You touch it.** Continue pointing to it until the student finds it. If needed, physically guide the student to find the word.

Repeat with the content for each lesson; see **Level 9 Content** on p. 107.

ERSB Teacher's Guide ■ Level 9

Segmenting I

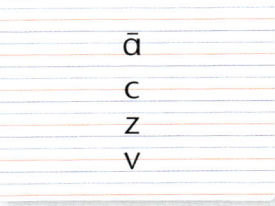

Objective 3
Segment the first and middle sounds in words.
Pronunciation: /eɪ/ as in <u>a</u>pe

Prompting
- Lesson 1: Time delay 0 seconds
- Lessons 2–5: Time delay 4 seconds

Activity directions
I'll say a word. You show me the first/middle sound you hear in the word.

Teaching moment
✔ Up to this level, students listened for the initial sound in words. Level 9 introduces listening for the middle sound. To make it easier for the student, emphasize or prolong the middle sound in the word.

✔ Pause for one second between the direction ("What is the first/middle sound in") and the target word to prepare the student for the target word.

✔ To practice without the software, provide more words with /eɪ/ in the beginning or middle of words and soft c (/s/) at the beginning or end of words.

✔ If the student chooses an incorrect response, give a reminder to not guess but to wait and you will help. You can also add to the directions, **If you are not sure of the answer, don't guess. Wait for me to help you.**

✔ **Note:** From this level forward, for the first six activities, the cue and the prompts in the lesson plans represent those used for time delay at 4 seconds. Refer to the software (or to earlier levels) for demonstrations and prompts using time delay of 0 seconds.

Cue	Student's independent response	If student needs help
(Lessons 1, 2, and 5) **What is the middle sound in <u>race</u>?**	Finds <u>ā</u> to say /eɪ/.	If no response after 4 seconds or an incorrect response, model finding <u>ā</u>. Say, **The middle sound is /eɪ/. You touch it.** If needed, physically guide the student to find /eɪ/.
(Lessons 3 and 4) **What is the first sound in <u>ace</u>?**	Finds <u>ā</u> to say /eɪ/.	If no response after 4 seconds or an incorrect response, model finding <u>ā</u>. Say, **The first sound is /eɪ/. You touch it.** If needed, physically guide the student to find /eɪ/.

Repeat with the <u>content</u> for each lesson; see **Level 9 Content** on p. 107.

Segmenting II

f | a | ce

Objective 4
Segment the sounds in CVC and CVCe words.
Pronunciation: /eɪ/ as in <u>a</u>pe

Prompting
- Lesson 1: Time delay 0 seconds
- Lessons 2–5: Time delay 4 seconds

Activity directions
Use the sounds you learned to sound out some words. I'll say a word, and you sound it out.

Teaching moment

✔ To help the student segment all of the sounds in the word, hold up a finger for each sound the student needs to find. Remember to hold up fingers for sounds, not letters (e.g., the word *face* has 3 sounds but 4 letters).

✔ If the student needs help, divide the dry-erase board into sections based on the number of sounds in the word. Have the student sound out each sound one at a time while you write the letter/sound the student chooses on the software screen.

✔ If the student makes an error on even one sound, have the student listen as you segment **all** the sounds in the word in the correct sequence. Then restate to touch the sounds in the word.

✔ **Note:** From this level forward, for the first six activities, the cue and the prompts in the lesson plans represent those used for time delay at 4 seconds. Refer to the software (or to earlier levels) for demonstrations and prompts using time delay of 0 seconds for Lesson 1.

Cue	Student's independent response	If student needs help
Sound out the word <u>face</u>.	Touches <u>f</u>, <u>a</u>, and <u>c</u> for the sounds /<u>f</u>/, /<u>eɪ</u>/, and /<u>s</u>/.	If no response after 4 seconds or an incorrect response, say, **Listen, /<u>f</u>/ /<u>eɪ</u>/ /<u>s</u>/. Touch the sounds in <u>face</u>.** If still no response or an incorrect response, model segmenting the word by touching each letter and saying each sound. Then say, **Your turn. Touch the sounds in <u>face</u>.** If still no response or an incorrect response, say, **Let's touch the sounds in <u>face</u>.** Then physically guide the student to touch each sound while you say it.

Repeat with the <u>content</u> for each lesson; see **Level 9 Content** on p. 107.

Decoding

Objective 5
Decode VCe, CVC, and CVCe words and identify their meanings.
Pronunciation: /eɪ/ as in <u>a</u>pe

Prompting
- Lesson 1: Time delay 0 seconds
- Lessons 2–5: Time delay 4 seconds

Activity directions
Now, use the sounds and letters you learned to read a word and find its picture.

> **Teaching moment**
>
> ✔ Be certain the student knows the name of each picture.
>
> ✔ Students may need you to continue to demonstrate how to sound out/decode the word. Point to the word, sound it out and prolong (if possible) each letter sound as you say it. Then blend the sounds, say the word, and find the picture representing it. Be sure to follow this demonstration with independent responding by the student.
>
> ✔ **Note:** From this level forward, for the first six activities, the cue and the prompts in the lesson plans represent those used for time delay at 4 seconds. Refer to the software (or to earlier levels) for demonstrations and prompts using time delay of 0 seconds for Lesson 1.

Cue	Student's independent response	If student needs help
First, let's hear each picture's name.	Listens as each picture is named.	
Say, **Your turn. Read the word and find the picture.**	Finds the picture of <u>cane</u>.	If no response after 4 seconds, point to the word and say, **This is /<u>k</u>/ /<u>eɪ</u>/ /<u>n</u>/.** Then touch the picture and say, **Here is <u>cane</u>. Now you read <u>cane</u> and find the picture.** Physically guide the student's hand if needed. If an incorrect response, point to the letters in the word as you say, **This says <u>cane</u>.** Touch the picture and say, **Here is the picture of <u>cane</u>.** Remove your finger and say, **Now you read <u>cane</u> and find the picture.** Physically guide the student's hand if needed.

Repeat with the <u>content</u> for each lesson; see **Level 9 Content** on p. 107.

Sight words

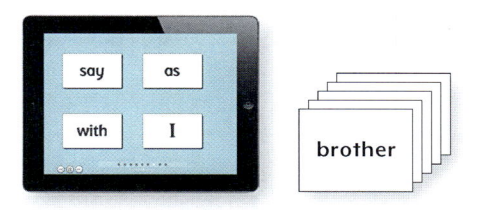

Objective 6
Read 9 new sight words.

Prompting
- Lesson 1: Time delay 0 seconds
- Lessons 2–5: Time delay 4 seconds

Activity directions
Sight words are tricky because you can't sound them out. You have to remember what they look like. Find the word.

Teaching moment
✔ The pace between the presentation of words should be rapid to keep the student motivated.

✔ Use the sight word flashcards to provide extra practice of sight word reading. Provide up to 4 response options for students to choose from.

✔ If the student chooses an incorrect response, give a reminder to not guess but to wait and you will help. You can also add to the directions, **If you are not sure of the answer, don't guess. Wait for me to help you.**

✔ **Note:** From this level forward, for the first six activities, the cue and the prompts in the lesson plans represent those used for time delay at 4 seconds. Refer to the software (or to earlier levels) for demonstrations and prompts using time delay of 0 seconds for Lesson 1.

Cue	Student's independent response	If student needs help
Find the word brother.	Finds the word brother.	If no response after 4 seconds or an incorrect response, model finding the word and say, **This is brother. You touch it.** Physically guide the student to find the word if needed.

Repeat with the new sight words and review sight words, words required for reading the story for this level; see **Level 9 Content** on p. 107.

ERSB Teacher's Guide ■ Level 9

Reading text / Comprehension questions

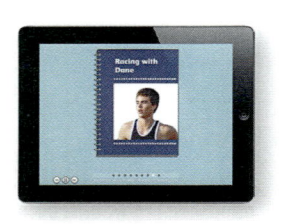

race
gaze
icy
rack

Objective 7 / Objective 8
Read connected text. / Answer comprehension questions about connected text.

Prompting
Least intrusive prompt

Activity directions
Now that you know how to read words, you can read a page from the story. Today you will read about Dane and his brother Jake.

Teaching moment
✔ One page of the story is read during each lesson, followed by the comprehension questions. This is the first level where only one story is provided for reading connected text.

✔ Use **Champion Reader 1** to show the title of the story and to point out the characters. It can also be used to give students additional reading practice. The comprehension questions that could be asked if not using the software and possible response options are listed in the **Level 9 Content** on p. 107. Write response options on the dry-erase board for students to read.

Cue	Student's independent response	If student needs help
Say, **Read this story silently in your head.** Do not read to the student or point to the words.	Reads the sentences silently.	

(Table continues)

ERSB Teacher's Guide ■ Level 9

Cue	Student's independent response	If student needs help
After the student silently reads the sentences on the page, say, **Let's answer some questions about the story. What does Dane like to do?**	Chooses the word <u>race</u>.	If no response or an incorrect response, say, **Read this sentence again.** Point to each word in the sentence that has the answer, then ask the question again.
		If still no response or an incorrect response, read the sentence with the answer to the student, **I like to race for my school.** Then ask, **What does Dane like to do?**
		If still no response or an incorrect response, physically guide the student to find <u>race</u>, and say, **Race. Dane likes to race for his school.**

Repeat with the <u>content</u> for each lesson; see **Level 9 Content** on p. 107.

Closing /Writing activity

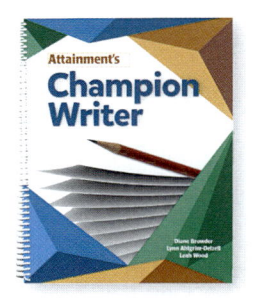

Objective 9
Write responses to activities that review level objectives.

Activity directions
Your lesson is over. GREAT reading today! Let's complete a page in your Champion Writer.

Teaching moment
✔ In order to keep the lesson from becoming too long, consider completing the writing activity at another time of the day.

✔ Some students may need adaptations to complete the writing page in **Champion Writer**; see p. 20 for ideas.

✔ Use the dry-erase board and an erasable marker to give the student practice in writing/forming sight words and words containing the letter/sounds of this level.

ERSB Teacher's Guide ■ Level 9

LEVEL 10

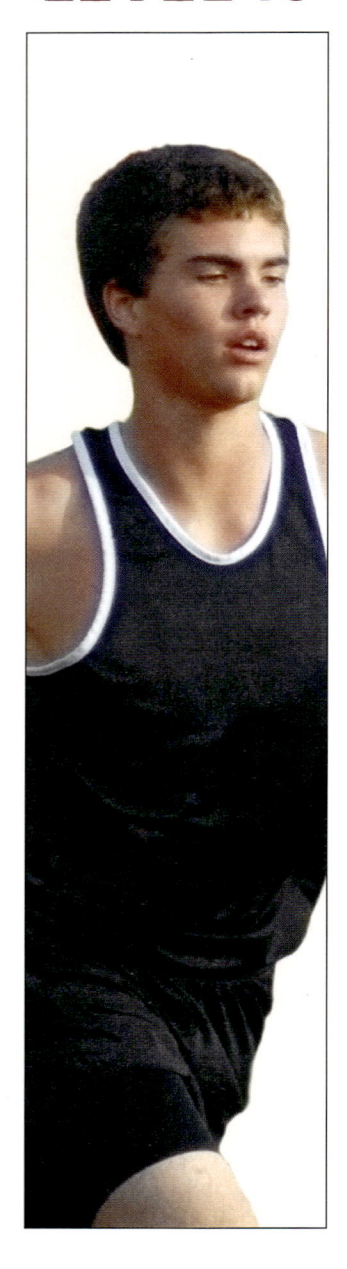

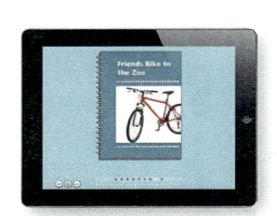

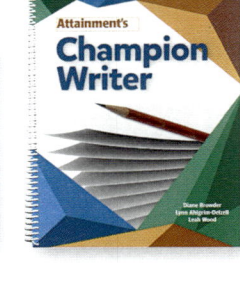

Focus
Long ī, soft g

Phonemic awareness
- Blend sounds for CVC, CVCe, and CVCC words
- Segment first, middle, and last sounds in words
- Segment sounds in CVC and CVCe words

Phonics
- Sounds /aɪ/ and /dʒ/ corresponding to graphemes ī and g (soft g)
- Decode CVC, CVCe, and CVCC words

Sight words
friends, funny, into, jump, jumps, look, then, there, this, zoo

Generalization words
ate, bikes, ride

Connected text
- ATOS level = 1.5
- Lexile level = 280L

Objectives
1. Identify ī and g (soft g) when given the sounds /aɪ/ and /dʒ/.
2. Blend sounds to form CVC, CVCe, and CVCC words.
3. Segment the first, middle, and last sounds in words.
4. Segment the sounds in CVC and CVCe words.
5. Decode CVC, CVCe, and CVCC words and identify their meanings.
6. Read 10 new sight words.
7. Read connected text.
8. Answer comprehension questions about connected text.
9. Write responses to activities that review level objectives.

Teaching notes
This level continues introducing students to long vowels. Students have learned that long vowels say their name. This level introduces long ī and how silent e makes the vowel long. Soft g is also introduced. Soft g says /dʒ/, the same sound as j, so g is placed in the corner of the j tile.

ERSB Teacher's Guide ■ Level 10

Level 10 Content

	Lesson 1	Lesson 2	Lesson 3	Lesson 4	Lesson 5
Letter/sound identification	**New:** long ī, soft g (on the j tile) **Review:** long ā, soft c (on the s tile)				
Blending	time, gels, Mike, line, kite, cane	**Optional demo:** time cage, bike, hide, page, hid	**Optional demo:** time side, page, pick, gel, pike	**Optional demo:** time wage, bike, kite, kit, cage	**Optional demo:** time gel, cane, side, cage, bike
Segmenting I	Listen for the *last* sound in each word: cage, lie, wage, pie, page, race	Listen for the *middle* sound in each word: **Optional demo:** nice page, hide, lip, like, made	Listen for the *first* sound in each word: **Optional demo:** ice gem, gentle, iPad, acorn, zoo	Listen for the *last* sound in each word: **Optional demo:** stage lace, huge, wedge, made, pie	Listen for the *last* sound in each word: **Optional demo:** huge lie, cage, tie, stage, price
Segmenting II	time, cape, cage, bite, dine, page	**Optional demo:** time page, fine, Mike, fin, bike	**Optional demo:** time pin, bite, rage, pine, cage	**Optional demo:** time line, cage, Mike, like, lick	**Optional demo:** time Mike, fine, gel, bike, cage
Decoding	bike, pipe, lime, cage, tap, page	**Optional demo:** bike lake, Gels, huge, lid, Mike	**Optional demo:** bike dive, bite, cage, rake, kit	**Optional demo:** bike Gels, bag, bite, page, hive	**Optional demo:** bike Gels, lid, Mike, kite, cage
Sight Words	**New:** friends, funny, into, jump, jumps, look, then, there, this, zoo **Review:** eat, have, hello, she, will, with, friend				
Comprehension questions (correct response in **bold**)	Where did the friends go? (like, school, **zoo**, zip) How do they get to the zoo? (zoo, **bikes**, bed, cars) Who went with Dane and Jane? (**Mike**, Tim, Mim, Gus)	Where is the ape? (**cage**, huge, cat, for) Who is funny? (cape, age, cat, **ape**) What does the ape have on? (**hat**, bit, can, gel)	Where do they want to eat? (Mels, **Gels**, Go, Does) What do they eat at Gels? (eat, **gel**, get, red) What size was the boy's bite? (bag, bit, not, **big**)	What does Dane want to go back to see? (**ape**, kite, bike, cat) What does Dane still have? (go, eat, **gel**, gem) Who does Dane give red gel to? (Mike, **Ape**, Kite, App)	Who yelled at Dane? (**Man**, Jane, Dane, More) The man said the ape is not what? (**tame**, to, race, came) What did the friends make Dane? (soon, **safe**, page, sad)

Letter/sound identification

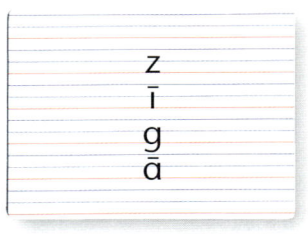

Objective 1
Identify long ī and g (soft g) when given the sounds /aɪ/ and /dʒ/.
Pronunciation: /aɪ/ as in m<u>i</u>ce, /dʒ/ as in pa<u>g</u>e, /ɪ/ as in b<u>i</u>n

Prompting
- Lesson 1: Time delay 0 seconds
- Lessons 2–5: Time delay 4 seconds

Activity directions
I'll say a sound, and you find the letter that makes that sound.

Teaching moment
✔ Review the concept of vowels. Say, **The letters a, e, i, o, and u are called vowels. Vowels can make different sounds. You already learned that i says /ɪ/.** Point to the tile on the software screen showing ī or write and point to it on the dry-erase board. **See ī with a line above it. The line means i says its name, /aɪ/. Remember, that's called a long vowel. Long vowels say their names.**

✔ Also introduce the soft g. Point to the tile on the software screen showing g on the corner of the j tile or write and point to it on the dry-erase board. Say, Say, **Notice the g on the j tile. Sometimes g says /dʒ/ like j.**

✔ If the student chooses an incorrect response, give a reminder to not guess but to wait and you will help. You can also add to the directions, **If you are not sure of the answer, don't guess. Wait for me to help you.**

Cue	Student's independent response	If student needs help
What letter says /aɪ/?	Finds the letter ī to make the /aɪ/ sound.	If no response after 4 seconds or an incorrect response, model finding the letter/sound, and continue pointing to it until the student finds it. If needed, physically guide the student to find the letter and say, **This is /aɪ/. You touch it.**

Repeat with soft g, and Level 9 review: ā and c (soft c).

ERSB Teacher's Guide ■ Level 10

Blending

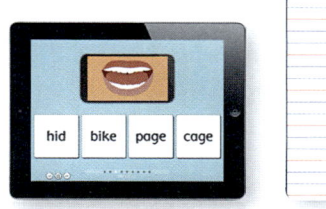

Objective 2
Blend sounds to form CVC, CVCe, and CVCC words.
Pronunciation: /aɪ/ as in m<u>i</u>ce, /ʌ/ as in <u>u</u>p

Prompting
- Lesson 1: Time delay 0 seconds
- Lessons 2–5: Time delay 4 seconds

Activity directions
I'll say some sounds. You blend the sounds together and find the word they make.

Teaching moment
✔ Review the silent e rule. Say, **Notice this word has an e at the end. You don't say the e; it is silent. Silent e makes the vowel i say its name: /aɪ/.**

✔ Prolong or emphasize the sounds at the beginning, middle, or end to help the student identify the word. Note that when you segment the sounds in words, do not add additional sounds to consonants (e.g., for t, say, /t/ not /tʌ/.

✔ Provide a one-second pause between the sounds to help the student process them.

Cue	Student's independent response	If student needs help
/t/ /aɪ/ /m/. Which word am I saying?	Finds the word <u>time</u>.	If no response after 4 seconds or an incorrect response, model finding the word and say, **This is <u>time</u>. You touch it.** Continue pointing to it until the student finds it. If needed, physically guide the student to find the word.

Repeat with the <u>content</u> for each lesson; see **Level 10 Content** on p. 117.

ERSB Teacher's Guide ■ **Level 10**

Segmenting I

Objective 3
Segment the first, middle, and last sounds in words.
Pronunciation: /aɪ/ as in m<u>i</u>ce, /ʤ/ as in pa<u>g</u>e

Prompting
- Lesson 1: Time delay 0 seconds
- Lessons 2–5: Time delay 4 seconds

Activity directions
I'll say a word. You show me the first/middle/last sound you hear in the word.

Teaching moment

✔ Up to Level 8, students listened for the initial sound in words. Level 9 introduced listening for the middle sound. Level 10 introduces listening for the last sound in words. To make it easier for the student, emphasize or prolong the last sound in the word when appropriate.

✔ Pause for one second between the direction ("What is the first/middle/last sound in") and the target word to prepare the student for the target word.

✔ If the student chooses an incorrect response, give a reminder to not guess but to wait and you will help. You can also add to the directions, **If you are not sure of the answer, don't guess. Wait for me to help you.**

Cue	Student's independent response	If student needs help
(Lesson 1, 4, and 5) **What is the last sound in <u>cage</u>?**	Activates the <u>g</u> to say /ʤ/.	If no response after 4 seconds or an incorrect response, model finding <u>g</u>. Say, **The last sound is /ʤ/. You touch it.** If needed, physically guide the student to find /ʤ/.
(Lesson 2) **What is the middle sound in <u>nice</u>?**	Activates the <u>ī</u> to say /aɪ/.	If no response after 4 seconds or an incorrect response, model finding <u>ī</u>. Say, **The middle sound is /aɪ/. You touch it.** If needed, physically guide the student to find /aɪ/.
(Lesson 3) **What is the first sound in <u>ice</u>?**	Activates the <u>ī</u> to say /aɪ/.	If no response after 4 seconds or an incorrect response, model finding <u>ī</u>. Say, **The first sound is /aɪ/. You touch it.** If needed, physically guide the student to find /aɪ/.

Repeat with the <u>content</u> for each lesson; see **Level 10 Content** on p. 117.

Segmenting II

t	i	me

Objective 4
Segment the sounds in CVC and CVCe words and identify their meanings.
Pronunciation: /aɪ/ as in m<u>i</u>ce

Prompting
- Lesson 1: Time delay 0 seconds
- Lessons 2–5: Time delay 4 seconds

Activity directions
Use the sounds you learned to sound out some words. I'll say a word, and you sound it out.

Teaching moment

✔ To help the student segment all of the sounds in the word, hold up a finger for each sound the student needs to find. Remember to hold up fingers for sounds, not letters (e.g., the word *time* has 3 sounds but 4 letters; the word *gel* has 3 sounds and 3 letters).

✔ Or if the student needs help, divide the dry-erase board into sections based on the number of sounds in the word. Have the student sound out the word by choosing one sound at a time on the software screen, while you write the letter/sound the student chooses on the dry-erase board (one sound per section).

✔ If the student chooses an incorrect response, give a reminder to not guess but to wait and you will help. Add to the directions, **If you are not sure of the answer, don't guess. Wait for me to help you.**

✔ If the student makes an error on even one sound, have the student listen as you segment **all** the sounds in the word in the correct sequence. Then restate to touch the sounds in the word.

Cue	Student's independent response	If student needs help
Sound out the word <u>time</u>.	Touches <u>t</u>, <u>i</u>, and <u>m</u> for the sounds /t/, /aɪ/, and /m/.	If no response after 4 seconds or an incorrect response, say, **Listen, /<u>t</u>/ /<u>aɪ</u>/ /<u>m</u>/. Touch the sounds in <u>time</u>.**
		If still no response or an incorrect response, model segmenting the word by touching each letter and saying each sound. Then say, **Your turn. Touch the sounds in <u>time</u>.**
		If still no response or an incorrect response, say, **Let's touch the sounds in <u>time</u>.** Then physically guide the student to touch each sound while you say it.

Repeat with the <u>content</u> for each lesson; see **Level 10 Content** on p. 117.

ERSB Teacher's Guide ■ Level 10

Decoding

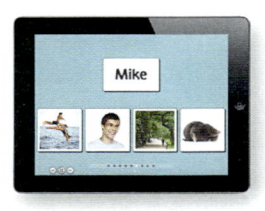

Objective 5
Decode CVC, CVCe, and CVCC words and identify their meanings.
Pronunciation: /aɪ/ as in m<u>i</u>ce

Prompting
- Lesson 1: Time delay 0 seconds
- Lessons 2–5: Time delay 4 seconds

Activity directions
Now, use the sounds and letters you learned to read a word and find its picture.

Teaching moment
✔ Be certain the student knows the name of each picture.

✔ Students may need you to continue to demonstrate how to sound out/decode the word. Point to the word, sound it out and prolong (if possible) each letter sound as you say it. Then blend the sounds, say the word, and find the picture representing it. Be sure to follow this demonstration with independent responding by the student.

Cue	Student's independent response	If student needs help
First, let's hear each picture's name.	Listens as each picture is named.	
Say, **Your turn. Read the word and find the picture.**	Finds the picture of <u>bike</u>.	If no response after 4 seconds, point to the word and say, **This is /b/ /aɪ/ /k/.** Then touch the picture and say, **Here is <u>bike</u>. Now you read <u>bike</u> and find the picture.** Physically guide the student's hand if needed.
		If an incorrect response, point to the letters in the word as you say, **This says <u>bike</u>.** Touch the picture and say, **Here is the picture of <u>bike</u>.** Remove your finger and say, **Now you read <u>bike</u> and find the picture.** Physically guide the student's hand if needed.

Repeat with the <u>content</u> for each lesson; see **Level 10 Content** on p. 117.

Sight words

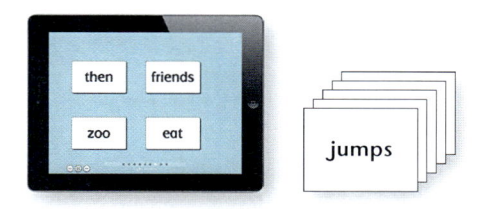

Objective 6
Read 10 new sight words.

Prompting
- Lesson 1: Time delay 0 seconds
- Lessons 2–5: Time delay 4 seconds

Activity directions
Sight words are tricky because you can't sound them out. You have to remember what they look like. **Find the word.**

Teaching moment
- ✔ The pace between the presentation of words is purposely rapid to keep the student motivated.
- ✔ Use the sight word flashcards to provide extra practice of sight word reading. Provide up to 4 response options for students to choose from.
- ✔ If the student chooses an incorrect response, give a reminder to not guess but to wait and you will help. You can also add to the directions, **If you are not sure of the answer, don't guess. Wait for me to help you.**

Cue	Student's independent response	If student needs help
Find the word jumps.	Finds the word jumps.	If no response after 4 seconds or an incorrect response, model finding the word and say, **This is jumps. You touch it.** Physically guide the student to find the word if needed.

Repeat with the new sight words and review sight words, words required for reading the story for this level; see **Level 10 Content** on p. 117.

ERSB Teacher's Guide ■ Level 10

Reading text / Comprehension questions

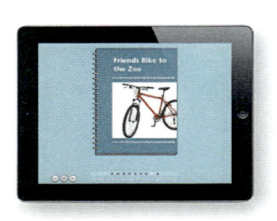

like
school
zoo
zip

Objective 7 / Objective 8
Read connected text. / Answer comprehension questions about connected text.

Prompting
Least intrusive prompt

Activity directions
Now that you know how to read words, you can read a page from the story.

Teaching moment
✔ One page of the story is read during each lesson, followed by the comprehension questions.

✔ Note that in this story, the word *gel* means gelato. Gel is used as a readable word in place of *gelato* (Italian ice cream).

✔ Use **Champion Reader 3** to show the title of the story and to point out the characters. It can also be used to give students additional reading practice. The comprehension questions that could be asked if not using the software and possible response options are listed in the **Level 10 Content** on p. 117. Write response options on the dry-erase board for students to read.

Cue	Student's independent response	If student needs help
Say, **Read this story silently in your head.** Do not read to the student or point to the words.	Reads the sentences silently.	

(Table continues)

Cue	Student's independent response	If student needs help
After the student silently reads the sentences on the page, say, **Let's answer some questions about the story. Where did the friends go?**	Chooses the word <u>zoo</u>.	If no response or an incorrect response, say, **Read this sentence again**. Point to each word in the sentence that has the answer, then ask the question again. If still no response or an incorrect response, read the sentence with the answer to the student, **Dane and Jane go to the zoo**. Then ask, **Where did the friends go?** If still no response or an incorrect response, physically guide the student to find <u>zoo</u>, and say, **Zoo. Dane and Jane go to the zoo**.

Repeat with the <u>content</u> for each lesson; see **Level 10 Content** on p. 117.

Closing / Writing activity

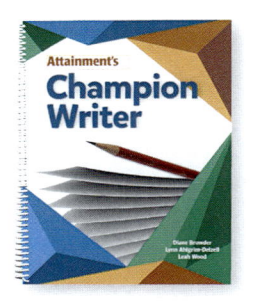

Objective 9
Write responses to activities that review level objectives.

Activity directions
Your lesson is over. GREAT reading today! Let's complete a page in your Champion Writer.

Teaching moment

✔ In order to keep the lesson from becoming too long, consider completing the writing activity at another time of the day.

✔ Some students may need adaptations to complete the writing page in **Champion Writer**; see p. 20 for ideas.

✔ Use the dry-erase board and an erasable marker to give the student practice in writing/forming sight words and words containing the letter/sounds of this level.

LEVEL 11

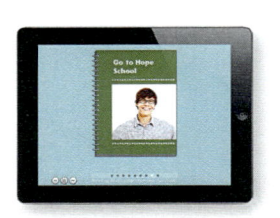

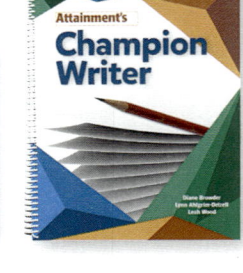

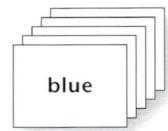

Focus
Long ō, long ū

Phonemic awareness
- Blend sounds for VCe, CVC, and CVCe words
- Segment first and middle sounds in words
- Segment sounds in CVC and CVCe words

Phonics
- Sounds /o/ and /ju/ corresponding to graphemes ō and ū
- Decode VCe, CVC, and CVCe words

Sight words
blue, cast, gives, here, new, now, wants

Generalization words
cope, mope, robe, tote, vote

Connected text
- ATOS level = .9
- Lexile level = 130L

Objectives
1 Identify ō and ū when given the sounds /o/ and /ju/.

2 Blend sounds to form VCe, CVC, and CVCe words.

3 Segment the first and middle sounds in words.

4 Segment the sounds in CVC and CVCe words.

5 Decode VCe, CVC, and CVCe words and identify their meanings.

6 Read 7 new sight words.

7 Read connected text.

8 Answer comprehension questions about connected text.

9 Write responses to activities that review level objectives.

Teaching notes
Level 11 continues to introduce students to long vowels. Students have learned that long vowels say their name. This level introduces long ū and long ō and reminds them that silent e makes the vowel long and makes the vowel say its name.

126

ERSB Teacher's Guide ■ Level 11

Level 11 Content

	Lesson 1	**Lesson 2**	**Lesson 3**	**Lesson 4**	**Lesson 5**
Letter/sound identification	**New:** long ō and long ū **Review:** soft g, long ī				
Blending	joke, mole, bone, mule, Mike, nope	Optional demo: joke nose, hope, cute, ape, coke	Optional demo: joke note, jute, nope, hop, time	Optional demo: joke jute, name, cut, hope, mute	Optional demo: mute nose, joke, cute, coke, nope
Segmenting I	Listen for the *first* sound in each word: ocean, use, open, ace, old, unity	Listen for the *middle* sound in each word: Optional demo: bone mute, pope, wave, nope, cute	Listen for the *first* sound in each word: Optional demo: old ache, uniform, open, icicle, ocean	Listen for the *middle* sound in each word: Optional demo: bone nope, time, cute, joke, bake	Listen for the *middle* sound in each word: Optional demo: bone pope, cute, nope, lime, joke
Segmenting II	cute, nope, name, bone, hole, mute	Optional demo: bone note, mute, joke, cot, fume	Optional demo: bone nose, mute, wave, hope, cut	Optional demo: bone jade, cute, fume, note, hop	Optional demo: bone mute, cut, wave, cute, hope
Decoding	fume, rope, mule, note, cube, nose	Optional demo: jute coke, note, time, mule, ape	Optional demo: jute Mike, mole, tub, note, mule	Optional demo: jute cube, time, home, note, cub	Optional demo: jute Mike, note, home, tub, mule
Sight Words	**New:** blue, cast, gives, here, new, now, wants **Review:** be, for, has, says, school, you				
Comprehension questions (correct response in **bold**)	To what school will Mike have to go? (Note, Hip, **Hope**, Pope) Who else got a note? (**Dane**, Dug, Jane, Tim) Will Dane go to Hope School? (will, **nope**, yup, hope)	Who does Mike give the note to? (dad, **Mom**, top, man) What school does Mike not like? (Joke, Mule, **Hope**, Him) Does Mike get a vote? (vote, **nope**, yup, pole)	What color is Mike's robe? (**blue**, robe, red, sock) What does Mike want to do? (mad, run, **mope**, be) Mom tells Mike, do not be what? (tube, **mule**, cast, robe)	What does Mike get on? (tub, **bus**, eat, bug) What does the girl do? (mule, **waves**, gives, with) What does the girl have on? (robe, cap, **cast**, has)	What does Jen let Mike use? (**pen**, pin, tube, ape) Is Mike still sad? (**nope**, nut, yup, mad) What helps Mike cope with his new school? (bug, **friend**, cast, fig)

Letter/sound identification

Objective 1
Identify ō and ū when given the sounds /o/ and /ju/.
Pronunciation: /o/ as in j<u>o</u>ke, /ju/ as in c<u>u</u>be

Prompting
- Lesson 1: Time delay 0 seconds
- Lessons 2–5: Time delay 4 seconds

Activity directions
I'll say a sound, and you find the letter that makes that sound.

Teaching moment
✔ Review the concept of vowels. Say, **The letters a, e, i, o, and u are called vowels. Remember that vowels can make different sounds.** Point to the tile on the software screen showing ō or write and point to it on the dry-erase board. **Today, see ō has a line above it. That line means o says its name, /o/.** Point to the tile on the software screen showing ū or write and point to it on the dry-erase board. **Here is ū with a line above it. That line means u says its name, /ju/. Long vowels say their name.**

✔ If the student chooses an incorrect response, give a reminder to not guess but to wait and you will help. You can also add to the directions, **If you are not sure of the answer, don't guess. Wait for me to help you.**

Cue	Student's independent response	If student needs help
What letter says /ju/?	Finds the letter ū to make the /ju/ sound.	If no response after 4 seconds or an incorrect response, model finding the letter/sound, and continue pointing to it until the student finds it. If needed, physically guide the student to find the letter and say, **This is /ju/. You touch it.**

Repeat with long ō, and Level 10 review: long ī and soft g.

Blending

Objective 2
Blend sounds to form VCe, CVC, and CVCe words.
Pronunciation: /o/ as in j<u>o</u>ke, /ju/ as in c<u>u</u>be

Prompting
- Lesson 1: Time delay 0 seconds
- Lessons 2–5: Time delay 4 seconds

Activity directions
I'll say some sounds. You blend the sounds together and find the word they make.

Teaching moment
✔ Review silent e. Point to the word *joke* on the software screen or write and point to it on the dry-erase board. Say, **Notice this word has an e at the end. You don't say the e; it is silent. Silent e makes the vowel say its name: /o/ or /ju/. This word says joke.**

✔ Prolong or emphasize the sounds at the beginning, middle, or end to help the student identify the word. Note that when you segment the sounds in words, do not add additional sounds to consonants (e.g., for k, say, /k/ not /kʌ/.

✔ Provide a one-second pause between the sounds to help students process them.

Cue	Student's independent response	If student needs help
/ʤ/ /o/ /k/. Which word am I saying?	Finds the word j<u>o</u>ke.	If no response after 4 seconds or an incorrect response, model finding the word and say, **This is j<u>o</u>ke. You touch it.** Continue pointing to it until the student finds it. If needed, physically guide the student to find the word.

Repeat with the <u>content</u> for each lesson; see **Level 11 Content** on p. 127.

Segmenting I

Objective 3
Segment the first and middle sounds in words.
Pronunciation: /o/ as in j<u>o</u>ke, /ju/ as in c<u>u</u>be

Prompting
- Lesson 1: Time delay 0 seconds
- Lessons 2–5: Time delay 4 seconds

Activity directions
I'll say a word. You show me the first/middle sound you hear in the word.

Teaching moment
✔ To practice without the software, provide more words with /o/ or /ju/ in the beginning or middle of words.

✔ Pause for one second between the direction ("What is the first/middle sound in") and the target word to prepare the student for the target word.

✔ To make it easier for the student, emphasize or prolong the target sound in the word.

✔ If the student chooses an incorrect response, give a reminder to not guess but to wait and you will help. You can also add to the directions, **If you are not sure of the answer, don't guess. Wait for me to help you.**

Cue	Student's independent response	If student needs help
(Lessons 1 and 3) **What is the first sound in <u>o</u>cean?**	Finds ō to say /o/.	If no response after 4 seconds or an incorrect response, model finding ō. Say, **The first sound is /o/. You touch it.** If needed, physically guide the student to find /o/.
(Lesson 2, 4, and 5) **What is the middle sound in m<u>u</u>te?**	Finds ū to say /ju/.	If no response after 4 seconds or an incorrect response, model finding ū. Say, **The first sound is /ju/. You touch it.** If needed, physically guide the student to find /ju/.

Repeat with the <u>content</u> for each lesson; see **Level 11 Content** on p. 127.

Segmenting II

Objective 4
Segment the sounds in CVC and CVCe words.
Pronunciation: /ju/ as in c<u>u</u>be

Prompting
- Lesson 1: Time delay 0 seconds
- Lessons 2–5: Time delay 4 seconds

Activity directions
Use the sounds you learned to sound out some words. I'll say a word, and you sound it out.

Teaching moment

✔ To help the student segment all of the sounds in the word, hold up a finger for each sound the student needs to find. Remember to hold up fingers for sounds, not letters (e.g., the word *hole* has 3 sounds but 4 letters; the word *cube* has 3 sounds but 4 letters).

✔ Or if the student needs help, divide the dry-erase board into sections based on the number of sounds in the word. Have the student sound out the word by choosing one sound at a time on the software screen, while you write the letter/sound the student chooses on the dry-erase board (one sound per section).

✔ If the student chooses an incorrect response, give a reminder to not guess but to wait and you will help. Add to the directions, **If you are not sure of the answer, don't guess. Wait for me to help you.**

✔ If the student makes an error on even one sound, have the student listen as you segment **all** the sounds in the word in the correct sequence. Then restate to touch the sounds in the word.

Cue	Student's independent response	If student needs help
Sound out the word <u>cute</u>.	Touches <u>c</u>, <u>ū</u>, and <u>t</u> for the sounds /<u>k</u>/, /<u>ju</u>/, and /<u>t</u>/.	If no response after 4 seconds or an incorrect response, say, **Listen, /<u>k</u>/ /<u>ju</u>/ /<u>t</u>/. Touch the sounds in <u>cute</u>.**
		If still no response or an incorrect response, model segmenting the word by touching each letter and saying each sound. Then say, **Your turn. Touch the sounds in <u>cute</u>.**
		If still no response or an incorrect response, say, **Let's touch the sounds in <u>cute</u>.** Then physically guide the student to touch each sound while you say it.

Repeat with the <u>content</u> for each lesson; see **Level 11 Content** on p. 127.

Decoding

Objective 5
Decode VCe, CVC, and CVCe words and identify their meanings.
Pronunciation: /o/ as in j<u>o</u>ke

Prompting
- Lesson 1: Time delay 0 seconds
- Lessons 2–5: Time delay 4 seconds

Activity directions
Now, use the sounds and letters you learned to read a word and find its picture.

Teaching moment
✔ Be certain the student knows the name of each picture.

✔ Students may need you to continue to demonstrate how to sound out/decode the word. Point to the word, sound it out and prolong (if possible) each letter sound as you say it. Then blend the sounds, say the word, and find the picture representing it. Be sure to follow this demonstration with independent responding by the student.

Cue	Student's independent response	If student needs help
First, let's hear each picture's name.	Listens as each picture is named.	
Say, **Your turn. Read the word and find the picture.**	Finds the picture of <u>rope</u>.	If no response after 4 seconds, point to the word and say, **This is /r/ /o/ /p/**. Then touch the picture and say, **Here is <u>rope</u>. Now you read <u>rope</u> and find the picture.** Physically guide the student's hand if needed. If an incorrect response, point to the letters in the word as you say, **This says <u>rope</u>**. Touch the picture and say, **Here is the picture of <u>rope</u>**. Remove your finger and say, **Now you read <u>rope</u> and find the picture.** Physically guide the student's hand if needed.

Repeat with the <u>content</u> for each lesson; see **Level 11 Content** on p. 127.

Sight words

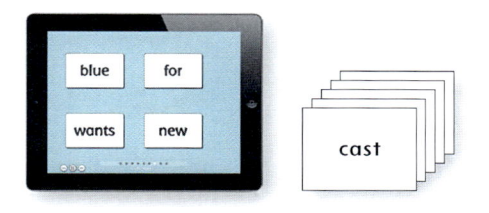

Objective 6
Read 7 new sight words.

Prompting
- Lesson 1: Time delay 0 seconds
- Lessons 2–5: Time delay 4 seconds

Activity directions
Sight words are tricky because you can't sound them out. You have to remember what they look like. **Find the word.**

Teaching moment
✔ The pace between the presentation of words is purposely rapid to keep the student motivated.

✔ Use the sight word flashcards to provide extra practice of sight word reading. Provide up to 4 response options for students to choose from.

✔ If the student chooses an incorrect response, give a reminder to not guess but to wait and you will help. You can also add to the directions, **If you are not sure of the answer, don't guess. Wait for me to help you.**

Cue	Student's independent response	If student needs help
Find the word cast.	Finds the word cast.	If no response after 4 seconds or an incorrect response, model finding the word and say, **This is cast. You touch it.** Physically guide the student to find the word if needed.

Repeat with the new sight words and review sight words, words required for reading the story for this level; see **Level 11 Content** on p. 127.

Reading text / Comprehension questions

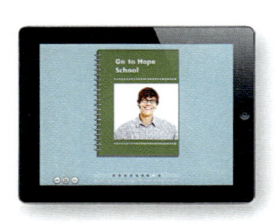

Objective 7 / Objective 8
Read connected text. / Answer comprehension questions about connected text.

Prompting
Least intrusive prompt

Activity directions
Now that you know how to read words, you can read a page from the story. Today you will read about Mike's new school.

Teaching moment
✔ One page of the story is read during each lesson, followed by the comprehension questions.

✔ Use **Champion Reader 3** to show the title of the story and to point out the characters. It can also be used to give students additional reading practice. The comprehension questions that could be asked if not using the software and possible response options are listed in the **Level 11 Content** on p. 127. Write response options on the dry-erase board for students to read.

Cue	Student's independent response	If student needs help
Say, **Read this story silently in your head.** Do not read to the student or point to the words.	Reads the sentences silently.	

(Table continues)

Cue	Student's independent response	If student needs help
After the student silently reads the sentences on the page, say, **Let's answer some questions about the story. To what school will Mike have to go?**	Chooses the word Hope.	If no response or an incorrect response, say, **Read this sentence again**. Point to each word in the sentence that has the answer, then ask the question again. If still no response or an incorrect response, read the sentence with the answer to the student, **It says he will go to a new school, Hope**. Then ask, **To what school will Mike have to go?** If still no response or an incorrect response, physically guide the student to find Hope, and say, **Hope. Mike will have to go to Hope School**.

Repeat with the content for each lesson; see **Level 11 Content** on p. 127.

Closing / Writing activity

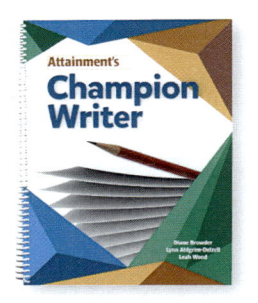

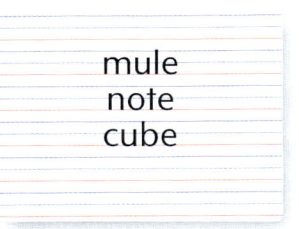

Objective 9
Write responses to activities that review level objectives.

Activity directions
Your lesson is over. GREAT reading today! Let's complete a page in your Champion Writer.

mule
note
cube

Teaching moment

✔ In order to keep the lesson from becoming too long, consider completing the writing activity at another time of the day.

✔ Some students may need adaptations to complete the writing page in **Champion Writer**; see p. 20 for ideas.

✔ Use the dry-erase board and an erasable marker to give the student practice in writing/forming sight words and words containing the letter/sounds of this level.

LEVEL 12

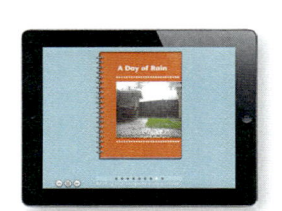

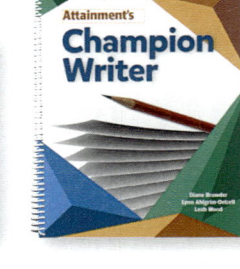

Focus
Long ē; digraphs—ee, ea, ai, ay

Phonemic awareness
- Blend sounds for CV, CVC, CVvC, and CVCe words
- Segment first, middle, and last sounds in words
- Segment sounds in CV, CVCe, and CVvC words

Phonics
- Sounds /i/ and /eɪ/ corresponding to graphemes ē, ee, ea, and ai, ay
- Decode CV, CVCe, and CVvC words

Sight words
about, all, bracelet, by, first, girls, next, was, yellow

Generalization words
beat, Jean, may, ray, read, reads, seat, way

Connected text
- ATOS level = 1.7
- Lexile level = 330L

Objectives
1. Identify ē, ee, ea and ai, ay when given the sounds /i/ and /eɪ/.
2. Blend sounds to form CV, CVC, CVvC, and CVCe words.
3. Segment the first, middle, and last sounds in words.
4. Segment the sounds in CV, CVC, CVCe, and CVvC words.
5. Decode CV, CVCe, and CVvC words and identify their meanings.
6. Read 9 new sight words.
7. Read connected text.
8. Answer comprehension questions about connected text.
9. Write responses to activities that review level objectives.

Teaching notes
This level introduces long ē and digraphs ee, ea, ai, and ay. A digraph is a sound represented by two letters (e.g., ee). Note that these digraphs are pronounced like long ē or long ā and therefore the letters are placed on the tiles for long ē (/i/) and long ā /eɪ/.

Level 12 Content

	Lesson 1	Lesson 2	Lesson 3	Lesson 4	Lesson 5
Letter/sound identification	**New:** long ē, ee, ea (on the long ē tile); ai, ay (on the long ā tile) **Review:** long ō, long ū				
Blending	rain, day, deal, peep, rope, bail	**Optional demo:** rain hay, lead, jeep, cube, pay	**Optional demo:** rain day, neat, deed, met, heal	**Optional demo:** rain lay, bead, keep, man, feel	**Optional demo:** rain met, jeep, bail, day, feel
Segmenting I	Listen for the *middle* sound in each word: fail, lame, bead, peep, hope, mule	Listen for the *first* sound in each word: **Optional demo:** aim open, acorn, over, use, ice, unicorn	Listen for the *middle* sound in each word: **Optional demo:** bait fail, maid, bead, beet, mope, cube	Listen for the *last* sound in each word: **Optional demo:** play say, may, snow, tree, bay, tray	Listen for the *middle* sound in each word: **Optional demo:** bait mope, cube, mice, cute, fail
Segmenting II	pain, day, seal, bee, home, mail	**Optional demo:** pail say, bead, jeep, cube, mean	**Optional demo:** pail rain, bead, need, pole, keep	**Optional demo:** pail lay, neat, jeep, made, bay	**Optional demo:** pail paid, neat, peep, bone, bee
Decoding	feet, lay, bead, jeep, bone, bait	**Optional demo:** feet day, meal, weed, mule, hay	**Optional demo:** feet hay, bead, bee, rope, pail	**Optional demo:** feet day, seal, peep, hose, rain	**Optional demo:** feet seal, meat, bead, bee, hose
Sight Words	**New:** about, all, bracelet, by, first, girls, next, was, yellow **Review:** are, blue, do, of, so, that, then, there, what				
Comprehension questions (correct response in **bold**)	What is beating on the pane? (beet, **rain**, pain, red) Who will lead the way to fun? (**Jane**, Dane, Gus, Jean	What is Jane reading about? (bike, read, **seal**, sail) What is Jean reading about? (jam, peep, **jeep**, pigs)	What does Jean like to do? (take, give, **bake**, bead) Who has the red and blue beads? (**Jane**, Dane, Jean, Mim)	What are the girls going to bake? (blue, **cake**, sake, good) Who will beat the cake? (Jean, Jake, **Jane**, Gus) Who will keep it neat? (Tim, **Jean**, Jane, Dane)	Who ate cake with Jean and Jane? (Don, **Dane**, Tim, Gus) What do the girls like to do? (bug, **read**, run, rain) What did Jean and Jane eat with Dane? (beet, bracelet, **cake**, rain)

Letter/sound identification

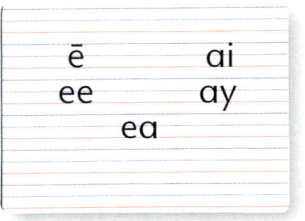

ē   ai
ee   ay
ea

Objective 1
Identify ē, ee, ea and ai, ay when given the sounds /i/ and /eɪ/.
Pronunciation: /i/ as in p<u>ee</u>p, /eɪ/ as in r<u>ai</u>n

Prompting
- Lesson 1: Time delay 0 seconds
- Lessons 2–5: Time delay 4 seconds

Activity directions
I'll say a sound, and you find the letter that makes that sound.

Teaching moment
✓ Introduce ē, ee, and ea. **Today we are going to read words that have sounds made by two vowels together.** Point to the long ē tile on the software screen showing the ee and ea in the corners or write and point to them on the dry-erase board. Tell students, **These vowels together—ee and ea—say /i/, like long ē.**

✓ Point to the long a tile on the software screen showing the ai and ay in the corners or write and point to them on the dry-erase board. Tell students, **These sounds together—ai and ay—say /eɪ/ like long ā.**

✓ If the student chooses an incorrect response, give a reminder to not guess but to wait and you will help. You can also add to the directions, **If you are not sure of the answer, don't guess. Wait for me to help you.**

Cue	Student's independent response	If student needs help
What letters says /<u>i</u>/?	Finds the letters ē, ee, ea to make the /<u>i</u>/ sound.	If no response after 4 seconds or an incorrect response, model finding the letter/sound, and continue pointing to it until the student finds it. If needed, physically guide the student to find the letter and say, **This is /<u>i</u>/. You touch it.**

Repeat with ai, ay, and Level 11 review: long ō and long ū.

Blending

Objective 2
Blend sounds to form CV, CVC, and CVvC, and CVCe words.
Pronunciation: /eɪ/ as in r<u>ai</u>n

Prompting
- Lesson 1: Time delay 0 seconds
- Lessons 2–5: Time delay 4 seconds

Activity directions
I'll say some sounds. You blend the sounds together and find the word they make.

Teaching moment
✔ Prolong or emphasize the sounds at the beginning, middle, or end to help the student identify the word. Note that when you segment the sounds in words, do not add additional sounds to consonants (e.g., for d, say, /d/ not /dʌ/.

✔ Provide a one-second pause between the sounds to help students process the sounds.

✔ Remind students, **Remember, ee and ea together make e say its name and ai and ay together make a say its name.**

✔ If the student chooses an incorrect response, give a reminder to not guess but to wait and you will help. You can also add to the directions, **If you are not sure of the answer, don't guess. Wait for me to help you.**

Cue	Student's independent response	If student needs help
/r/ /eɪ/ /n/. Which word am I saying?	Finds the word <u>rain</u>.	If no response after 4 seconds or an incorrect response, model finding the word and say, **This is <u>rain</u>. You touch it.** Continue pointing to it until the student finds it. If needed, physically guide the student to find the word.

Repeat with the <u>content</u> for each lesson; see **Level 12 Content** on p. 137.

Segmenting I

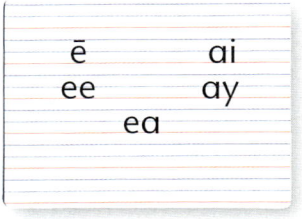

Objective 3
Segment the first, middle, and last sounds in words.
Pronunciation: /eɪ/ as in r<u>ai</u>n

Prompting
- Lesson 1: Time delay 0 seconds
- Lessons 2–5: Time delay 4 seconds

Activity directions
I'll say a word. You show me the first/middle/ending sound you hear in the word.

Teaching moment
✔ To practice without the software, provide more words with /i/ and /eɪ/ in the beginning, middle, or end of the word.

✔ Pause for one second between the direction ("What is the first/middle/last sound in") and the target word to prepare the student for the target word.

✔ If the student chooses an incorrect response, give a reminder to not guess but to wait and you will help. You can also add to the directions, **If you are not sure of the answer, don't guess. Wait for me to help you.**

✔ To make it easier for the student, emphasize or prolong the first, middle, or last sound.

Cue	Student's independent response	If student needs help
(Lessons 1, 3, and 5) **What is the middle sound in f<u>ai</u>l?**	Touches <u>ai</u> to say /<u>eɪ</u>/.	If no response after 4 seconds or an incorrect response, model finding <u>ai</u>. Say, **The middle sound is /eɪ/. You touch it.** If needed, physically guide the student to find /eɪ/.
(Lesson 2) **What is the first sound in <u>ai</u>m?**	Touches <u>ai</u> to say /<u>eɪ</u>/.	If no response after 4 seconds or an incorrect response, model finding <u>ai</u>. Say, **The first sound is /eɪ/. You touch it.** If needed, physically guide the student to find /eɪ/.
(Lesson 4) **What is the last sound in pl<u>ay</u>?**	Touches <u>ay</u> to say /<u>eɪ</u>/.	If no response after 4 seconds or an incorrect response, model finding <u>ay</u>. Say, **The ending sound is /eɪ/. You touch it.** If needed, physically guide the student to find /eɪ/.

Repeat with the <u>content</u> for each lesson; see **Level 12 Content** on p. 137.

Segmenting II

Objective 4
Segment the sounds in CV, CVC, CVCe, and CVvC words.
Pronunciation: /eɪ/ as in r<u>ai</u>n

Prompting
- Lesson 1: Time delay 0 seconds
- Lessons 2–5: Time delay 4 seconds

Activity directions
Use the sounds you learned to sound out some words. I'll say a word, and you sound it out.

Teaching moment

✔ To help the student segment all of the sounds in the word, hold up a finger for each sound the student needs to find. Remember to hold up fingers for sounds, not letters (e.g., the word *pain* has 3 sounds but 4 letters).

✔ Or if the student needs help, divide the dry-erase board into sections based on the number of sounds in the word. Have the student sound out the word by choosing one sound at a time on the software screen, while you write the letter/sound the student chooses on the dry-erase board (one sound per section).

✔ If the student chooses an incorrect response, give a reminder to not guess but to wait and you will help. Add to the directions, **If you are not sure of the answer, don't guess. Wait for me to help you.**

✔ If the student makes an error on even one sound, have the student listen as you segment **all** the sounds in the word in the correct sequence. Then restate to touch the sounds in the word.

Cue	Student's independent response	If student needs help
Sound out the word <u>pain</u>.	Touches <u>p</u>, <u>ai</u>, and <u>n</u> for the sounds /<u>p</u>/, /<u>eɪ</u>/, and /<u>n</u>/.	If no response after 4 seconds or an incorrect response, say, **Listen, /<u>p</u>/ /<u>eɪ</u>/ /<u>n</u>/. Touch the sounds in <u>pain</u>.** If still no response or an incorrect response, model segmenting the word by touching each letter and saying each sound. Then say, **Your turn. Touch the sounds in <u>pain</u>.** If still no response or an incorrect response, say, **Let's touch the sounds in <u>pain</u>.** Then physically guide the student to touch each sound while you say it.

Repeat with the <u>content</u> for each lesson; see **Level 12 Content** on p. 137.

Decoding

Objective 5
Decode CV, CVCe, and CVvC words and identify their meanings.
Pronunciation: /i/ as in p<u>ee</u>p

Prompting
- Lesson 1: Time delay 0 seconds
- Lessons 2–5: Time delay 4 seconds

Activity directions
Now, use the sounds and letters you learned to read a word and find its picture.

Teaching moment
✔ Be certain the student knows the name of each picture.

✔ Students may need you to continue to demonstrate how to sound out/decode the word. Point to the word, sound it out and prolong (if possible) each letter sound as you say it. Then blend the sounds by saying the word and find the picture representing it. Be sure to follow this demonstration with independent responding by the student.

Cue	Student's independent response	If student needs help
First, let's hear each picture's name.	Listens as each picture is named.	
Say, **Your turn. Read the word and find the picture.**	Finds the picture of <u>feet</u>.	If no response after 4 seconds, point to the word and say, **This is /<u>f</u>/ /<u>i</u>/ /<u>t</u>/.** Then touch the picture and say, **Here is a picture of <u>feet</u>. Now you read <u>feet</u> and find the picture.** Physically guide the student's hand if needed. If an incorrect response, point to the letters in the word as you say, **This says <u>feet</u>.** Touch the picture and say, **Here is the picture of <u>feet</u>.** Remove your finger and say, **Now you read <u>feet</u> and find the picture.** Physically guide the student's hand if needed.

Repeat with the <u>content</u> for each lesson; see **Level 12 Content** on p. 137.

Sight words

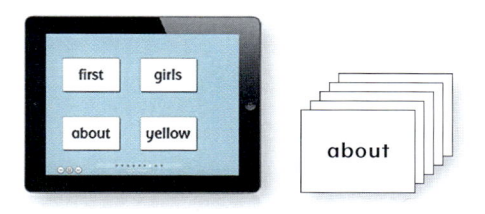

Objective 6
Read 9 new sight words.

Prompting
- Lesson 1: Time delay 0 seconds
- Lessons 2–5: Time delay 4 seconds

Activity directions
Sight words are tricky because you can't sound them out. You have to remember what they look like. Find the word.

Teaching moment
- ✔ The pace between the presentation of words is purposely rapid to keep the student motivated.
- ✔ Use the sight word flashcards to provide extra practice of sight word reading. Provide up to 4 response options for students to choose from.
- ✔ If the student chooses an incorrect response, give a reminder to not guess but to wait and you will help. You can also add to the directions, **If you are not sure of the answer, don't guess. Wait for me to help you.**

Cue	Student's independent response	If student needs help
Find the word about.	Finds the word about.	If no response after 4 seconds or an incorrect response, model finding the word and say, **This is about. You touch it.** Physically guide the student to find the word if needed.

Repeat with the new sight words and review sight words, words required for reading the story for this level; see **Level 12 Content** on p. 137.

Reading text / Comprehension questions

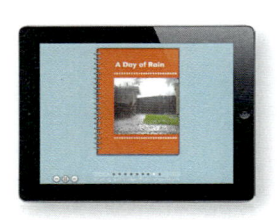

Objective 7 / Objective 8
Read connected text. / Answer comprehension questions about connected text.

Prompting
Least intrusive prompt

Activity directions
Now that you know how to read words, you can read a page from the story. Today you will read about Jean and Jane.

Teaching moment
✔ One page of the story is read during each lesson, followed by the comprehension questions.

✔ Use **Champion Reader 3** to show the title of the story and to point out the characters. It can also be used to give students additional reading practice. The comprehension questions that could be asked if not using the software and possible response options are listed in the **Level 12 Content** on p. 137. Write response options on the dry-erase board for students to read.

Cue	Student's independent response	If student needs help
Say, **Read this story silently in your head.** Do not read to the student or point to the words.	Reads the sentences silently.	

(Table continues)

Cue	Student's independent response	If student needs help
After the student silently reads the sentences on the page, **Let's answer some questions about the story. What is beating on the pane?**	Choose the word rain.	If no response or an incorrect response, say, **Read this sentence again.** Point to each word in the sentence that has the answer, then ask the question again.
		If still no response or an incorrect response, read the sentence with the answer to the student, **The rain beat on the pane.** Then ask, **What is beating on the pane?**
		If still no response or an incorrect response, physically guide the student to find rain, and say, **Rain. The rain beat on the pane.** Point to the words as you read the sentence.

Repeat with the content for each lesson; see **Level 12 Content** on p. 137.

Closing/Writing activity

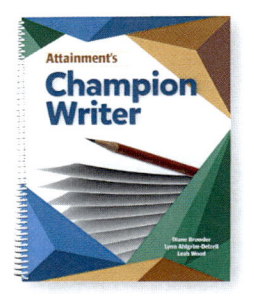

Objective 9
Write responses to activities that review level objectives.

Activity directions
Your lesson is over. GREAT reading today! Let's complete a page in your Champion Writer.

Teaching moment
✔ In order to keep the lesson from becoming too long, consider completing the writing activity at another time of the day.

✔ Some students may need adaptations to complete the writing page in **Champion Writer**; see p. 20 for ideas.

✔ Use the dry-erase board and an erasable marker to give the student practice in writing/forming sight words and words containing the letter/sounds of this level.

LEVEL 13

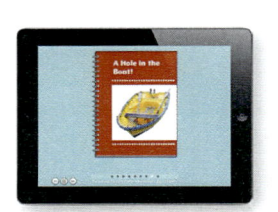

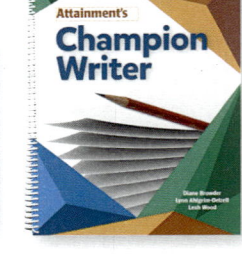

Focus
Digraphs—ie, oa, ow; compound words

Phonemic awareness
- Blend sounds for CVv and CVvC words, and blend words for compound words
- Segment first, middle, and last sounds in words
- Segment sounds in VvC, CVv, and CVvC words

Phonics
- Sounds /aɪ/ and /o/ corresponding to graphemes ie (long ī) and oa, ow (long ō)
- Decode VvC, CVv, and CVvC words, and compound words

Sight words
after, away, each, help, laugh, throw, together, while, white

Generalization words
boat, die, inside, load, road, tow, uphill

Connected text
- ATOS level = 1.6
- Lexile level = 290L

Objectives
1. Identify ie (long ī) and oa, ow (long ō) when given the sounds /aɪ/ and /o/.
2. Blend sounds to form CVv and CVvC words, and blend words to form compound words.
3. Segment the first, middle, and last sounds in words.
4. Segment the sounds in VvC, CVv, and CVvC words.
5. Decode VvC, CVv, CVvC words and compound words and identify their meanings.
6. Read 9 new sight words.
7. Read connected text.
8. Answer comprehension questions about connected text.
9. Write responses to activities that review level objectives.

Teaching notes
This level introduces the digraphs ie, oa, and ow. A digraph is a sound represented by two letters (e.g., ie). Note that these digraphs are pronounced like long ī and long ō and therefore the letters are placed on the tiles for long ī (/aɪ/) and long ō (/o/). Simple compound words (CVC+VC or CVC+CVC) are also introduced in this level.

Level 13 Content

	Lesson 1	Lesson 2	Lesson 3	Lesson 4	Lesson 5
Letter/sound identification	**New**: ie (on long ī tile); oa, ow (on the long ō tile) **Review**: long ē, ee, ea, ai, ay				
Blending	bow, tie, coat, goal, into*, boyfriend* Compound words are demonstrated	**Optional demo**: coal vie, soak, row, today*, cannot*	**Optional demo**: coal low, soap, pie, onto*, rowboat*	**Optional demo**: coal coat, pie, foam, upon*, into*	**Optional demo**: coal rowboat*, coat, tie, into*, bow
Segmenting I	Listen for the *last* sound in each word: pie, flow, mow, lie, sow, row	**Optional demo**: ice Listen for the *first* sound in each word: oar, idle, ivy, apron, oak, over	**Optional demo**: flow Listen for the *last* sound in each word: row, tie, mow, lie, low, pie	**Optional demo**: toad Listen for the *middle* sound in each word: soak, right, coat, hope, rate, hide	**Optional demo**: mow Listen for the *last* sound in each word: flow, tie, pie, row, stow
Segmenting II	tie, soap, row, lie, coat, bow	**Optional demo**: loan oar, row, pie, foam, mow, vie	**Optional demo**: loan bow, tie, coat, row, pie, goal	**Optional demo**: loan moan, mow, vie, oar, row, pie	**Optional demo**: loan coat, pie, goal, bow, oar
Decoding	coat, soap, pie, rowboat, bow, coal	**Optional demo**: coal coat, goal, hotdog, oar, bow	**Optional demo**: coal bow, oak, toad, caveman, foam	**Optional demo**: coal soak, rowboat, goal, tie, mow	**Optional demo**: coal soap, tie, toad, oar, hotdog
Sight Words	**New**: after, away, each, help, laugh, throw, together, while, white **Review**: boys, eat, funny, girls, jump, out, there, we, what, yellow				
Comprehension questions (correct response in **bold**)	What do the girls run to? (**rowboat**, rain, sailboat, uphill) What did the girls get before they jumped into the boat? (oak, bow, **oar**, soap)	What do the girls do with the boat? (was, **row**, run, lie) What is on the white oak tree? (**toad**, coat, fun, tow)	What does the boat have? (hope, yellow, **hole**, sail) What is low in the water? (oak, **rowboat**, boys, toad)	What do the girls not want to do? (**die**, lie, den, funny) What do the girls need? (row, **tow**, foam, today) Where are the boys? (**road**, hope, boat, pie)	What did the girls throw? (boat, tie, **rope**, load) What do the boys do with the boat? (yell, **tow**, pole, row) Where do the boys lug the boat? (**uphill**, inside, downhill, bug) What kind of tree did the boys tie the boat to? (boat, pine, **oak**, coat)

* first sound

Letter/sound identification

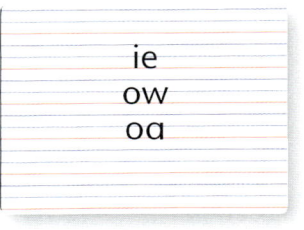

ie
ow
oa

Objective 1
Identify ie (long ī) and oa, ow (long ō) when given the sounds /aɪ/ and /o/.
Pronunciation: /aɪ/ as in t<u>ie</u>, /o/ as in b<u>oa</u>t

Prompting
- Lesson 1: Time delay 0 seconds
- Lessons 2–5: Time delay 4 seconds

Activity directions
I'll say a sound, and you find the letter that makes that sound.

Teaching moment
✔ Introduce ie, **Today we are going to read words that have sounds made by two vowels together.** Point to the long ī tile on the software screen showing the ie in the corner or write and point to it on the dry-erase board. Tell students, **These vowels—ie— together say /aɪ/, like long ī.**

✔ Introduce oa and ow. Point to the long ō tile on the software screen showing the oa and ow in the corners or write and point to them on the dry-erase board. Tell students, **These vowels—oa and ow—together say /o/ like long ō.**

✔ If the student chooses an incorrect response, give a reminder to not guess but to wait and you will help. You can also add to the directions, **If you are not sure of the answer, don't guess. Wait for me to help you.**

Cue	Student's independent response	If student needs help
What letters say /<u>aɪ</u>/?	Finds the letters <u>ie</u> to make the /<u>aɪ</u>/ sound.	If no response after 4 seconds or an incorrect response, model finding the letter/sound, and continue pointing to it until the student finds it. If needed, physically guide the student to find the letter and say, **This is /aɪ/. You touch it.**

Repeat with oa, ow and Level 12 review: long ē, ee, ea and ai, ay.

Blending

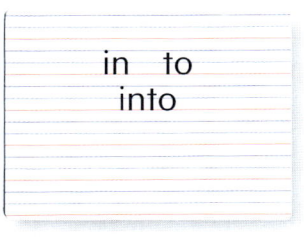

Objective 2
Blend sounds to form CVv and CVvC words, and blend words to form compound words.
Pronunciation: /o/ as in b<u>oa</u>t

Prompting
- Lesson 1: Time delay 0 seconds
- Lessons 2–5: Time delay 4 seconds

Activity directions
I'll say some sounds. You blend the sounds together and find the word they make.

Teaching moment
✔ Prolong or emphasize the sounds at the beginning, middle, or end to help the student identify the word. Note that when you segment the sounds in words, do not add additional sounds to consonants (e.g., for b, say, /b/ not /bʌ/.

✔ Introduce compound words at the first occurrence of a compound word. Using the dry-erase board with the compound word written on it, tell students, **Some words are two words in one, like into.** Cover the word *to* and say, **You sound out** *in* (then cover *in*), **and then you sound out** *to*. **Then you put them together:** *into*.

✔ Note that <u>oar</u> in this level is considered a long ō (/o/) followed by a consonantal /r/, even though it might be considered an r-controlled vowel (or).

Cue	Student's independent response	If student needs help
/b/ /o/. **Which word am I saying?**	Finds the word <u>bow</u>.	If no response after 4 seconds or an incorrect response, model finding the word and say, **This is** <u>bow</u>. **You touch it.** Continue pointing to it until the student finds it. If needed, physically guide the student to find the word.

Repeat with the <u>content</u> for each lesson; see **Level 13 Content** on p. 147.

Segmenting I

Objective 3
Segment the first, middle, and last sounds in words.
Pronunciation: /aɪ/ as in t<u>ie</u>, /o/ as in b<u>oa</u>t

Prompting
- Lesson 1: Time delay 0 seconds
- Lessons 2–5: Time delay 4 seconds

Activity directions
I'll say a word. You show me the first/middle/last sound you hear in the word.

Teaching moment
✔ To practice without the software, provide more words with /aɪ/ and /o/ in the beginning, middle, or end of the word.

✔ Pause for one second between the direction ("What is the first/middle/last sound in") and the target word to prepare the student for the target word.

✔ To make it easier for the student, emphasize or prolong the first, middle, or last sound.

✔ If the student chooses an incorrect response, give a reminder to not guess but to wait and you will help. You can also add to the directions, **If you are not sure of the answer, don't guess. Wait for me to help you.**

Cue	Student's independent response	If student needs help
(Lessons 1, 3, and 5) **What is the last sound in <u>flow</u>?**	Finds <u>ow</u> to say /o/.	If no response after 4 seconds or an incorrect response, model finding <u>ow</u>. Say, **The middle sound is /o/. You touch it.** If needed, physically guide the student to find /o/.
(Lessons 2) **What is the first sound in <u>ice</u>?**	Finds ī to say /aɪ/.	If no response after 4 seconds or an incorrect response, model finding ī. Say, **The first sound is /aɪ/. You touch it.** If needed, physically guide the student to find /aɪ/.
(Lesson 4) **What is the middle sound in <u>toad</u>?**	Finds <u>oa</u> to say /o/.	If no response after 4 seconds or an incorrect response, model finding <u>oa</u>. Say, **The middle sound is /o/. You touch it.** If needed, physically guide the student to find /o/.

Repeat with the <u>content</u> for each lesson; see **Level 13 Content** on p. 147.

Segmenting II

t	ie

Objective 4
Segment the sounds in VvC, CVv, and CVvC words.
Pronunciation: /aɪ/ as in t<u>ie</u>

Prompting
- Lesson 1: Time delay 0 seconds
- Lessons 2–5: Time delay 4 seconds

Activity directions
Use the sounds you learned to sound out some words. I'll say a word, and you sound it out.

Teaching moment

✔ To help the student segment all of the sounds in the word, hold up a finger for each sound the student needs to find. Remember to hold up fingers for sounds, not letters (e.g., the word *soap* has 3 sounds but 4 letters; the word *lie* has 2 sounds and 3 letters).

✔ Or if the student needs help, divide the dry-erase board into sections based on the number of sounds in the word. Have the student sound out the word by choosing one sound at a time on the software screen, while you write the letter/sound the student chooses on the dry-erase board (one sound per section).

✔ If the student chooses an incorrect response, give a reminder to not guess but to wait and you will help. Add to the directions, **If you are not sure of the answer, don't guess. Wait for me to help you.**

Cue	Student's independent response	If student needs help
Sound out the word t<u>ie</u>.	Touches t and ie for the sounds /t/ and /aɪ/.	If no response after 4 seconds or an incorrect response, say, **Listen, /t/ /aɪ/. Touch the sounds in t<u>ie</u>.**
		If still no response or an incorrect response, model segmenting the word by touching each letter and saying each sound. Then say, **Your turn. Touch the sounds in t<u>ie</u>.**
		If still no response or an incorrect response, say, **Let's touch the sounds in t<u>ie</u>.** Then physically guide the student to touch each sound while you say it.

Repeat with the <u>content</u> for each lesson; see **Level 13 Content** on p. 147.

ERSB Teacher's Guide ■ Level 13

Decoding

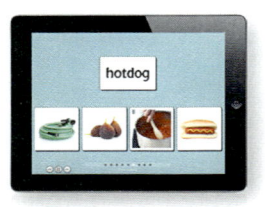

Objective 5
Decode VvC, CVv, CVvC words and compound words and identify their meanings.
Pronunciation: /o/ as in b<u>oa</u>t

Prompting
- Lesson 1: Time delay 0 seconds
- Lessons 2–5: Time delay 4 seconds

Activity directions
Now, use the sounds and letters you learned to read a word and find its picture.

Teaching moment
✔ Be certain the student knows the name of each picture.

✔ If students need help decoding, sound out the word by prolonging each letter sound as you say it. Then say the word (blending the sounds together); find the picture representing it. Be sure to follow this demonstration with independent responding by the student.

✔ Review how to decode a compound word if necessary.

Cue	Student's independent response	If student needs help
First, let's hear each picture's name.	Listens as each picture is named.	
Say, **Your turn. Read the word and find the picture.**	Finds the picture of <u>coat</u>.	If no response after 4 seconds, point to the word and say, **This is /k/ /o/ /t/**. Then touch the picture and say, **Here is <u>coat</u>. Now you read <u>coat</u> and find the picture**. Physically guide the student's hand if needed. If an incorrect response, point to the letters in the word as you say, **This says <u>coat</u>**. Touch the picture and say, **Here is the picture of <u>coat</u>**. Remove your finger and say, **Now you read <u>coat</u> and find the picture**. Physically guide the student's hand if needed.

Repeat with the <u>content</u> for each lesson; see **Level 13 Content** on p. 147.

Sight words

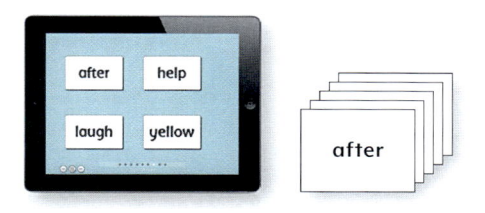

Objective 6
Read 9 new sight words.

Prompting
- Lesson 1: Time delay 0 seconds
- Lessons 2–5: Time delay 4 seconds

Activity directions
Sight words are tricky because you can't sound them out. You have to remember what they look like. **Find the word.**

Teaching moment
✔ The pace between the presentation of words is purposely rapid to keep the student motivated.

✔ Use the sight word flashcards to provide extra practice of sight word reading. Provide up to 4 response options for students to choose from.

✔ If the student chooses an incorrect response, give a reminder to not guess but to wait and you will help. You can also add to the directions, **If you are not sure of the answer, don't guess. Wait for me to help you.**

Cue	Student's independent response	If student needs help
Find the word after.	Finds the word after.	If no response after 4 seconds or an incorrect response, model finding the word and say, **This is after. You touch it.** Physically guide the student to find the word if needed.

Repeat with the new sight words and review sight words, words required for reading the story for this level; see **Level 13 Content** on p. 147.

Reading text / Comprehension questions

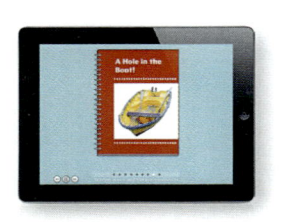

rowboat
rain
sailboat
uphill

Objective 7 / Objective 8
Read connected text. / Answer comprehension questions about connected text.

Prompting
Least intrusive prompt

Activity directions
Now that you know how to read words, you can read a page from the story. Today you will read about Jane and Jean.

Teaching moment
✔ One page of the story is read during each lesson, followed by the comprehension questions.

✔ Compound words are embedded in this level's story. Remind students that these words are made of two smaller words and they can read them by breaking the larger word apart.

✔ Use **Champion Reader 3** to give students additional reading practice. The comprehension questions that could be asked if not using the software and possible response options are listed in the **Level 13 Content** on p. 147. Write response options on the dry-erase board for students to read.

Cue	Student's independent response	If student needs help
Say, **Read this story silently in your head.** Do not read to the student or point to the words.	Reads the sentences silently.	

(Table continues)

Cue	Student's independent response	If student needs help
After the student reads the sentences on the page, say, **Let's answer some questions about the story. What do the girls run to?**	Chooses the word rowboat.	If no response or an incorrect response, say, **Read this sentence again.** Point to each word in the sentence that has the answer, then ask the question again.
		If still no response or an incorrect response, read the sentence with the answer to the student, **Jean and Jane run to the rowboat.** Then ask, **What do the girls run to?**
		If still no response or an incorrect response, physically guide the student to find rowboat, and say, **Rowboat. Jean and Jane run to the rowboat.**

Repeat with the content for each lesson; see **Level 13 Content** on p. 147.

Closing / Writing activity

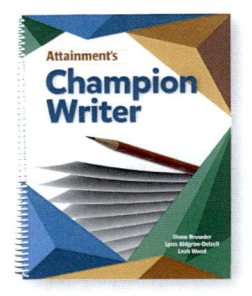

Objective 9
Write responses to activities that review level objectives.

Activity directions
Your lesson is over. GREAT reading today! Let's complete a page in your Champion Writer.

Teaching moment

✔ In order to keep the lesson from becoming too long, consider completing the writing activity at another time of the day.

✔ Some students may need adaptations to complete the writing page; see p. 20 for ideas.

✔ Use the dry-erase board (lined side) and an erasable marker to give the student practice in writing/forming sight words and words containing the letter/sounds of this level.

LEVEL 14

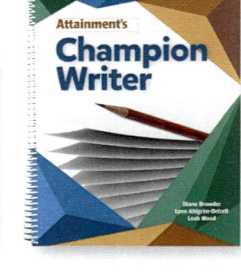

Focus
Consonant blends (final)—st, nt, mp, nd

Phonemic awareness
- Blend sounds for VCC and CVCC words
- Segment the last two sounds in words
- Segment sounds in CCVC, CCVvC, and CCVCe words

Phonics
- Sounds /st/, /nt/, /mp/, and /nd/ corresponding to graphemes st, nt, mp, and nd
- Decode CCVC, CCVvC, and CCVCe words

Sight words
class, comes, good, green, Mr., play, plays, rally, walk

Generalization words
Demp, hunt, fist, just, pump

Connected text
- ATOS level = 1.4
- Lexile level = 180L

Objectives
1. Identify st, nt, mp, and nd when given the sounds /st/, /nt/, /mp/, and /nd/.
2. Blend sounds to form VCC and CVCC words.
3. Segment the last two sounds in words.
4. Segment the sounds in CCVC, CCVvC, and CCVCe words.
5. Decode CCVC, CCVvC, and CCVCe words and identify their meanings.
6. Read 9 new sight words.
7. Read connected text.
8. Answer comprehension questions about connected text.
9. Write responses to activities that review level objectives.

Teaching notes
This level introduces students to consonant blends. A consonant blend is a group of two or three consonants in a word that make a distinct consonant sound. Each letter within the blend is pronounced individually, but quickly, so they blend together. The focus in this level is on blends in the final position of words for st, nt, mp, and nd. Each blend is presented together on a tile but it is also correct if, when segmenting, the student chooses the two sounds in the blend individually.

Level 14 Content

	Lesson 1	Lesson 2	Lesson 3	Lesson 4	Lesson 5
Letter/sound identification	**New:** st, nt, mp, nd (final) **Review:** ie, oa, ow				
Blending	pest, tent, end, fast, bump, and	**Optional demo:** land mast, tent, camp, went, mint	**Optional demo:** land wind, cast, mint, band, pond	**Optional demo:** land best, pant, pond, dust, mint	**Optional demo:** land tent, pant, pond, jump, best
Segmenting I	Listen for the *last two* sounds in each word: wind, stamp, pant, band, cast, mint	Listen for the *last two* sounds in each word: **Optional demo:** wind pest, tent, end, fast, bent	Listen for the *last two* sounds in each word: **Optional demo:** wind best, send, pond, dump, mint	Listen for the *last two* sounds in each word: **Optional demo:** wind send, fast, bunt, band, damp	These words have four sounds. Listen for the *last two* sounds in each word: **Optional demo:** wind pant, tent, mast, band, jump
Segmenting II	best, send, pond, must, mint, fast	**Optional demo:** dust wind, fast, sent, band, jump	**Optional demo:** dust pest, tent, end, fast, bent	**Optional demo:** dust mast, pant, band, cast, mint	**Optional demo:** dust tent, pond, camp, bunt, fast
Decoding	hand, tent, jump, mint, dust, cast	**Optional demo:** hand best, ramp, send, band, bend	**Optional demo:** hand band, dust, fast, jump, tent	**Optional demo:** hand lump, tent, cast, bent, end	**Optional demo:** wind end, tent, send, ant, fast
Sight Words	**New:** class, comes, good, green, Mr., play, plays, rally, walk **Review:** friend, girls, here, next, school, there, was, with				
Comprehension questions (correct response in **bold**)	What do the fans want to send to the team? (land, duck, **luck,** sun) Who is the rally for? (meat, time, **team,** ducks) How did Kim walk? (fun, **fast,** past, slow)	What does Kim look for when she gets to the pep rally? (heat, fast, **seat,** land) Who does Kim want to sit with? (**Tam,** Tim, Kim, Gus) Where in the row does Kim sit? (tent, **end,** bend, top)	Who is with the team? (team, land, **band,** dogs) What does Ben have? (pant, dust, **cast,** can) Which row does Mr. Demp sit in? (pop, tent, **top,** end)	Who plays the music? (bus, pest, **band,** team) What did the girls make for the team? (pond, **tent,** must, team) Who do Tam and Kim wave to? (tent, end, **team,** meat)	Does Kim want to go back to class? (yes, all, **no,** mint) Where would Kim rather be? (**friends,** first, school, pond) What will Kim have to take when she gets back? (dust, team, **test,** must)

Letter/sound identification

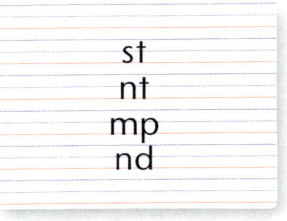

st
nt
mp
nd

Objective 1
Identify st, nt, mp, and nd when given the sounds /st/, /nt/, /mp/, and /nd/.
Pronunciation: /st/ as in ca<u>st</u>

Prompting
- Lesson 1: Time delay 0 seconds
- Lessons 2–5: Time delay 4 seconds

Activity directions
I'll say sounds and you find the letters that make those sounds.

Teaching moment
✔ The blends students learn in this level are at the end of words. Introduce /st/, /nt/, /mp/, and /nd/. **Today we are going to read more words that blend two sounds together.**

✔ Point to the tiles on the software screen showing the st, nt, mp, and nd tiles or write and point to them on the dry-erase board. Tell students, **These letters blend together to say /st/, /nt/, /mp/, and /nd/.**

✔ If the student chooses an incorrect response, give a reminder to not guess but to wait and you will help. You can also add to the directions, **If you are not sure of the answer, don't guess. Wait for me to help you.**

Cue	Student's independent response	If student needs help
What letters say /st/?	Finds the letters <u>st</u> to make the /<u>st</u>/ sound.	If no response after 4 seconds or an incorrect response, model finding the letter/sound, and continue pointing to it until the student finds it. If needed, physically guide the student to find the letters and say, **This says /<u>st</u>/. You touch it.**

Repeat with nt, mp, nd and Level 13 review: ie, oa, ow.

Blending

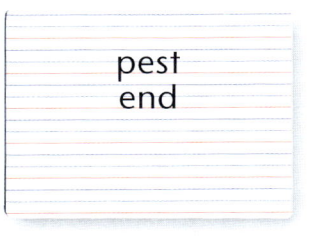

Objective 2
Blend sounds to form VCC and CVCC words.
Pronunciation: /ɛ/ as in p<u>e</u>st, /ʌ/ as in d<u>u</u>g

Prompting
- Lesson 1: Time delay 0 seconds
- Lessons 2–5: Time delay 4 seconds

Activity directions
I'll say some sounds. You blend the sounds together and find the word they make.

Teaching moment
✔ Prolong or emphasize the sounds at the beginning, middle, or end to help the student identify the word. Note that when you segment the sounds in words, do not add additional sounds to consonants (e.g., for p, say, /p/ not /pʌ/.

✔ Provide a one-second pause between the sounds to help students process them.

Cue	Student's independent response	If student needs help
/p/ /ɛ/ /st/. Which word am I saying?	Finds the word <u>pest</u>.	If no response after 4 seconds or an incorrect response, model finding the word and say, **This is <u>pest</u>. You touch it**. Continue pointing to it until the student finds it. If needed, physically guide the student to find the word.

Repeat with the <u>content</u> for each lesson; see **Level 14 Content** on p. 157.

ERSB Teacher's Guide ■ **Level 14**

Segmenting I

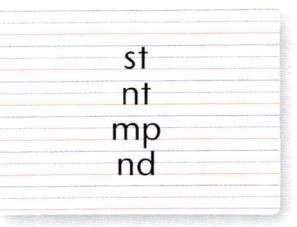

st
nt
mp
nd

Objective 3
Segment the last two sounds in words.
Pronunciation: /nd/ as in ba<u>nd</u>

Prompting
- Lesson 1: Time delay 0 seconds
- Lessons 2–5: Time delay 4 seconds

Activity directions
I'll say a word. You show me the last two sounds you hear in the word.

Teaching moment
✔ To practice without the software, provide more words with /st/, /nt/, /mp/, and /nd/ at the end of words.

✔ Pause for one second between the direction ("What are the last two sounds in") and the target word to prepare the student for the target word.

✔ To make it easier for the student, emphasize or prolong the last two sounds in the word.

✔ If the student chooses an incorrect response, give a reminder to not guess but to wait and you will help. You can also add to the directions, **If you are not sure of the answer, don't guess. Wait for me to help you.**

Cue	Student's independent response	If student needs help
What are the last two sounds in <u>wind</u>?	Finds <u>nd</u> to say /<u>nd</u>/.	If no response after 4 seconds or an incorrect response, model finding <u>nd</u>. Say, **The last two sounds are /<u>nd</u>/. You touch them.** If needed, physically guide the student to find /<u>nd</u>/.

Repeat with the <u>content</u> for each lesson; see **Level 14 Content** on p. 157.

Segmenting II

Objective 4
Segment the sounds in CCVC, CCVvC, and CCVCe words.
Pronunciation: /st/ as in ca<u>st</u>, /ɛ/ as in b<u>e</u>st

Prompting
- Lesson 1: Time delay 0 seconds
- Lessons 2–5: Time delay 4 seconds

Activity directions
Use the sounds you learned to sound out some words. I'll say a word, and you sound it out.

Teaching moment
✔ If the student needs help, divide the dry-erase board into sections based on the number of sounds in the word. Have the student sound out the word by choosing one sound at a time on the software screen, while you write the letter/sound the student chooses on the dry-erase board (one sound per section).

✔ Remember that even though the consonant blends are presented as a unit, they are two distinct sounds.

✔ If the student chooses an incorrect response, give a reminder to not guess but to wait and you will help. You can also add to the directions, **If you are not sure of the answer, don't guess. Wait for me to help you.**

✔ If the student makes an error on even one sound, have the student listen as you segment **all** the sounds in the word in the correct sequence. Then restate to touch the sounds in the word.

Cue	Student's independent response	If student needs help
Sound out the word <u>best</u>.	Touches <u>b</u>, <u>e</u>, and <u>st</u> for the sounds /b/, /ɛ/, and /st/.	If no response after 4 seconds or an incorrect response, say, **Listen, /b/, /ɛ/, and /st/. Touch the sounds in <u>best</u>.**
		If still no response or an incorrect response, model segmenting the word by touching each letter and saying each sound. Then say, **Your turn. Touch the sounds in <u>best</u>.**
		If still no response or an incorrect response, say, **Let's touch the sounds in <u>best</u>.** Then physically guide the student to touch each sound while you say it.

Repeat with the <u>content</u> for each lesson; see **Level 14 Content** on p. 157.

ERSB Teacher's Guide ■ Level 14

Decoding

Objective 5
Decode CCVC, CCVvC, and CCVCe words and identify their meanings.
Pronunciation: /nd/ as in ba<u>nd</u>, /æ/ as in <u>h</u>and

Prompting
- Lesson 1: Time delay 0 seconds
- Lessons 2–5: Time delay 4 seconds

Activity directions
Now, use the sounds and letters you learned to read a word and find its picture.

Teaching moment
✓ Be certain the student knows the name of each picture.

✓ If students need help decoding, sound out the word by prolonging each letter sound as you say it. Then say the word (blending the sounds together); find the picture representing it. Be sure to follow this demonstration with independent responding by the student.

Cue	Student's independent response	If student needs help
First, let's hear each picture's name.	Listens as each picture is named.	
Say, **Your turn. Read the word and find the picture.**	Finds the picture of <u>hand</u>.	If no response after 4 seconds, point to the word and say, **This is /h/ /æ/ /nd/.** Then touch the picture and say, **Here is hand. Now you read <u>hand</u> and find the picture.** Physically guide the student's hand if needed. If an incorrect response, point to the letters in the word as you say, **This says <u>hand</u>.** Touch the picture and say, **Here is the picture of <u>hand</u>.** Remove your finger and say, **Now you read <u>hand</u> and find the picture.** Physically guide the student's hand if needed.

Repeat with the <u>content</u> for each lesson; see **Level 14 Content** on p. 157.

Sight words

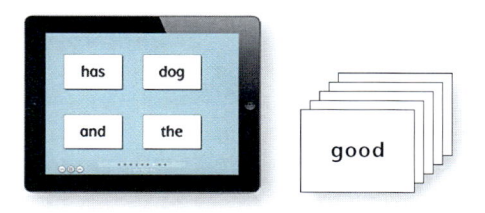

Objective 6
Read 9 new sight words.

Prompting
- Lesson 1: Time delay 0 seconds
- Lessons 2–5: Time delay 4 seconds

Activity directions
Sight words are tricky because you can't sound them out. You have to remember what they look like. Find the word.

Teaching moment

✔ The pace between the presentation of words is purposely rapid to keep the student motivated.

✔ Use the sight word flashcards to provide extra practice of sight word reading. Provide up to 4 response options for students to choose from.

✔ Note that the word *green* is included as a sight word since students have not learned the consonant blend gr. This is a good opportunity to help the student generalize reading other consonant blends.

✔ If the student chooses an incorrect response, give a reminder to not guess but to wait and you will help. You can also add to the directions, **If you are not sure of the answer, don't guess. Wait for me to help you.**

Cue	Student's independent response	If student needs help
Find the word good.	Finds the word good.	If no response after 4 seconds or an incorrect response, model finding the word and say, **This is good. You touch it.** Physically guide the student to find the word if needed.

Repeat with the new sight words and review sight words, words required for reading the story for this level; see **Level 14 Content** on p. 157.

Reading text / Comprehension questions

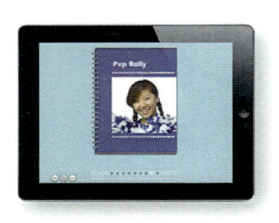

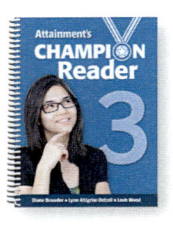

Objective 7 / Objective 8
Read connected text. / Answer comprehension questions about connected text.

Prompting
Least intrusive prompt

Activity directions
Now that you know how to read words, you can read a page from the story. Today you will read about Kim at a pep rally.

Teaching moment
✔ One page of the story is read during each lesson, followed by the comprehension questions.

✔ Use **Champion Reader 3** to give students additional reading practice. The comprehension questions that could be asked if not using the software and possible response options are listed in the **Level 14 Content** on p. 157. Write response options on the dry-erase board for students to read.

✔ Explain what a pep rally is if students are not aware.

Cue	Student's independent response	If student needs help
Say, **Read this story silently in your head.** Do not read to the student or point to the words.	Reads the sentences silently.	

(Table continues)

ERSB Teacher's Guide ■ Level 14

Cue	Student's independent response	If student needs help
After reading the sentences on the page, say, **Let's answer some questions about the story. What do the fans want to send to the team?**	Chooses the word luck.	If no response or an incorrect response, say, **Read this sentence again.** Point to each word in the sentence that has the answer, then ask the question again.
		If still no response or an incorrect response, read the sentence with the answer to the student, **We want to send them good luck for their game**. Then ask, **What do the fans want to send to the team?**
		If still no response or an incorrect response, physically guide the student to find luck, and say, **Luck. They want to send luck to the team**.

Repeat with the content for each lesson; see **Level 14 Content** on p. 157.

Closing / Writing activity

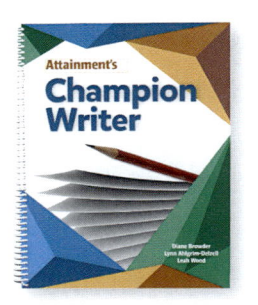

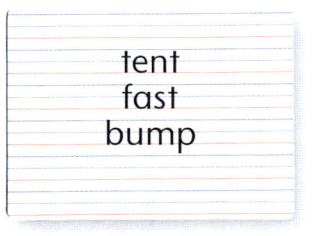

tent
fast
bump

Objective 9
Write responses to activities that review level objectives.

Activity directions
Your lesson is over. GREAT reading today! Let's complete a page in your Champion Writer.

Teaching moment

✔ In order to keep the lesson from becoming too long, consider completing the writing activity at another time of the day.

✔ Some students may need adaptations to complete the writing page in **Champion Writer**; see p. 20 for ideas.

✔ Use the dry-erase board and an erasable marker to give the student practice in writing/forming sight words and words containing the letter/sounds of this level.

LEVEL 15

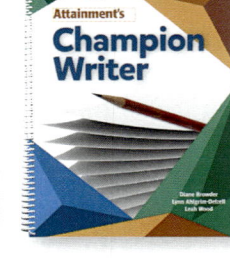

Focus
Consonant blends (initial)—sl, br, bl, st

Phonemic awareness
- Blend sounds for CCVC, CCVvC, and CCVCe words
- Segment the first two sounds in words
- Segment sounds in VCC and CVCC words

Phonics
- Sounds /sl/, /br/, /bl/, and /st/ corresponding to graphemes sl, br, bl, and st
- Decode VCC and CVCC words

Sight words
alone, brow, dance, door, hair, hi, shoes, soon, when

Generalization words
brake, brave, cannot, slam, slap, slip, still

Connected text
- ATOS level = 1
- Lexile level = 230L

Objectives
1. Identify sl, br, bl, and st when given the sounds /sl/, /br/, /bl/, and /st/.
2. Blend sounds to form CCVC, CCVvC, and CCVCe words.
3. Segment the first two sounds in words.
4. Segment the sounds in VCC and CVCC words.
5. Decode VCC and CVCC words and identify their meanings.
6. Read 9 new sight words.
7. Read connected text.
8. Answer comprehension questions about connected text.
9. Write responses to activities that review level objectives.

Teaching notes
This level presents the students with four additional consonant blends. A consonant blend is a group of two or three consonants in a word that make a distinct consonant sound. Each letter within the blend is pronounced individually, but quickly, so they blend together. The focus in this level is on blends in the initial position of words for sl, br, bl, and st. Each blend is presented together but it is also correct if, when segmenting, the student chooses the two sounds in the blend individually.

Level 15 Content

	Lesson 1	**Lesson 2**	**Lesson 3**	**Lesson 4**	**Lesson 5**
Letter/sound identification	**New**: br, sl, bl, st (initial) **Review**: st, nt, mp, nd (final)				
Blending	braid, stick, slim, brace, stone, slide	**Optional demo**: stub Brad, slick, step, slop, bleed	**Optional demo**: stub Sloan, step, braid, slack, stone	**Optional demo**: stub Brad, step, Sloan, slim, brick	**Optional demo**: stub Sloan, braid, black, slip, step
Segmenting I	*Listen for the first two sounds in each word:* braid, slide, stick, brim, slope, brain	*Listen for the first two sounds in each word:* **Optional demo**: brick step, blow, bridge, stop, stone	*Listen for the first two sounds in each word:* **Optional demo**: brick stick, Brad, store, slug, blue	*Listen for the first two sounds in each word:* **Optional demo**: brick braid, slide, slick, black, step	*Listen for the first two sounds in each word:* **Optional demo**: brick Brad, store, slide, broke, blue
Segmenting II	stick, Brad, slid, brim, slim, sled	**Optional demo**: sled step, Sloan, braid, stack, blob	**Optional demo**: sled Brad, stick, slick, brace, stone	**Optional demo**: sled step, Brad, slow, stab, slug	**Optional demo**: sled step, brim, stick, slick, blame
Decoding	stack, step, slick, braid, stem, block	**Optional demo**: stack Brad, slide, stick, brick, blow	**Optional demo**: stack slow, step, Sloan, brain, stone	**Optional demo**: stack slide, braid, stick, brain, stem	**Optional demo**: stack blow, slow, Brad, black, stick
Sight Words	**New**: alone, brow, dance, door, hair, hi, shoes, soon, when **Review**: away, class, does, friend, look, out, walk				
Comprehension questions (correct response in **bold**)	What did Sloan stick in her dance bag? (**shoes**, bags, dance, door) What did Sloan see? (ran, coat, **cat**, sat) What did Sloan's mom slam on? (brim, cake, hair, **brake**)	What did Sloan do with her hair? (broke, **braid**, cut, sun) Who does Sloan see? (Ben, **Brad**, Dane, Sloan) What does Brad not take? (stem, hip, **step**, dance)	What did Sloan see to know Brad was sad? (**brow**, stow, brag, help) What does Brad not want to do? (tip, sled, **slip**, braid) What did Sloan tell Brad to be? (sad, **brave**, brow, brag) Sloan will help Brad so he does not do what? (**slip**, help, sled, not)	Who does Sloan dance with? (Gus, **Brad**, Ben, Tim) What do Sloan and Brad's shoes not do? (step, dance, **stick**, shoe) What does Sloan like to do? (sleep, eat, **slide**, ride) What doesn't Sloan want to do? (stem, top, sled, **stop**)	What does Brad do alone? (do, **dance**, eat, damp) Who is brave? (**Brad**, Ben, Tad, Sloan) How does Brad step? (**fast**, funny, slow, go) What do Brad and Sloan do with their hands? (**slap**, tap, slide, when)

Letter/sound identification

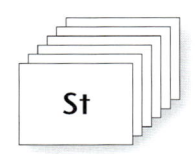

Objective 1
Identify sl, br, bl, and st when given the sounds /sl/, /br/, /bl/, and /st/.
Pronunciation: /br/ as in brain, /bl/ as in blame

Prompting
- Lesson 1: Time delay 0 seconds
- Lessons 2–5: Time delay 4 seconds

Activity directions
I'll say sounds, and you find the letters that make the sounds.

Teaching moment

✔ Introduce /sl/, /br/, and /bl/ and review /st/. Tell students, **You learned about blends at the ends of words. Today you will learn to read blends at the beginning of words.** Point to the tiles on the software screen showing the sl, br, and bl tiles or write and point to them on the dry-erase board. Tell students, **These two letters blend together to say /sl/, these two say /br/, and these two say /bl/. You already know that s and t blend together to say /st/.**

✔ If the student chooses an incorrect response, give a reminder to not guess but to wait and you will help. You can also add to the directions, **If you are not sure of the answer, don't guess. Wait for me to help you.**

Cue	Student's independent response	If student needs help
What letters say /br/?	Finds the letters br to make the /br/ sound.	If no response after 4 seconds or an incorrect response, model finding the letter/sound, and continue pointing to it until the student finds it. If needed, physically guide the student to find the letters and say, **This says /br/. You touch it.**

Repeat with sl, bl, st and Level 14 review: st, nt, mp, nd.

Blending

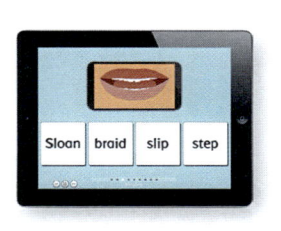

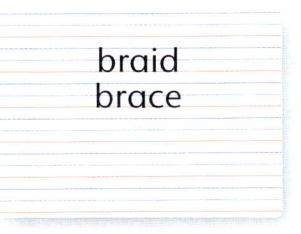

Objective 2
Blend sounds to form CCVC, CCVvC, and CCVCe words.
Pronunciation: /br/ as in brain, /eɪ/ as in braid

Prompting
- Lesson 1: Time delay 0 seconds
- Lessons 2–5: Time delay 4 seconds

Activity directions
I'll say some sounds. You blend the sounds together and find the word they make.

Teaching moment
✔ Prolong or emphasize the beginning blend, and the middle, or ending sounds to help the student identify the word.

✔ Provide a one-second pause between the sounds to help students process them.

Cue	Student's independent response	If student needs help
/br/ /eɪ/ /d/. **Which word am I saying?**	Finds the word braid.	If no response after 4 seconds or an incorrect response, model finding the word and say, **This is braid. You touch it.** Continue pointing to it until the student finds it. If needed, physically guide the student to find the word.

Repeat with the content for each lesson; see **Level 15 Content** on p. 167.

ERSB Teacher's Guide ■ Level 15

Segmenting I

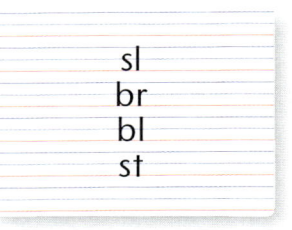

sl
br
bl
st

Objective 3
Segment the first two sounds in words.
Pronunciation: /br/ as in brain

Prompting
- Lesson 1: Time delay 0 seconds
- Lessons 2–5: Time delay 4 seconds

Activity directions
I'll say a word. You show me the first two sounds you hear in the word.

Teaching moment
✔ To practice without the software, provide more words with /sl/, /br/, /bl/, and /st/ at the beginning of words.

✔ Pause for one second between the direction ("What are the first two sounds in") and the target word to prepare the student for the target word.

✔ To make it easier for the student, emphasize or prolong the first two sounds in the word.

✔ If the student chooses an incorrect response, give a reminder to not guess but to wait and you will help. You can also add to the directions, **If you are not sure of the answer, don't guess. Wait for me to help you.**

Cue	Student's independent response	If student needs help
What are the first two sounds in braid?	Finds br to say /br/.	If no response after 4 seconds or an incorrect response, model finding br. Say, **The first sounds are /br/. You touch it.** If needed, physically guide the student to find /br/.

Repeat with the content for each lesson; see **Level 15 Content** on p. 167.

Segmenting II

Objective 4
Segment the sounds in VCC and CVCC words.
Pronunciation: /ɪ/ as in st<u>i</u>ck

Prompting
- Lesson 1: Time delay 0 seconds
- Lessons 2–5: Time delay 4 seconds

Activity directions
Use the sounds you learned to sound out some words. I'll say a word, and you sound it out.

Teaching moment

✔ If the student needs help, divide the dry-erase board into sections based on the number of sounds in the word. Have the student sound out the word by choosing one sound at a time on the software screen, while you write the letter/sound the student chooses on the dry-erase board (one sound per section).

✔ Remember that even though the consonant blends are presented as a unit, they are two sounds.

✔ If the student chooses an incorrect response, give a reminder to not guess but to wait and you will help. Add to the directions, **If you are not sure of the answer, don't guess. Wait for me to help you.**

✔ If the student makes an error on even one sound, have the student listen as you segment **all** the sounds in the word in the correct sequence. Then restate to touch the sounds in the word.

Cue	Student's independent response	If student needs help
Sound out the word <u>stick</u>.	Touches <u>st</u>, <u>i</u> and <u>k</u> for the sounds /<u>st</u>/, /<u>ɪ</u>/, and /<u>k</u>/.	If no response after 4 seconds or an incorrect response, say, **Listen, /<u>st</u>/ /<u>ɪ</u>/ /<u>k</u>/. Touch the sounds in <u>stick</u>.** If still no response or an incorrect response, model segmenting the word by touching each letter and saying each sound. Then say, **Your turn. Touch the sounds in <u>stick</u>.** If still no response or an incorrect response, say, **Let's touch the sounds in <u>stick</u>.** Then physically guide the student to touch each sound while you say it.

Repeat with the <u>content</u> for each lesson; see **Level 15 Content** on p. 167.

Decoding

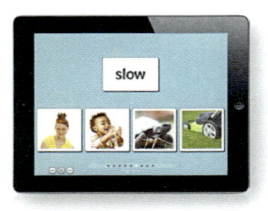

Objective 5
Decode VCC and CVCC words and identify their meanings.
Pronunciation: /æ/ as in st<u>a</u>ck

Prompting
- Lesson 1: Time delay 0 seconds
- Lessons 2–5: Time delay 4 seconds

Activity directions
Now, use the sounds and letters you learned to read a word and find its picture.

Teaching moment
✔ Be certain the student knows the name of each picture.

✔ If students need help decoding, sound out the word by prolonging each letter sound as you say it. Then say the word (blending the sounds together); find the picture representing it. Be sure to follow this demonstration with independent responding by the student.

Cue	Student's independent response	If student needs help
First, let's hear each picture's name.	Listens as each picture is named.	
Say, **Your turn. Read the word and find the picture.**	Finds the picture of <u>stack</u>.	If no response after 4 seconds, point to the word and say, **This is /<u>st</u>/ /<u>æ</u>/ /<u>k</u>/.** Then touch the picture and say, **Here is <u>stack</u>. Now you read <u>stack</u> and find the picture.** Physically guide the student's hand if needed. If an incorrect response, point to the letters in the word as you say, **This says <u>stack</u>.** Touch the picture and say, **Here is the picture of <u>stack</u>.** Remove your finger and say, **Now you read <u>stack</u> and find the picture.** Physically guide the student's hand if needed.

Repeat with the <u>content</u> for each lesson; see **Level 15 Content** on p. 167.

Sight words

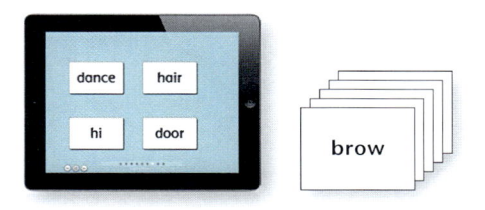

Objective 6
Read 9 new sight words.

Prompting
- Lesson 1: Time delay 0 seconds
- Lessons 2–5: Time delay 4 seconds

Activity directions
Sight words are tricky because you can't sound them out. You have to remember what they look like. Find the word.

Teaching moment
✔ The pace between the presentation of words is purposely rapid to keep the student motivated.

✔ Use the sight word flashcards to provide extra practice of sight word reading. Provide up to 4 response options for students to choose from.

✔ If the student chooses an incorrect response, give a reminder to not guess but to wait and you will help. You can also add to the directions, **If you are not sure of the answer, don't guess. Wait for me to help you.**

✔ Note that the word *brow* is included as a sight word since students have not learned to decode the dipthong ow.

Cue	Student's independent response	If student needs help
Find the word brow.	Finds the word brow.	If no response after 4 seconds or an incorrect response, model finding the word and say, **This is brow. You touch it.** Physically guide the student to find the word if needed.

Repeat with the new sight words and review sight words, words required for reading the story for this level; see **Level 15 Content** on p. 167.

ERSB Teacher's Guide ■ Level 15

Reading text / Comprehension questions

shoes
bags
dance
door

Objective 7 / Objective 8
Read connected text. / Answer comprehension questions about connected text.

Prompting
Least intrusive prompt

Activity directions
Now that you know how to read words, you can read a page from the story. Today you will read about Sloan's dance class.

Teaching moment
✔ One page of the story is read during each lesson, followed by the comprehension questions.

✔ Use **Champion Reader 3** to give students additional reading practice. The comprehension questions that could be asked if not using the software and possible response options are listed in the **Level 15 Content** on p. 167. Write response options on the dry-erase board for students to read.

Cue	Student's independent response	If student needs help
Say, **Read this story silently in your head.** Do not read to the student or point to the words.	Reads the sentences silently.	

(Table continues)

Cue	Student's independent response	If student needs help
After reading the sentences on the page, say, **Let's answer some questions about the story. What did Sloan stick in her dance bag?**	Chooses the word <u>shoes</u>.	If no response or an incorrect response, say, **Read this sentence again.** Point to each word in the sentence that has the answer, then ask the question again.
		If still no response or an incorrect response, read the sentence with the answer to the student, **I get my dance bag and stick my shoes in it**. Then ask, **What did Sloan stick in her dance bag?**
		If still no response or an incorrect response, physically guide the student to find <u>shoes</u>, and say, **Shoes. Sloan stuck her shoes in her dance bag.**

Repeat with the <u>content</u> for each lesson; see **Level 15 Content** on p. 167.

Closing / Writing activity

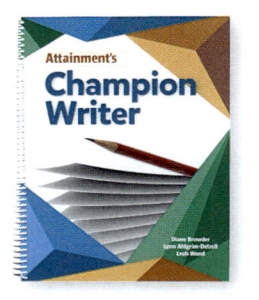

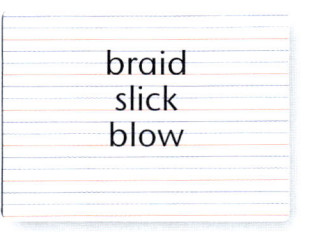

Objective 9
Write responses to activities that review level objectives.

Activity directions
Your lesson is over. GREAT reading today! Let's complete a page in your Champion Writer.

Teaching moment
✔ In order to keep the lesson from becoming too long, consider completing the writing activity at another time of the day.

✔ Some students may need adaptations to complete the writing page in **Champion Writer**; see p. 20 for ideas.

✔ Use the dry-erase board and an erasable marker to give the student practice in writing/forming sight words and words containing the letter/sounds of this level.

ERSB Teacher's Guide ■ **Level 15**

LEVEL 16

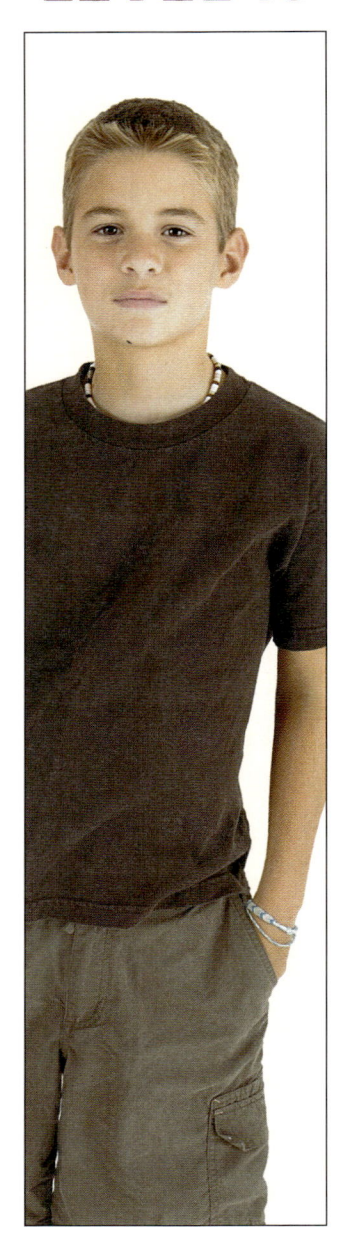

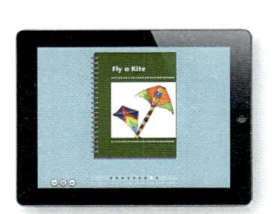

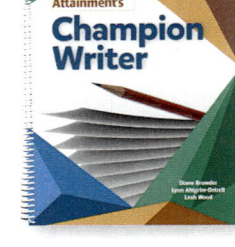

Focus
Consonant blends—tr, fl, sk, sp; y (long ī)

Phonemic awareness
- Blend sounds for CV, CCV, CCVC, CVCC, and CCVvC words
- Segment the first two sounds and last sound in words
- Segment sounds in CV, CCV, CCVC, CVCC, and CCVvC words

Phonics
- Sounds /tr/, /fl/, /sk/, /sp/, and /aɪ/ corresponding to graphemes tr, fl, sk, sp, and y (long ī)
- Decode CV, CCV, CCVC, CVCC, and CCVvC words

Sight words
our, loves, your, today, two, their, oh, free, again

Generalization words
trust, trek, float, flop, flip

Connected text
- ATOS level = 1.2
- Lexile level = 350L

Objectives
1. Identify tr, fl, sk, sp, and y (long ī) when given the sounds /tr/, /fl/, /sk/, /sp/, and /aɪ/.
2. Blend sounds to form CV, CCV, CCVC, CVCC, and CCVvC words.
3. Segment the first two sounds and the last sound in words.
4. Segment the sounds in CV, CCV, CCVC, CVCC, and CCVvC words.
5. Decode CV, CCV, CCVC, CVCC, and CCVvC words and identify their meanings.
6. Read 9 new sight words.
7. Read connected text.
8. Answer comprehension questions about connected text.
9. Write responses to activities that review level objectives.

Teaching notes
This level introduces students to more consonant blends: tr, fl, sk, and sp. The focus is on these blends in the initial position of words. Though each blend is presented together on one tile, the student should learn that they are separate sounds that "blend" together. It is also correct if, when segmenting, the student chooses the two sounds of the blend individually. Students are also introduced to a new sound for y. Sometimes y makes the long ī sound /aɪ/ and so it is placed on the ī tile.

Level 16 Content

	Lesson 1	Lesson 2	Lesson 3	Lesson 4	Lesson 5
Letter/sound identification	**New:** tr, fl, sk, sp, y (on the long ī tile) **Review:** br, sl, bl, st				
Blending	trail, fly, Ty, land, flat, dust	**Optional demo:** flag flat, land, spy, trim, fly	**Optional demo:** flag trip, flap, Ty, sty, land	**Optional demo:** flag trail, flat, dust, sky, pant	**Optional demo:** flag sky, trim, flab, fly, trip
Segmenting I	Listen for the *first two* sounds in each word: trim, flap, stick, spin, trail, flap	Listen for the *last* sound in each word: **Optional demo:** flea tree, stay, spy, sky, play	Listen for the *first two* sounds in each word: **Optional demo:** brave flat, trample, trail, stump, skip	Listen for the *last* sound in each word: **Optional demo:** spy stay, Ty, tree, flea, sky	Listen for the *first two* sounds in each word: **Optional demo:** brave flat, skin, trim, spin, trail
Segmenting II	trap, flap, spy, land, trail, fly	**Optional demo:** spin try, trip, Ty, trail, sky	**Optional demo:** try trail, fly, trim, spin, spy	**Optional demo:** spin sky, trail, land, try, flap	**Optional demo:** spin tree, fast, trail, trick, flap
Decoding	tree, flag, spin, fly, sky	**Optional demo:** try spin, sky, flea, trail, flag	**Optional demo:** try train, flap, step, sky, truck	**Optional demo:** try Ty, flat, land, trap, trip	**Optional demo:** try trim, tree, fast, fly, trick
Sight Words	**New:** our, loves, your, today, two, their, oh, free, again **Review:** boys, new, blue, says, good, day, they, want, now				
Comprehension questions (correct response in **bold**)	Who loves to fly kites? (Ron, Tim, **Ty**, Mom) What is fast? (run, **wind**, bike, when) What does Ty want to try and fly? (bug, **kite**, bite, kit)	What do the boys do with the rope? (**trim**, truck, that, him) What does Ty think his kite will do? (**float**, flag, boat, rope) What does Brad think his kite will do? (stem, spike, **spin**, land)	Where do Ty and Brad ride bikes? (**trail**, lake, tree, rain) What do the boys do at the top of the hill? (sleep, call, step, **stop**) What kind of land does Brad spy? (flop, fly, **flat**, hat)	What do the kite tails do in the wind? (**flap**, flat, sky, sap) How did Brad and Ty run? (slow, **fast**, funny, past) Where did the kites float? (skip, **sky**, say, flat) What will trap Ty's kite? (**tree**, truck, float, bee)	Where is the kite? (train, trail, **tree**, free) Who freed the kite from the tree? (Tim, Ty, Ben, **Brad**) What did the kites do in the sky? (**flip**, sip, flat, fast) What did the boys get the kites to do? (friend, **fly**, flag, dry)

Letter/sound identification

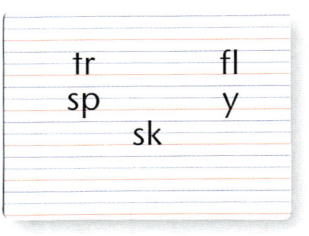

Objective 1
Identify tr, fl, sk, sp, and y (long ī) when given the sounds /tr/, /fl/, /sk/, /sp/, and /aɪ/.
Pronunciation: /aɪ/ as in tr<u>y</u>

Prompting
- Lesson 1: Time delay 0 seconds
- Lessons 2–5: Time delay 4 seconds

Activity directions
I'll say a sound(s) and you find the letter(s) that make that sound.

Teaching moment
✔ Introduce /tr/, /fl/, /sk/, and /sp/. **Today we are going to read more words that blend two sounds together.** Point to the tiles on the software screen showing the tr, fl, sk, and sp tiles or write and point to them on the dry-erase board. Tell students, **These letters blend together to say /tr/, /fl/, /sk/, and /sp/.**

✔ Introduce y (/aɪ/). Point to the y in the corner of the long ī tile on the software screen or write and point to y on the dry-erase board. Tell students, **You already learned the y sound /j/ but sometimes y says /aɪ/. Here it is on the long ī tile.**

✔ If the student chooses an incorrect response, give a reminder to not guess but to wait and you will help. You can also add to the directions, **If you are not sure of the answer, don't guess. Wait for me to help you.**

Cue	Student's independent response	If student needs help
What letters say /<u>tr</u>/?	Finds the letters <u>tr</u> to make the /<u>tr</u>/ sound.	If no response after 4 seconds or an incorrect response, model finding the letter/sound, and continue pointing to it until the student finds it. If needed, physically guide the student to find the letters and say, **This is /<u>tr</u>/.**

Repeat with fl, sk, sp, and y (long ī) and Level 15 review: sl, br, st, and bl.

Blending

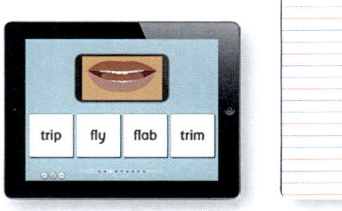

Objective 2
Blend sounds to form CV, CCV, CCVC, CVCC, and CCVvC words.
Pronunciation: /eɪ/ as in tr<u>ai</u>l

Prompting
- Lesson 1: Time delay 0 seconds
- Lessons 2–5: Time delay 4 seconds

Activity directions
I'll say some sounds. You blend the sounds together and find the word they make.

Teaching moment
✔ Prolong or emphasize the sounds at the beginning, middle, or end to help the student identify the word.

✔ Provide a one-second pause between the sounds to help students process the sounds.

Cue	Student's independent response	If student needs help
/tr/ /eɪ/ /l/. **Which word am I saying?**	Finds the word <u>trail</u>.	If no response after 4 seconds or an incorrect response, model finding the word and say, **This is <u>trail</u>. You touch it.** Continue pointing to it until the student finds it. If needed, physically guide the student to find the word.

Repeat with the <u>content</u> for each lesson; see **Level 16 Content** on p. 177.

Segmenting I

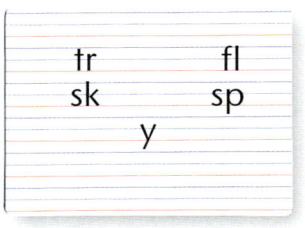

Objective 3
Segment the first two sounds and the last sound in words.
Pronunciation: /aɪ/ as in try

Prompting
- Lesson 1: Time delay 0 seconds
- Lessons 2–5: Time delay 4 seconds

Activity directions
I'll say a word. You show me the first two sounds/last sound you hear in the word.

Teaching moment
✔ To practice without the software, provide more words with /tr/, /fl/, /sk/, and /sp/ in the initial position; also provide more words with y pronounced as /aɪ/ at the end of the words.

✔ Pause for one second between the direction ("What are the first two sounds/is the last sound in") and the target word to prepare the student for the target word.

✔ To make it easier for the student, emphasize or prolong the first two sounds/last sound in the word.

✔ If the student chooses an incorrect response, give a reminder to not guess but to wait and you will help. You can also add to the directions, **If you are not sure of the answer, don't guess. Wait for me to help you.**

Cue	Student's independent response	If student needs help
(Lessons 1, 3, and 5) **What are the first two sounds in trim?**	Finds tr to say /tr/.	If no response after 4 seconds or an incorrect response, model finding tr. Say, **The first two sounds are /tr/. You touch them.** If needed, physically guide the student to find /tr/.
(Lessons 2 and 4) **What is the last sound in sky?**	Finds y to say /aɪ/.	If no response after 4 seconds or an incorrect response, model finding y. Say, **The last sound is /y/. You touch it.** If needed, physically guide the student to find /aɪ/.

Repeat with the content for each lesson; see **Level 16 Content** on p. 177.

Segmenting II

t	r	a	p

Objective 4
Segment the sounds in CV, CCV, CCVC, CVCC, and CCVvC words.
Pronunciation: /æ/ as in tr**a**p

Prompting
- Lesson 1: Time delay 0 seconds
- Lessons 2–5: Time delay 4 seconds

Activity directions
Use the sounds you learned to sound out some words. I'll say a word, and you sound it out.

Teaching moment

✔ To help the student segment all of the sounds in the word, hold up a finger for each sound the student needs to find. Remember to hold up fingers for sounds, not letters (e.g., the word *trail* has 4 sounds but 5 letters).

✔ Or if the student needs help, divide the dry-erase board into sections based on the number of sounds in the word. Have the student sound out the word by choosing one sound at a time on the software screen, while you write the letter/sound the student chooses on the dry-erase board (one sound per section).

✔ If the student chooses an incorrect response, give a reminder to not guess but to wait and you will help. Add to the directions, **If you are not sure of the answer, don't guess. Wait for me to help you.**

✔ If the student makes an error on even one sound, have the student listen as you segment **all** the sounds in the word in the correct sequence. Then restate to touch the sounds in the word.

Cue	Student's independent response	If student needs help
Sound out the word trap.	Touches tr, a, and p for the sounds /tr/, /æ/, and /p/.	If no response after 4 seconds or an incorrect response, say, **Listen, /tr/ /æ/ /p/. Touch the sounds in trap.**
		If still no response or an incorrect response, model segmenting the word by touching each letter and saying each sound. Then say, **Your turn. Touch the sounds in trap.**
		If still no response or an incorrect response, say, **Let's touch the sounds in trap.** Then physically guide the student to touch each sound while you say it.

Repeat with the content for each lesson; see **Level 16 Content** on p. 177.

ERSB Teacher's Guide ■ Level 16

Decoding

Objective 5
Decode CV, CCV, CCVC, CVCC, and CCVvC words and identify their meanings.
Pronunciation: /i/ as in tr<u>ee</u>

Prompting
- Lesson 1: Time delay 0 seconds
- Lessons 2–5: Time delay 4 seconds

Activity directions
Now, use the sounds and letters you learned to read a word and find its picture.

Teaching moment
✔ Be certain the student knows the name of each picture.

✔ If students need help decoding, sound out the word by prolonging each letter sound as you say it. Then say the word (blending the sounds together); find the picture representing it. Be sure to follow this demonstration with independent responding by the student.

Cue	Student's independent response	If student needs help
First, let's hear each picture's name.	Listens as each picture is named.	
Say, **Your turn. Read the word and find the picture.**	Finds the picture of <u>tree</u>.	If no response after 4 seconds, point to the word and say, **This is /tr/ /i/**. Then touch the picture and say, **Here is <u>tree</u>. Now you read <u>tree</u> and find the picture.** Physically guide the student's hand if needed.
		If an incorrect response, point to the letters in the word as you say, **This says <u>tree</u>.** Touch the picture and say, **Here is the picture of <u>tree</u>.** Remove your finger and say, **Now you read <u>tree</u> and find the picture.** Physically guide the student's hand if needed.

Repeat with the <u>content</u> for each lesson; see **Level 16 Content** on p. 177.

Sight words

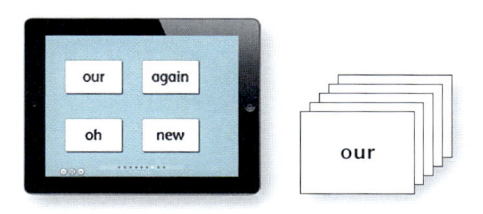

Objective 6
Read 9 new sight words.

Prompting
- Lesson 1: Time delay 0 seconds
- Lessons 2–5: Time delay 4 seconds

Activity directions
Sight words are tricky because you can't sound them out. You have to remember what they look like. Find the word.

Teaching moment
✔ The pace between the presentation of words is purposely rapid to keep the student motivated.

✔ Use the sight word flashcards to provide extra practice of sight word reading. Provide up to 4 response options for students to choose from.

✔ Note that the word *free* is included as a sight word since students have not learned to decode the consonant blend /fr/. However, this is a good opportunity to help the student generalize reading other consonant blends.

✔ If the student chooses an incorrect response, give a reminder to not guess but to wait and you will help. You can also add to the directions, **If you are not sure of the answer, don't guess. Wait for me to help you.**

Cue	Student's independent response	If student needs help
Find the word our.	Finds the word our.	If no response after 4 seconds or an incorrect response, physically guide the student to press our. Say, **This is our.**

Repeat with the new sight words and review sight words, words required for reading the story for this level; see **Level 16 Content** on p. 177.

ERSB Teacher's Guide ■ Level 16

Reading text / Comprehension questions

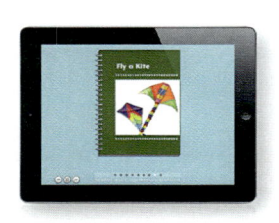

Ron
Tim
Ty
mom

Objective 7 / Objective 8
Read connected text. / Answer comprehension questions about connected text.

Prompting
Least intrusive prompt

Activity directions
Now that you know how to read words, you can read a page from the story. Today you will read about Ty and Brad and their kite-flying adventure.

Teaching moment
✔ One page of the story is read during each lesson, followed by the comprehension questions.

✔ Use **Champion Reader 3** to give students additional reading practice. The comprehension questions that could be asked if not using the software and possible response options are listed in the **Level 16 Content** on p. 177. Write response options on the dry-erase board for students to read.

Cue	Student's independent response	If student needs help
Say, **Read this story silently in your head.** Do not read to the student or point to the words.	Reads the sentences silently.	Reads the sentences silently.
After the student reads the sentences on the page, say, **Let's answer some questions about the story. Who loves to fly kites?**	Chooses the word Ty.	If no response or an incorrect response, say, **Read this sentence again**. Point to each word in the sentence that has the answer, then ask the question again. If still no response or an incorrect response, read the sentence with the answer to the student, **Ty loves to fly kites**. Then ask, **Who loves to fly kites?** If still no response or an incorrect response, physically guide the student to find Ty, and say, **Ty. Ty loves to fly kites.**

Repeat with the content for each lesson; see **Level 16 Content** on p. 177.

Closing /Writing activity

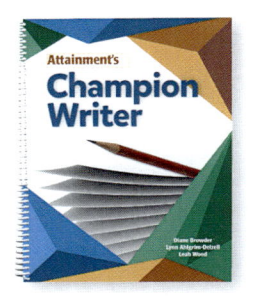

trail
flap
sky

Objective 9
Write responses to activities that review level objectives.

Activity directions
Your lesson is over. GREAT reading today! Let's complete a page in your Champion Writer.

Teaching moment
✔ In order to keep the lesson from becoming too long, consider completing the writing activity at another time of the day.

✔ Some students may need adaptations to complete the writing page in **Champion Writer**; see p. 20 for ideas.

✔ Use the dry-erase board and an erasable marker to give the student practice in writing/forming sight words and words containing the letter/sounds of this level.

LEVEL 17

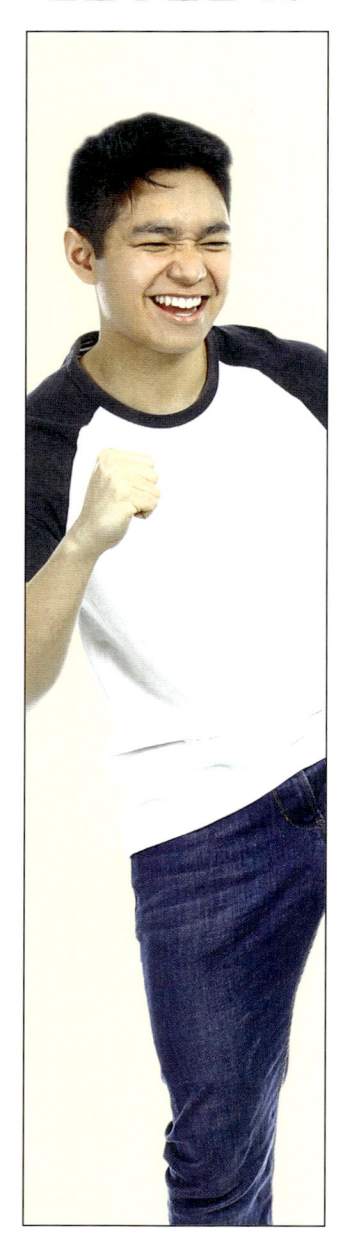

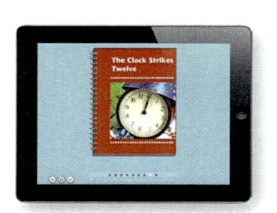

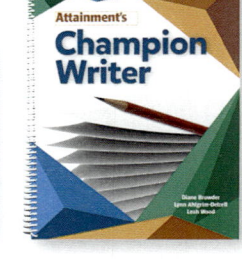

Focus
Consonant clusters—scr, str

Phonemic awareness
- Blend sounds for CCV, CCVC, CCCVC, CCCVCe, and CCCVvC words
- Segment the first two or three sounds in words
- Segment sounds in CCVC, CCVvC, CCCVC, CCCVCe, and CCCVvC words

Phonics
- Sounds /skr/ and /str/ corresponding to graphemes scr and str
- Decode CCVC, CCCVC, CCVvC, CCVCe, CCCVCe, and CCCVvC words and identify their meanings

Sight words
year, twelve, tonight, happy, party, other, night, were

Generalization words
scram, strike, strikes, stress, clock, drum

Connected text
- ATOS level = 1.7
- Lexile level = 300L

Objectives
1. Identify scr and str when given the sounds /skr/ and /str/.
2. Blend sounds to form CCV, CCVC, CCCVC, CCCVCe, and CCCVvC words.
3. Segment the first two or three sounds in words.
4. Segment the sounds in CCVC, CCVvC, CCCVC, CCCVCe, and CCCVvC words.
5. Decode CCVC, CCCVC, CCVvC, CCVCe, CCCVCe, and CCCVvC words and identify their meanings.
6. Read 8 new sight words.
7. Read connected text.
8. Answer comprehension questions about connected text.
9. Write responses to activities that review level objectives.

Teaching notes
This level introduces students to consonant clusters, scr and str. Consonant clusters are there consonants that blend together. The focus is on these clusters in the initial position of words. Though each cluster is presented together on one tile, the student should learn that they are three separate sounds that "blend" together. It is also correct if, when segmenting, the student chooses the three sounds of the cluster individually.

Level 17 Content

	Lesson 1	**Lesson 2**	**Lesson 3**	**Lesson 4**	**Lesson 5**
Letter/sound identification	**New:** scr, str **Review:** tr, fl, sk, sp, y (ī)				
Blending	strum, scream, struck, scrub, street, scrape	**Optional demo:** scrub strap, slim, screen, stripe, stay	**Optional demo:** scrub tram, screen, street, fly, strap	**Optional demo:** scrub scream, strum, stuck, strut, spud	**Optional demo:** scrub tram, skin, screen, strap, spin
Segmenting I	Listen for the *first three* sounds in each word: strong, scrap, scream, strip, straight, strum	Listen for the *first two/three* sounds in each word: **Optional demo:** street flag, stripe, scratch, skunk, tree	Listen for the *first two/three* sounds in each word: **Optional demo:** street scrub, struck, flip, strap, spin	Listen for the *first two/three* sounds in each word: **Optional demo:** street scrap, strum, skate, screen, trim	Listen for the *first three* sounds in each word: **Optional demo:** street scream, scrap, struck, strum, screen
Segmenting II	scream, strap, scrub, trap, screen, struck	**Optional demo:** stripe strap, stream, screen, fled, strum	**Optional demo:** strap stripe, Sloan, strum, flag, street	**Optional demo:** stripe stuck, scream, skid, steam, strap	**Optional demo:** stripe strum, spin, screen, steam, scream
Decoding	scream, scrub, stream, screen, stripe, steam	**Optional demo:** stripe street, scream, skate, flag, strap	**Optional demo:** stripe screen, train, spin, street, strap	**Optional demo:** stripe strap, stream, flag, scream, screen	**Optional demo:** stripe street, strap, scream, skip, trick
Sight Words	**New:** year, twelve, tonight, happy, party, other, night, were **Review:** friends, walk, door, new, dance, there				
Comprehension questions (correct response in **bold**)	Who will go to the party with Brad and Ty? (Slim, Loan, **Sloan**, Gus) What will the friends do when the clock strikes twelve? (stream, **scream**, scrunch, sleep)	What does Ty say not to do? (stem, tess, **stress**, yell) Where do the friends scram to? (**street**, tweet, stem, walk)	What kind of door do the friends see? (**screen**, blue, scram, seen) Who is on the other side of the door? (**friends**, bugs, bands, fry) What looks like fun? (stay, star, year, **party**)	What do Zack and Sam beat on? (strum, stripe, **drum**, stem) What do the friends do? (Brad, **dance**, down, friends) Brad said there is not a what? (dance, **scrap**, strap, scram) Who thinks the friends were late to the party? (Brim, **Brad**, Sloan, Tad)	What speed is the beat? (slow, fly, **fast**, mast) What will the clock do at twelve? (scream, **strike**, bike, door) What did the clock strike? (two, **twelve**, boys, ten) What do the friends do when the clock strikes twelve? (stress, screen, **scream**, dance)

Letter/sound identification

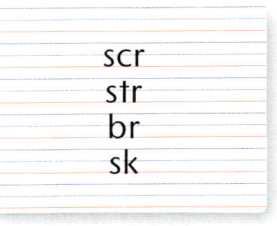

scr
str
br
sk

Objective 1
Identify scr and str when given the sound /skr/ and /str/.
Pronunciation: /skr/ as in scream

Prompting
- Lesson 1: Time delay 0 seconds
- Lessons 2–5: Time delay 4 seconds

Activity directions
I'll say sounds and you find the letters that make those sounds.

Teaching moment
✓ Introduce /skr/ and /str/. **Today we are going to read words that blend three sounds together.**

✓ Point to the tiles on the software screen showing the scr and str tiles or write and point to them on the dry-erase board. Tell students, **These letters blend together to say /skr/ and /str/.**

✓ If the student chooses an incorrect response, give a reminder to not guess but to wait and you will help. You can also add to the directions, **If you are not sure of the answer, don't guess. Wait for me to help you.**

Cue	Student's independent response	If student needs help
What letters say /skr/?	Finds the letters scr to make the /skr/ sound.	If no response after 4 seconds or an incorrect response, model finding the letter/sound, and continue pointing to it until the student finds it. If needed, physically guide the student to find the letters and say, **This says /skr/. You touch it.**

Repeat with str and Level 16 review: tr, fl, sk, sp, y (ī).

Blending

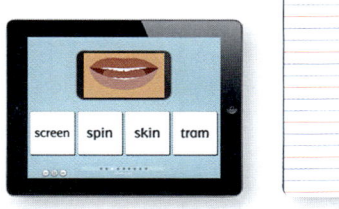

Objective 2
Blend sounds to form CCV, CCVC, CCCVC, CCCVCe, and CCCVvC words.
Pronunciation: /ʌ/ as in str**u**m

Prompting
- Lesson 1: Time delay 0 seconds
- Lessons 2–5: Time delay 4 seconds

Activity directions
I'll say some sounds. You blend the sounds together and find the word they make.

Teaching moment
✔ Prolong or emphasize the sounds at the beginning, middle, or end to help the student identify the word.

✔ Provide a one-second pause between the sounds to help students process the sounds.

Cue	Student's independent response	If student needs help
/str/ /ʌ/ /m/. **Which word am I saying?**	Finds the word strum.	If no response after 4 seconds or an incorrect response, model finding the word and say, **This is strum. You touch it.** Continue pointing to it until the student finds it. If needed, physically guide the student to find the word.

Repeat with the content for each lesson; see **Level 17 Content** on p. 187.

ERSB Teacher's Guide ■ Level 17

Segmenting I

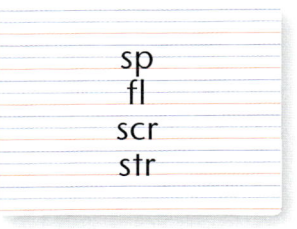

Objective 3
Segment the first two or three sounds in words.
Pronunciation: /str/ as in strap

Prompting
- Lesson 1: Time delay 0 seconds
- Lessons 2–5: Time delay 4 seconds

Activity directions
I'll say a word. You show me the first sound you hear in the word.

Teaching moment
✔ To practice without the software, provide more words with /skr/ and /str/ in the initial position of words.

✔ Pause for one second between the direction ("What are the first three sounds in") and the target word to prepare the student for the target word.

✔ To make it easier for the student, emphasize or prolong the first sounds in the word.

✔ If the student chooses an incorrect response, give a reminder to not guess but to wait and you will help. You can also add to the directions, **If you are not sure of the answer, don't guess. Wait for me to help you.**

Cue	Student's independent response	If student needs help
What are the first three sounds in strong?	Finds str to say /str/.	If no response after 4 seconds or an incorrect response, model finding str. Say, **The first three sounds are /str/. You touch them.** If needed, physically guide the student to find /str/.
What are the first two sounds in flag?	Finds fl to say /fl/.	If no response after 4 seconds or an incorrect response, model finding fl. Say, **The first two sounds are /fl/. You touch them.** If needed, physically guide the student to find /fl/.

Repeat with the content for each lesson; see **Level 17 Content** on p. 187.

Segmenting II

Objective 4
Segment the sounds in CCVC, CCVvC, CCCVC, CCCVCe, and CCCVvC words.
Pronunciation: /skr/ as in scream, /i/ as in scream

Prompting
- Lesson 1: Time delay 0 seconds
- Lessons 2–5: Time delay 4 seconds

Activity directions
Use the sounds you learned to sound out some words. I'll say a word, and you sound it out.

Teaching moment
✔ To help the student segment all of the sounds in the word, hold up a finger for each sound the student needs to find. Remember to hold up fingers for sounds, not letters (e.g., the word *scream* has 5 sounds but 6 letters; *street* has 5 sounds but 6 letters).

✔ Or if the student needs help, divide the dry-erase board into sections based on the number of sounds in the word. Have the student sound out the word by choosing one sound at a time on the software screen, while you write the letter/sound the student chooses on the dry-erase board (one sound per section).

✔ If the student chooses an incorrect response, give a reminder to not guess but to wait and you will help. Add to the directions, **If you are not sure of the answer, don't guess. Wait for me to help you.**

✔ If the student makes an error on even one sound, have the student listen as you segment **all** the sounds in the word in the correct sequence. Then restate to touch the sounds in the word.

Cue	Student's independent response	If student needs help
Sound out the word scream.	Touches scr, ea, and m for the sounds /skr/, /i/, and /m/.	If no response after 4 seconds or an incorrect response, say, **Listen, /scr/ /i/ /m/. Touch the sounds in scream.**
		If still no response or an incorrect response, model segmenting the word by touching each letter and saying each sound. Then say, **Your turn. Touch the sounds in scream.**
		If still no response or an incorrect response, say, **Let's touch the sounds in scream.** Then physically guide the student to touch each sound while you say it.

Repeat with the content for each lesson; see **Level 17 Content** on p. 187.

Decoding

Objective 5
Decode CCVC, CCCVC, CCVvC, CCVCe, CCCVCe, and CCCVvC words and identify their meanings.
Pronunciation: /i/ as in scr<u>ea</u>m

Prompting
- Lesson 1: Time delay 0 seconds
- Lessons 2–5: Time delay 4 seconds

Activity directions
Now, use the sounds and letters you learned to read a word and find its picture.

Teaching moment
✔ Be certain the student knows the name of each picture.

✔ If students need help decoding, sound out the word by prolonging each letter sound as you say it. Then say the word (blending the sounds together); find the picture representing it. Be sure to follow this demonstration with independent responding by the student.

Cue	Student's independent response	If student needs help
First, let's hear each picture's name.	Listens as each picture is named.	
Say, **Your turn. Read the word and find the picture.**	Finds the picture of <u>scream</u>.	If no response after 4 seconds, point to the word and say, **This is /scr/ /i/ /m/**. Then touch the picture and say, **Here is <u>scream</u>. Now you read <u>scream</u> and find the picture.** Physically guide the student's hand if needed.
		If an incorrect response, point to the letters in the word as you say, **This says <u>scream</u>.** Touch the picture and say, **Here is the picture of <u>scream</u>.** Remove your finger and say, **Now you read <u>scream</u> and find the picture.** Physically guide the student's hand if needed.

Repeat with the <u>content</u> for each lesson; see **Level 17 Content** on p. 187.

Sight words

Objective 6
Read 8 new sight words.

Prompting
- Lesson 1: Time delay 0 seconds
- Lessons 2–5: Time delay 4 seconds

Activity directions
Sight words are tricky because you can't sound them out. You have to remember what they look like. **Find the word.**

Teaching moment

✔ The pace between the presentation of words is purposely rapid to keep the student motivated.

✔ Use the sight word flashcards to provide extra practice of sight word reading. Provide up to 4 response options for students to choose from.

✔ Note that the word *twelve* is included is included as a sight word since students have not learned to decode the tw consonant blend, nor the rule of the silent e at the end of this word. However, this is a good opportunity to help the student generalize reading other consonant blends (tw).

✔ If the student chooses an incorrect response, give a reminder to not guess but to wait and you will help. You can also add to the directions, **If you are not sure of the answer, don't guess. Wait for me to help you.**

Cue	Student's independent response	If student needs help
Find the word year.	Finds the word year.	If no response after 4 seconds or an incorrect response, model finding the word and say, **This is year. You touch it.** Physically guide the student to find the word if needed.

Repeat with the new sight words and review sight words, words required for reading the story for this level; see **Level 17 Content** on p. 187.

ERSB Teacher's Guide ■ Level 17

Reading text / Comprehension questions

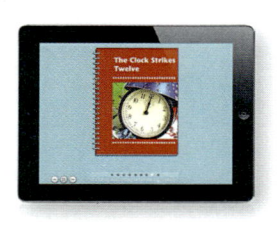

Slim
Loan
Sloan
Gus

Objective 7 / Objective 8
Read connected text. / Answer comprehension questions about connected text.

Prompting
Least intrusive prompt

Activity directions
Now that you know how to read words, you can read a page from the story. Today you will read about Sloan, Brad, and Ty celebrating New Year's Eve at a party.

Teaching moment
✔ One page of the story is read during each lesson, followed by the comprehension questions.

✔ Use **Champion Reader 3** to give students additional reading practice. The comprehension questions that could be asked if not using the software and possible response options are listed in the **Level 17 Content** on p. 187. Write response options on the dry-erase board for students to read.

Cue	Student's independent response	If student needs help
Say, **Read this story silently in your head.** Do not read to the student or point to the words.	Reads the sentences silently.	

(Table continues)

Cue	Student's independent response	If student needs help
After the student reads the sentences on the page, say, **Let's answer some questions about the story. Who will go to the party with Brad and Ty?**	Chooses the word Sloan.	If no response or an incorrect response, say, **Read this sentence again.** Point to each word in the sentence that has the answer, then ask the question again. If still no response or an incorrect response, read the sentence with the answer to the student, **Sloan, Ty, and Brad want to go to a party.** Then ask, **Who will go to the party with Brad and Ty?** If still no response or an incorrect response, physically guide the student to find Sloan, and say, **Sloan. Sloan, Ty, and Brad want to go to a party.**

Repeat with the content for each lesson; see **Level 17 Content** on p. 187.

Closing /Writing activity

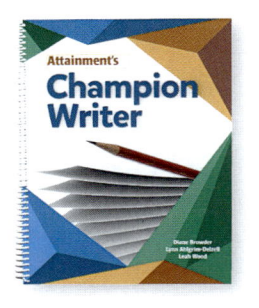

scream
street
screen

Objective 9
Write responses to activities that review level objectives.

Activity directions
Your lesson is over. GREAT reading today! Let's complete a page in your Champion Writer.

Teaching moment

✔ In order to keep the lesson from becoming too long, consider completing the writing activity at another time of the day.

✔ Some students may need adaptations to complete the writing page in **Champion Writer**; see p. 20 for ideas.

✔ Use the dry-erase board and an erasable marker to give the student practice in writing/forming sight words and words containing the letter/sounds of this level.

LEVEL 18

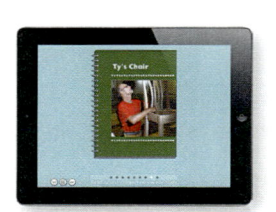

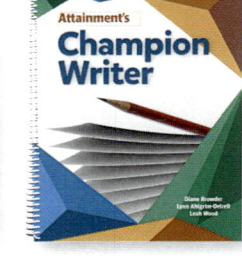

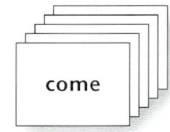

Focus
Consonant digraphs—th, sh, ch

Phonemic awareness
- Blend sounds for CVC, CVvC, CCCVC, and CVCe words
- Segment first and last sounds in words
- Segment sounds in CVC, CVvC, CCCVC, and CVCe words

Phonics
- Sounds /θ/, /ʃ/, and /tʃ/ corresponding to graphemes th, sh, and ch
- Decode CVC, CVvC, CCCVC, and CVCe words and identify their meanings

Sight words
come, both, from, more, one, done, pretty, use, breaks, push

Generalization words
shock, faith

Connected text
- ATOS level = 1.7
- Lexile level = 330L

Objectives
1. Identify th, sh, and ch when given the sounds /θ/, /ʃ/, and /tʃ/.
2. Blend sounds to form CVC, CVvC, CCCVC, and CVCe words.
3. Segment the first and last sounds in words.
4. Segment the sounds in CVC, CVvC, CCCVC, and CVCe words.
5. Decode CVC, CVvC, CCCVC, and CVCe words and identify their meanings.
6. Read 10 new sight words.
7. Read connected text.
8. Answer comprehension questions about connected text.
9. Write responses to activities that review level objectives.

Teaching notes
This level introduces the digraphs th, sh, and ch. A digraph is a single sound represented by two letters (e.g., th). Note that th can be produced with voicing from the larynx (as in the word *the*) or without voicing (as in the word *thin*). This level will only introduce the unvoiced th /θ/, since many words with the voiced th are introduced as sight words (e.g., *there, then, them*).

Level 18 Content

	Lesson 1	Lesson 2	Lesson 3	Lesson 4	Lesson 5
Letter/sound identification	**New:** th, sh, ch **Review:** scr, str				
Blending	chair, thin, shin, shed, teach, thud	**Optional demo:** mush thin, chill, path, scram, shape	**Optional demo:** thin chime, mush, Chet, math, thick	**Optional demo:** mush thug, chair, sheet, street, teach	**Optional demo:** mush thud, chair, thick, shape, sheet
Segmenting I	Listen for the *first* sound in each word: thud, shed, Chet, shadow, chin, thick	Listen for the *last* sound in each word: **Optional demo:** math teach, push, much, flash, path	Listen for the *first* sound in each word: **Optional demo:** thick shed, thin, channel, shelter, thank	Listen for the *last* sound in each word: **Optional demo:** math much, breath, teach, bath, push	Listen for the *first* sound in each word: **Optional demo:** thick Chet, thirsty, chin, shelter, think
Segmenting II	shut, wish, thin, path, sheet, chin	**Optional demo:** chin much, bath, sheet, chat, scrap	**Optional demo:** chin path, shine, strap, chair, chip	**Optional demo:** chin shed, shut, much, thin, wish	**Optional demo:** chin much, thin, cheek, path, teeth
Decoding	trash, teeth, sheet, chair, path, chin	**Optional demo:** trash shave, strap, path, Chet, flash	**Optional demo:** trash shine, chair, bath, sheet, chin	**Optional demo:** trash chin, bath, chair, Chet, path	**Optional demo:** trash scrub, path, sheet, flash, chair
Sight Words	**New:** come, both, from, more, one, done, pretty, use, breaks, push **Review:** says, yellow, walk, down, now, right, their				
Comprehension questions (correct response in **bold**)	Where does Dad take Ty? (shine, chop, **shop**, chair) Where do they go to get the oak? (**shed**, oak, chip, bed)	What does the nail make on the oak? (big, ship, **gash**, good) What kind of nails does Ty need? (dip, **big**, bug, now)	What does Ty make? (**chair**, shine, chin, make) What color does Ty paint the chair? (green, blue, yet, **yellow**) Who will sit on Mom's lap? (**Chet**, Chad, Ben, Mom)	What is wrong with one leg on the chair? (thick, blue, **thin**, chin) What happens when Ty sits on the chair? (**breaks**, braid, fix, brim) After Dad sands the chair, what does Ty do to it? (chair, **paints**, path, pat)	Where does Ty hide the chair? (**shed**, tree, ship, chat) What does Mom do when she sees her new chair? (**likes**, smell, shine, much) How does she thank Ty? (kit, miss, thank, **kiss**)

Letter/sound identification

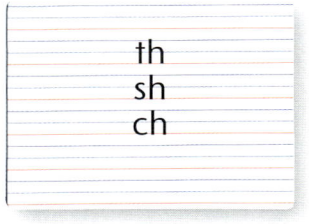

Objective 1
Identify th, sh, and ch when given the sounds /θ/, /ʃ/, and /ch/.
Pronunciation: /θ/ as in <u>th</u>in, /ʃ/ as in <u>sh</u>in, /tʃ/ as in <u>ch</u>in

Prompting
- Lesson 1: Time delay 0 seconds
- Lessons 2–5: Time delay 4 seconds

Activity directions
I'll say a sound, and you find the letter that makes that sound.

Teaching moment

✓ Introduce /θ/, /ʃ/, and /tʃ/. **Today we are going to learn to read letters that together make one sound.**

✓ Point to the tile on the software screen showing th or write and point to the letters on the dry-erase board. Tell students, **These letters make one sound. Even though there are two letters, together they make one sound. The letters th say /th/; to say th the tongue goes between our teeth.**

✓ Point to the tiles on the software screen showing the sh and ch tiles or write and point to them on the dry-erase board. Tell students, **These letters also make one sound. The letters sh say /ʃ/. The letters ch say /tʃ/. To say sh and ch, your tongue is on the top of your mouth. Ch pops out and sh is like saying to be quiet, shhhh.**

✓ If the student chooses an incorrect response, give a reminder to not guess but to wait and you will help. You can also add to the directions, **If you are not sure of the answer, don't guess. Wait for me to help you.**

Cue	Student's independent response	If student needs help
What letters say /θ/?	Finds the letters <u>th</u> to make the /θ/ sound.	If no response after 4 seconds or an incorrect response, model finding the letter/sound, and continue pointing to it until the student finds it. If needed, physically guide the student to find the letter and say, **This is /θ/. You touch it.**

Repeat with sh, ch and Level 17 review: scr and str.

Blending

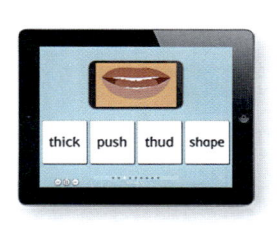

Objective 2
Blend sounds to form CVC, CVvC, CCCVC, and CVCe words.
Pronunciation: /tʃ/ as in <u>ch</u>in, /eɪ/ as in p<u>a</u>ne

Prompting
- Lesson 1: Time delay 0 seconds
- Lessons 2–5: Time delay 4 seconds

Activity directions
I'll say some sounds. You blend the sounds together and find the word they make.

Teaching moment
✔ Prolong or emphasize the sounds at the beginning or end to help the student identify the word.

✔ Provide a one-second pause between the sounds to help students process the sounds.

✔ Note that *air* in the word *chair* in this level is considered a long ā (/eɪ/) followed by a consonantal /r/, even though it might be considered an r-controlled vowel (air).

Cue	Student's independent response	If student needs help
/<u>ch</u>/ /<u>eɪ</u>/ /<u>r</u>/. Which word am I saying?	Finds the word <u>chair</u>.	If no response after 4 seconds or an incorrect response, model finding the word and say, **This is <u>chair</u>. You touch it.** Continue pointing to it until the student finds it. If needed, physically guide the student to find the word.

Repeat with the <u>content</u> for each lesson; see **Level 18 Content** on p. 197.

ERSB Teacher's Guide ■ Level 18

Segmenting I

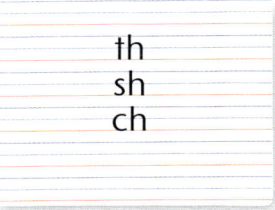

Objective 3
Segment the first and last sounds in words.
Pronunciation: /θ/ as in thin, /ʃ/ as in shin, /tʃ/ as in chin

Prompting
- Lesson 1: Time delay 0 seconds
- Lessons 2–5: Time delay 4 seconds

Activity directions
I'll say a word. You show me the first/last sound you hear in the word.

Teaching moment
✔ To practice without the software, provide more words containing unvoiced /θ/, /ʃ/, and /tʃ/.

✔ Pause for one second between the direction ("What is the first/last sound in") and the target word to prepare the student for the target word.

✔ To make it easier for the student, emphasize or prolong the first/last sound in the word.

✔ If the student chooses an incorrect response, give a reminder to not guess but to wait and you will help. You can also add to the directions, **If you are not sure of the answer, don't guess. Wait for me to help you.**

Cue	Student's independent response	If student needs help
(Lessons 1, 3, and 5) **What is the first sound in thud?**	Finds th to say /θ/.	If no response after 4 seconds or an incorrect response, model finding th. Say, **The first sound is /θ/. You touch it.** If needed, physically guide the student to find /θ/.
(Lessons 2 and 4) **What is the last sound in math?**	Finds th to say /θ/.	If no response after 4 seconds or an incorrect response, model finding th. Say, **The first sound is /θ/. You touch it.** If needed, physically guide the student to find /θ/.

Repeat with the content for each lesson; see **Level 18 Content** on p. 197.

Segmenting II

sh	u	t

Objective 4
Segment the sounds in CVC, CVvC, CCCVC, and CVCe words.
Pronunciation: /ʃ/ as in <u>sh</u>in, /ʌ/ as in sh<u>u</u>t

Prompting
- Lesson 1: Time delay 0 seconds
- Lessons 2–5: Time delay 4 seconds

Activity directions
Use the sounds you learned to sound out some words. I'll say a word, and you sound it out.

Teaching moment

✔ To help the student segment all of the sounds in the word, hold up a finger for each sound the student needs to find. Remember to hold up fingers for sounds, not letters (e.g., the word *shut* has 3 sounds but 4 letters).

✔ Or if the student needs help, divide the dry-erase board into sections based on the number of sounds in the word. Have the student sound out the word by choosing one sound at a time on the software screen, while you write the letter/sound the student chooses on the dry-erase board (one sound per section).

✔ If the student chooses an incorrect response, give a reminder to not guess but to wait and you will help. Add to the directions, **If you are not sure of the answer, don't guess. Wait for me to help you.**

✔ If the student makes an error on even one sound, have the student listen as you segment **all** the sounds in the word in the correct sequence. Then restate to touch the sounds in the word.

Cue	Student's independent response	If student needs help
Sound out the word <u>shut</u>.	Touches <u>sh</u>, <u>u</u>, and <u>t</u> for the sounds /ʃ/, /ʌ/, and /t/.	If no response after 4 seconds or an incorrect response, say, **Listen, /ʃ/ /ʌ/ /t/. Touch the sounds in <u>shut</u>.** If still no response or an incorrect response, model segmenting the word by touching each letter and saying each sound. Then say, **Your turn. Touch the sounds in <u>shut</u>.** If still no response or an incorrect response, say, **Let's touch the sounds in <u>shut</u>.** Then physically guide the student to touch each sound while you say it.

Repeat with the <u>content</u> for each lesson; see **Level 18 Content** on p. 197.

ERSB Teacher's Guide ■ Level 18

Decoding

Objective 5
Decode CVC, CVvC, CCCVC, and CVCe words and identify their meanings.
Pronunciation: /ʃ/ as in <u>sh</u>in, /æ/ as in <u>a</u>m

Prompting
- Lesson 1: Time delay 0 seconds
- Lessons 2–5: Time delay 4 seconds

Activity directions
Now, use the sounds and letters you learned to read a word and find its picture.

Teaching moment
✔ Be certain the student knows the name of each picture.

✔ If students need help decoding, sound out the word by prolonging each letter sound as you say it. Then say the word (blending the sounds together); find the picture representing it. Be sure to follow this demonstration with independent responding by the student.

Cue	Student's independent response	If student needs help
First, let's hear each picture's name.	Listens as each picture is named.	
Say, **Your turn. Read the word and find the picture.**	Finds the picture of <u>trash</u>.	If no response after 4 seconds, point to the word and say, **This is /tr/ /æ/ /ʃ/.** Then touch the picture and say, **Here is <u>trash</u>. Now you read <u>trash</u> and find the picture.** Physically guide the student's hand if needed. If an incorrect response, point to the letters in the word as you say, **This says <u>trash</u>.** Touch the picture and say, **Here is the picture of <u>trash</u>.** Remove your finger and say, **Now you read <u>trash</u> and find the picture.** Physically guide the student's hand if needed.

Repeat with the <u>content</u> for each lesson; see **Level 18 Content** on p. 197.

Sight words

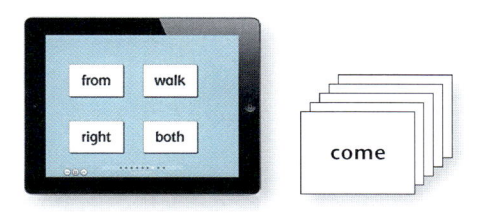

Objective 6
Read 10 new sight words.

Prompting
- Lesson 1: Time delay 0 seconds
- Lessons 2–5: Time delay 4 seconds

Activity directions
Sight words are tricky because you can't sound them out. You have to remember what they look like. Find the word.

Teaching moment
- ✔ The pace between the presentation of words is purposely rapid to keep the student motivated.
- ✔ Use the sight word flashcards to provide extra practice of sight word reading. Provide up to 4 response options for students to choose from.
- ✔ Note that the word *push* is included as a sight word since students have not yet learned the sound /ʊ/.
- ✔ If the student chooses an incorrect response, give a reminder to not guess but to wait and you will help. You can also add to the directions, **If you are not sure of the answer, don't guess. Wait for me to help you.**

Cue	Student's independent response	If student needs help
Find the word come.	Finds the word come.	If no response after 4 seconds or an incorrect response, model finding the word and say, **This is come. You touch it.** Physically guide the student to find the word if needed.

Repeat with the new sight words and review sight words, words required for reading the story for this level; see **Level 18 Content** on p. 197.

ERSB Teacher's Guide ■ Level 18

Reading text / Comprehension questions

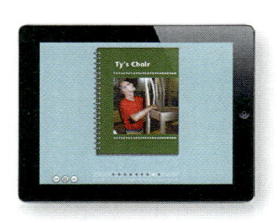

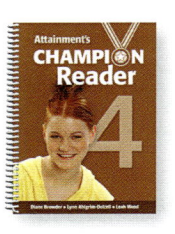

Objective 7 / Objective 8
Read connected text. / Answer comprehension questions about connected text.

Prompting
Least intrusive prompt

Activity directions
Now that you know how to read words, you can read a page from the story. Today you will read about a surprise Ty made for his mother.

Teaching moment
✔ One page of the story is read during each lesson, followed by the comprehension questions.

✔ Use **Champion Reader 4** to give students additional reading practice. The comprehension questions that could be asked if not using the software and possible response options are listed in the **Level 18 Content** on p. 197. Write response options on the dry-erase board for students to read.

Cue	Student's independent response	If student needs help
Say, **Read this story silently in your head.** Do not read to the student or point to the words.	Reads the sentences silently.	

(Table continues)

Cue	Student's independent response	If student needs help
After the student reads the sentences on the page, say, **Let's answer some questions about the story. Where does Dad take Ty?**	Chooses the word shop.	If no response or an incorrect response, say, **Read this sentence again**. Point to each word in the sentence that has the answer, then ask the question again. If still no response or an incorrect response, read the sentence with the answer to the student, **Dad says to Ty, "Come with me to my shop."** Then ask, **Where does Dad take Ty?** If still no response or an incorrect response, physically guide the student to find shop, and say, **Shop. Dad took Ty to the shop**.

Repeat with the content for each lesson; see **Level 18 Content** on p. 197.

Closing /Writing activity

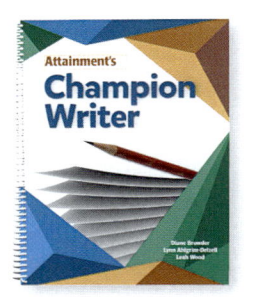

Objective 9
Write responses to activities that review level objectives.

Activity directions
Your lesson is over. GREAT reading today! Let's complete a page in your Champion Writer.

Teaching moment

✔ In order to keep the lesson from becoming too long, consider completing the writing activity at another time of the day.

✔ Some students may need adaptations to complete the writing page in **Champion Writer**; see p. 20 for ideas.

✔ Use the dry-erase board and an erasable marker to give the student practice in writing/forming sight words and words containing the letter/sounds of this level.

ERSB Teacher's Guide ■ Level 18

LEVEL 19

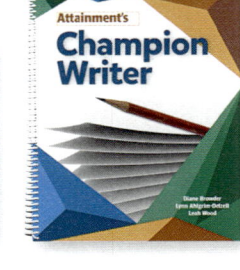

Focus
Consonant digraphs—wh, ph; consonant blend—gr

Phonemic awareness
- Blend sounds for CVC, CVCe, CCV, CCVC, and CVvC words
- Segment first and last sounds in words
- Segment sounds in CVC, CVCe, CCVC, and CCVvC words

Phonics
- Sounds /w/, /f/, and /gr/ corresponding to graphemes wh, ph, and gr
- Decode CVC, CVCe, CVvC, CCVvC, and CCVC words and identify their meanings

Sight words
said, text, break, only, think, should, great, fair, okay

Generalization words
whim, shack, whine, without

Connected text
- ATOS level = 2.2
- Lexile level = 370L

Objectives
1. Identify wh, ph, and gr when given the sounds /w/, /f/, and /gr/.
2. Blend sounds to form CVC, CVCe, CCV, CCVv, CCVC, and CVvC words.
3. Segment the first and last sounds in words.
4. Segment the sounds in CVC, CVCe, CCVC, and CCVvC words.
5. Decode CVC, CVCe, CVvC, CCVvC, and CCVC words and identify their meanings.
6. Read 9 new sight words.
7. Read connected text.
8. Answer comprehension questions about connected text.
9. Write responses to activities that review level objectives.

Teaching notes
This level introduces the digraphs wh and ph. A digraph is a single sound represented by two letters (e.g., wh) but both of these digraphs say sounds already introduced, thus wh is added to the /w/ tile and ph is added to the /f/ tile. Note that wh is often produced as /hw/, however, this level will not make that distinction for students.

Level 19 Content

	Lesson 1	Lesson 2	Lesson 3	Lesson 4	Lesson 5
Letter/sound identification	**New**: wh (on the w tile), ph (on the f tile), gr **Review**: sh, ch, th				
Blending	wham, Phan, pain, graph, ban, whip	**Optional demo**: thick which, phone, tree, graph, while	**Optional demo**: thick graph, wham, phone, Phan, grim	**Optional demo**: thick Phan, with, graph, buzz, which	**Optional demo**: thick while, maid, phone, wham, graph
Segmenting I	**Listen for the *first* sound in each word:** which, champ, phone, green, shelter, Phan	**Listen for the *last* sound in each word:** **Optional demo**: mush bath, graph, teeth, proof, buzz	**Listen for the *first* sound in each word:** **Optional demo**: photo whip, grape, which, Phan, chip	**Listen for the *last* sound in each word:** **Optional demo**: mush path, wish, push, which, graph	**Listen for the *first* sound in each word:** **Optional demo**: photo green, whip, which, shell, Phan
Segmenting II	which, phone, green, with, whip, math	**Optional demo**: whine graph, bath, whim, math, phone	**Optional demo**: whine phone, much, Phan, buzz, which	**Optional demo**: whine while, with, graph, whop, phone	**Optional demo**: whine Phan, buzz, graph, with, which
Decoding	whip, wheel, phone, teeth, graph, green	**Optional demo**: teeth trash, phone, whip, graph, wheel	**Optional demo**: trash whip, phone, graph, chin, green	**Optional demo**: trash wheel, path, chip, phone, whip	**Optional demo**: trash which, wheel, phone, whip, chin
Sight Words	**New**: said, text, break, only, think, should, great, fair, okay **Review**: one, two, both, have				
Comprehension questions (correct response in **bold**)	What class do the girls have together? (**math**, graph, path, mom) How many friends can Beth take to the fair? (two, **one**, tub, ten)	What does Beth have to make for math class? (class, **graph**, math, phone) How does Beth send a text message to Sloan? (cone, **phone**, whim, fine)	What does Tam send to Beth? (**text**, ten, next, each) Who does Beth want to go with her to the fair? (path, bath, **both**, math) Who says Beth can take only one friend? (Dad, **Mom**, Tam, Beth)	What does Beth think about? (**plan**, been, pine, flag) Does Beth have luck coming up with a plan? (**no**, yes, nut, plan) Who does Beth ask for help? (Dad, **Mom**, Mim, Tam) What does Beth do when she asks Mom to help? (**whine**, what, when, laugh)	What does Mom say about taking two friends? (**okay**, no, without, whine) What does Beth whip out fast? (fun, whip, **phone**, home) How are the girls talking to each other? (test, girl, ten, **text**) What does Tam's text say? (green, **great**, graph, not) Before Beth goes to the State Fair, what does she have to finish? (phone, **graph**, good, fair)

Letter/sound identification

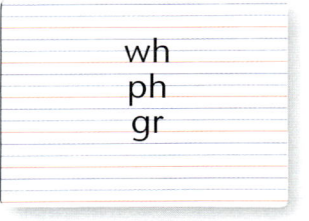

wh
ph
gr

Objective 1
Identify wh, ph, and gr when given the sounds /w/, /f/, and /gr/.
Pronunciation: /w/ as in <u>wh</u>oosh, /f/ as in <u>ph</u>one

Prompting
- Lesson 1: Time delay 0 seconds
- Lessons 2–5: Time delay 4 seconds

Activity directions
I'll say a sound, and you find the letters that makes that sound.

Teaching moment

✓ Introduce wh. **Today we are going to learn to read more letters that together make one sound.** Point to the tile on the software screen showing wh in the corner of the w tile or write and point to the letters on the dry-erase board. Tell students, **These letters make one sound. Even though there are two letters, together they make one sound. The letters wh say /w/, just like w.**

✓ Introduce ph. Point to the tile on the software screen showing ph in the corner of the f tile or write and point to the letters on the dry-erase board. Tell students, **These letters make one sound. Even though there are two letters, together they make one sound. The letters ph say /f/.**

✓ Introduce gr. Point to the tile on the software screen showing gr or write and point to the letters on the dry-erase board. Tell students, **These letters make two sounds, just like other consonant blends we learned. There are two letters and we blend them together to say /gr/.**

✓ If the student chooses an incorrect response, give a reminder to not guess but to wait and you will help. You can also add to the directions, **If you are not sure of the answer, don't guess. Wait for me to help you.**

Cue	Student's independent response	If student needs help
What letters says /<u>w</u>/?	Finds the letters <u>wh</u> to make the /<u>w</u>/ sound.	If no response after 4 seconds or an incorrect response, model finding the letter/sound, and continue pointing to it until the student finds it. If needed, physically guide the student to find the letter and say, **This is /<u>w</u>/. You touch it.**

Repeat with ph, gr, and Level 18 review: th, sh, and ch.

Blending

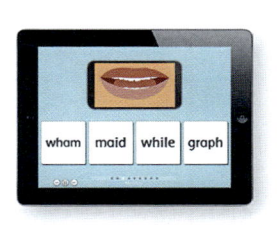

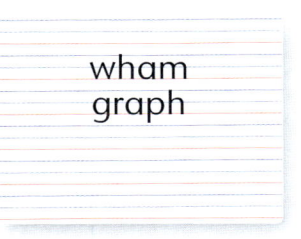

Objective 2
Blend sounds to form CVC, CVCe, CCV, CCVv, CCVC, and CVvC words.
Pronunciation: /æ/ as in <u>a</u>m

Prompting
- Lesson 1: Time delay 0 seconds
- Lessons 2–5: Time delay 4 seconds

Activity directions
I'll say some sounds. You blend the sounds together and find the word they make.

Teaching moment
✔ Prolong or emphasize the sounds at the beginning or end to help the student identify the word.

✔ Provide a one-second pause between the sounds to help students process the sounds.

Cue	Student's independent response	If student needs help
/w/ /æ/ /m/. Which word am I saying?	Finds the word <u>wham</u>.	If no response after 4 seconds or an incorrect response, model finding the word and say, **This is <u>wham</u>. You touch it.** Continue pointing to it until the student finds it. If needed, physically guide the student to find the word.

Repeat with the <u>content</u> for each lesson; see **Level 19 Content** on p. 207.

Segmenting I

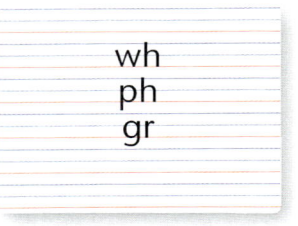

wh
ph
gr

Objective 3
Segment the first and last sounds in words.
Pronunciation: /ʃ/ as in mu<u>sh</u>

Prompting
- Lesson 1: Time delay 0 seconds
- Lessons 2–5: Time delay 4 seconds

Activity directions
I'll say a word. You show me the first/last sound(s) you hear in the word.

Teaching moment
✔ To practice without the software, provide more words containing /w/, /f/, and /gr/.

✔ Pause for one second between the direction ("What is the first/last sounds in") and the target word to prepare the student for the target word.

✔ To make it easier for the student, emphasize or prolong the first/last sound in the word.

✔ If the student chooses an incorrect response, give a reminder to not guess but to wait and you will help. You can also add to the directions, **If you are not sure of the answer, don't guess. Wait for me to help you.**

Cue	Student's independent response	If student needs help
(Lessons 1, 3, and 5) **What is the first sound in <u>which</u>?**	Finds <u>wh</u> to say /w/.	If no response after 4 seconds or an incorrect response, model finding <u>wh</u>. Say, **The first sound is /w/. You touch it.** If needed, physically guide the student to find /w/.
(Lessons 2 and 4) **What is the last sound in <u>mush</u>?**	Finds <u>sh</u> to say /ʃ/.	If no response after 4 seconds or an incorrect response, model finding <u>sh</u>. Say, **The last sound is /sh/. You touch it.** If needed, physically guide the student to find /ʃ/.

Repeat with the <u>content</u> for each lesson; see **Level 19 Content** on p. 207.

Segmenting II

wh	i	ch

Objective 4
Segment the sounds in CVC, CVCe, CCVC, and CCVvC words.
Pronunciation: /tʃ/ as in whi<u>ch</u>, /ɪ/ as in gr<u>i</u>n

Prompting
- Lesson 1: Time delay 0 seconds
- Lessons 2–5: Time delay 4 seconds

Activity directions
Use the sounds you learned to sound out some words. I'll say a word, and you sound it out.

Teaching moment

✔ To help the student segment all of the sounds in the word, hold up a finger for each sound the student needs to find. Remember to hold up fingers for sounds, not letters (e.g., the word *green* has 4 sounds but 5 letters; the word *which* has 3 sounds but 5 letters).

✔ Or if the student needs help, divide the dry-erase board into sections based on the number of sounds in the word. Have the student sound out the word by choosing one sound at a time on the software screen, while you write the letter/sound the student chooses on the dry-erase board (one sound per section).

✔ If the student chooses an incorrect response, give a reminder to not guess but to wait and you will help. Add to the directions, **If you are not sure of the answer, don't guess. Wait for me to help you.**

✔ If the student makes an error on even one sound, have the student listen as you segment **all** the sounds in the word in the correct sequence. Then restate to touch the sounds in the word.

Cue	Student's independent response	If student needs help
Sound out the word <u>which</u>.	Touches <u>wh</u>, <u>i</u>, and <u>ch</u> for the sounds /<u>w</u>/, /<u>ɪ</u>/, and /<u>tʃ</u>/.	If no response after 4 seconds or an incorrect response, say, **Listen, /w/ /ɪ/ /tʃ/. Touch the sounds in <u>which</u>.** If still no response or an incorrect response, model segmenting the word by touching each letter and saying each sound. Then say, **Your turn. Touch the sounds in <u>which</u>.** If still no response or an incorrect response, say, **Let's touch the sounds in <u>which</u>.** Then physically guide the student to touch each sound while you say it.

Repeat with the <u>content</u> for each lesson; see **Level 19 Content** on p. 207.

ERSB Teacher's Guide ■ Level 19

Decoding

Objective 5
Decode CVC, CVCe, CVvC, CCVvC, and CCVC words and identify their meanings.
Pronunciation: /ɪ/ as in gr<u>i</u>n

Prompting
- Lesson 1: Time delay 0 seconds
- Lessons 2–5: Time delay 4 seconds

Activity directions
Now, use the sounds and letters you learned to read a word and find its picture.

Teaching moment
✔ Be certain the students touch each picture to hear its name.
✔ If students need help decoding, sound out the word by prolonging each letter sound as you say it. Then say the word (blending the sounds together); find the picture representing it. Be sure to follow this demonstration with independent responding by the student.

Cue	Student's independent response	If student needs help
First, let's hear each picture's name.	Listens as each picture is named.	
Say, **Your turn. Read the word and find the picture.**	Finds the picture of <u>whip</u>.	If no response after 4 seconds, point to the word and say, **This is /w/ /ɪ/ /p/**. Then touch the picture and say, **Here is whip. Now you read <u>whip</u> and find the picture.** Physically guide the student's hand if needed. If an incorrect response, point to the letters in the word as you say, **This says <u>whip</u>**. Touch the picture and say, **Here is the picture of <u>whip</u>**. Remove your finger and say, **Now you read <u>whip</u> and find the picture.** Physically guide the student's hand if needed.

Repeat with the <u>content</u> for each lesson; see **Level 19 Content** on p. 207.

Sight words

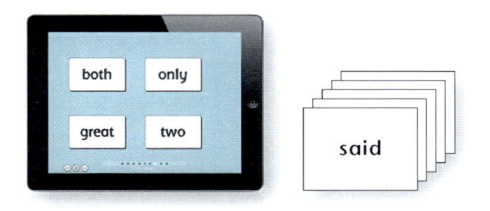

Objective 6
Read 9 new sight words.

Prompting
- Lesson 1: Time delay 0 seconds
- Lessons 2–5: Time delay 4 seconds

Activity directions
Sight words are tricky because you can't sound them out. You have to remember what they look like. **Find the word.**

> **Teaching moment**
> ✔ The pace between the presentation of words is purposely rapid to keep the student motivated.
>
> ✔ Use the sight word flashcards to provide extra practice of sight word reading. Provide up to 4 response options for students to choose from.
>
> ✔ If the student chooses an incorrect response, give a reminder to not guess but to wait and you will help. You can also add to the directions, **If you are not sure of the answer, don't guess. Wait for me to help you.**

Cue	Student's independent response	If student needs help
Find the word said.	Finds the word said.	If no response after 4 seconds or an incorrect response, model finding the word and say, **This is said. You touch it.** Physically guide the student to find the word if needed.

Repeat with the new sight words and review sight words, words required for reading the story for this level; see **Level 19 Content** on p. 207.

Reading text / Comprehension questions

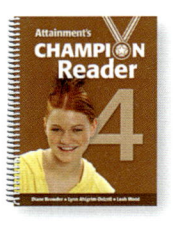

Objective 7 / Objective 8
Read connected text. / Answer comprehension questions about connected text.

Prompting
Least intrusive prompt

Activity directions
Now that you know how to read words, you can read a page from the story. Today you will read about Beth, Tam, and Sloan and their adventure to the State Fair.

Teaching moment
✔ One page of the story is read during each lesson, followed by the comprehension questions.

✔ Use **Champion Reader 4** to give students additional reading practice. The comprehension questions that could be asked if not using the software and possible response options are listed in the **Level 19 Content** on p. 207. Write response options on the dry-erase board for students to read.

Cue	Student's independent response	If student needs help
Say, **Read this story silently in your head.** Do not read to the student or point to the words.	Reads the sentences silently.	

(Table continues)

Cue	Student's independent response	If student needs help
After the student reads the sentences on the page, say, **Let's answer some questions about the story. What class do the girls have together?**	Chooses the word math.	If no response or an incorrect response, say, **Read this sentence again.** Point to each word in the sentence that has the answer, then ask the question again.
		If still no response or an incorrect response, read the sentence with the answer to the student, **We made a graph together in math class**. Then ask, **What class do the girls have together?**
		If still no response or an incorrect response, physically guide the student to find math, and say, **Math. The girls have math class together.**

Repeat with the content for each lesson; see **Level 19 Content** on p. 207.

Closing /Writing activity

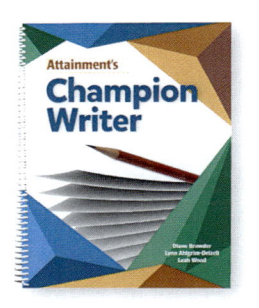

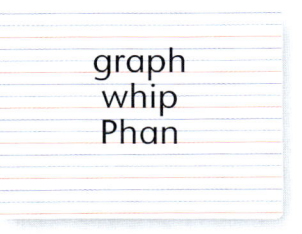

Objective 9
Write responses to activities that review level objectives.

Activity directions
Your lesson is over. GREAT reading today! Let's complete a page in your Champion Writer.

Teaching moment
✔ In order to keep the lesson from becoming too long, consider completing the writing activity at another time of the day.

✔ Some students may need adaptations to complete the writing page in **Champion Writer**; see p. 20 for ideas.

✔ Use the dry-erase board and an erasable marker to give the student practice in writing/forming sight words and words containing the letter/sounds of this level.

LEVEL 20

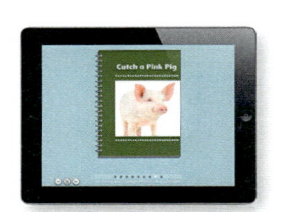

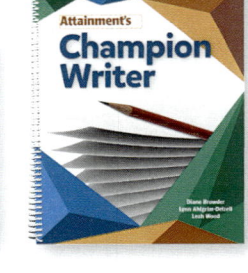

Focus
Consonant digraphs—ng, tch; consonant blend—nk

Phonemic awareness
- Blend sounds for CVC, CVCC, CCVCC, and CCCVvC words
- Segment the last sound/two sounds in words
- Segment sounds in CVC, CVCC, CCVCC, and CCCVvC words

Phonics
- Sounds /ŋk/, /ŋ/, and /tʃ/ corresponding to graphemes nk, ng, and tch
- Decode CVC, CVCC, and CCVC words and identify their meanings

Sight words
been, began, long, song, find, really

Generalization words
bank, sang, sank, thing, pink, batch, washtub

Connected text
- ATOS level = 2.2
- Lexile level = 330L

Objectives
1. Identify ng, tch, and nk when given the sounds /ŋ/, /tʃ/, and /ŋk/.
2. Blend sounds to form CVC, CVCC, CCVCC, and CCCVvC words.
3. Segment the last sound/two sounds in words.
4. Segment the sounds in CVC, CVCC, CCVCC, and CCCVvC words.
5. Decode CVC, CVCC, and CCVC words and identify their meanings.
6. Read 6 new sight words.
7. Read connected text.
8. Answer comprehension questions about connected text.
9. Write responses to activities that review level objectives.

Teaching notes
This level introduces the digraphs ng and tch. A digraph is a single sound represented by two letters (e.g., ng) or three letters (tch). Note /ŋ/ is a single sound produced in the back of the throat and emitted through the nose. The digraph tch makes the sound /tʃ/ and therefore it is in the corner of the ch tile. In addition, students are introduced to the consonant blend /ŋk/, which in this level will occur at the end of words. Students learn these are two separate sounds that "blend" to say nk.

Level 20 Content

	Lesson 1	**Lesson 2**	**Lesson 3**	**Lesson 4**	**Lesson 5**
Letter/sound identification	**New**: ng, nk, tch (on the ch tile) **Review**: wh, ph, gr				
Blending	rink, sung, latch, wing, catch, mink	Optional demo: mink stink, screen, rang, wing, pitch	Optional demo: mink sing, grunt, catch, match, rink	Optional demo: mink latch, rink, hutch, sing, wing	Optional demo: mink latch, rink, pitch, link, sunk
Segmenting I	Listen for the *last**/*last two*** sounds in each word: prank**, rink**, song*, wing*, blink**, hang*	Listen for the *last* sound in each word: Optional demo: wing long, hang, latch, graph, catch	Listen for the *last two* sounds in each word: Optional demo: blink sank, link, prank, wink, rink	Listen for the *last* sound in each word: Optional demo: wing math, long, ping, catch, myth	Listen for the *last**/*last two*** sounds in each word: Optional demo: blink** prank**, rang*, long*, wink**, hang*
Segmenting II	sing, hutch, stink, scream, patch, rang	Optional demo: tank match, link, hang, catch, mink	Optional demo: rang latch, sing, rink, stink, patch	Optional demo: tank hang, fang, catch, sing, stink	Optional demo: rang catch, tank, stink, patch, pang
Decoding	ring, tank, latch, hang, patch, link	Optional demo: tank hang, match, wing, ring, latch	Optional demo: tank latch, match, swing, sink, hang	Optional demo: tank wing, link, catch, patch, tank	Optional demo: link swing, tank, latch, sink, hang
Sight Words	**New**: been, began, long, song, find, really **Review**: about, all, funny, girls, how, okay, one, said, was, were, where				
Comprehension questions (correct response in **bold**)	Where did the girls go to get cash? (**bank**, off, stink, bed) What did they get at the bank? (cap, **cash**, trash, dog) What did they do on the way to the fair? (sad, hang, **sang**, flag)	What did the man put on them to keep them safe? (line, **latch**, catch, rode) What did the ride do that made Sloan scream? (sting, **swing**, swamp, crash) What did their seat do in the sky? (hide, fit, **hung**, fair)	Who did not like the ride? (Tam, **Sloan**, Beth, Chet) What kind of thing did Beth want to do? (okay, **funny**, sunny, catch) Where were the pigs? (sink, **rink**, pink, run) What do the boys and girls do with the pigs? (**catch**, latch, crash, stink)	What color were the pigs? (green, blink, red, **pink**) How many pigs were there? (pink, one, two, **five**) Where had the pigs been to get mud off of them? (washrag, bed, **washtub**, wash) What did Beth think about the pigs? (**stink**, swing, sink, hang)	Where were the pigs? (swing, ride, **rink**, sink) What did Beth say to do with the pig? (**catch**, latch, slick, match) Why did Tam not catch the pig? (screech, **slick**, stink, slim) What did the pig do to make the girls screech? (stunt, **grunt**, sing, great)

Letter/sound identification

th
sh
ch

Objective 1
Identify ng, tch, and nk when given the sounds /ŋ/, /tʃ/, and /ŋk/.
Pronunciation: /ŋ/ as in sa<u>ng</u>, /tʃ/ as ma<u>tch</u>, /ŋk/ as in dri<u>nk</u>

Prompting
- Lesson 1: Time delay 0 seconds
- Lessons 2–5: Time delay 4 seconds

Activity directions
I'll say a sound, and you find the letter that makes that sound.

Teaching moment

✔ Introduce ng and tch. **Today we are going to learn to read letters that together make one sound.** Point to the tile on the software screen showing ng or write and point to the letters on the dry-erase board. Tell students, **These letters make one sound. Even though there are two letters, together they make one sound. The letters ng say /ŋ/; this sound goes through the nose.**

✔ Point to the tiles on the software screen showing the ch with tch in the corner or write and point to them on the dry-erase board. Tell students, **These letters also make one sound. The letters tch say /tʃ/, just like ch.**

✔ Introduce nk. Say, **We also have another consonant blend, nk. These sounds blend together to say /ŋk/ and this blend is usually at the end of a word.**

✔ If the student chooses an incorrect response, give a reminder to not guess but to wait and you will help. You can also add to the directions, **If you are not sure of the answer, don't guess. Wait for me to help you.**

Cue	Student's independent response	If student needs help
What letters say /ŋk/?	Finds the letters <u>nk</u> to make the /ŋk/ sound.	If no response after 4 seconds or an incorrect response, model finding the letter/sound, and continue pointing to it until the student finds it. If needed, physically guide the student to find the letters and say, **This says /ŋk/. You touch it.**

Repeat with ng, tch and Level 19 review: wh, ph, and gr.

ERSB Teacher's Guide ■ Level 20

Blending

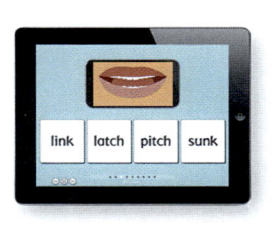

Objective 2
Blend sounds to form CVC, CVCC, CCVCC, and CCCVvC words.
Pronunciation: /ŋk/ as in dri<u>nk</u>, /ɪ/ as in r<u>i</u>nk

Prompting
- Lesson 1: Time delay 0 seconds
- Lessons 2–5: Time delay 4 seconds

Activity directions
I'll say some sounds. You blend the sounds together and find the word they make.

Teaching moment
✔ Prolong or emphasize the sounds at the beginning or end to help the student identify the word.

✔ Provide a one-second pause between the sounds to help students process the sounds.

Cue	Student's independent response	If student needs help
/r/ /ɪ/ /ŋk/. Which word am I saying?	Finds the word <u>rink</u>.	If no response after 4 seconds or an incorrect response, model finding the word and say, **This is <u>rink</u>. You touch it.** Continue pointing to it until the student finds it. If needed, physically guide the student to find the word.

Repeat with the <u>content</u> for each lesson; see **Level 20 Content** on p. 217.

Segmenting I

ng
tch
nk

Objective 3
Segment the last sound/two sounds in words.
Pronunciation: /ŋ/ as in sa<u>ng</u>, /tʃ/ as ma<u>tch</u>, /ŋk/ as in dri<u>nk</u>

Prompting
- Lesson 1: Time delay 0 seconds
- Lessons 2–5: Time delay 4 seconds

Activity directions
I'll say a word. You show me the last sound/two sounds you hear in the word.

Teaching moment
✔ To practice without the software, provide more words containing /ŋ/, /tʃ/, and /ŋk/.

✔ Pause for one second between the direction ("What is the last/last two sound(s) in") and the target word to prepare the student for the target word.

✔ To make it easier for the student, emphasize or prolong the last sound(s) in the word.

✔ If the student chooses an incorrect response, give a reminder to not guess but to wait and you will help. You can also add to the directions, **If you are not sure of the answer, don't guess. Wait for me to help you.**

Cue	Student's independent response	If student needs help
(Lessons 1, 3, and 5) **What are the last two sounds in <u>prank</u>?**	Finds nk to say /ŋk/.	If no response after 4 seconds or an incorrect response, model finding nk. Say, **The last two sounds are /ŋk/. You touch it.** If needed, physically guide the student to find /ŋk/.
(Lessons 1, 2, 4, 5) **What is the last sound in <u>wing</u>?**	Finds ng to say /ŋ/.	If no response after 4 seconds or an incorrect response, model finding ng. Say, **The last sound is /ŋ/. You touch it.** If needed, physically guide the student to find /ŋ/.

Repeat with the <u>content</u> for each lesson; see **Level 20 Content** on p. 217.

Segmenting II

s	i	ng

Objective 4
Segment the sounds in CVC, CVCC, CCVCC, and CCCVvC words.
Pronunciation: /ŋ/ as in s<u>a</u>n<u>g</u>, /ɪ/ as in s<u>i</u>ng

Prompting
- Lesson 1: Time delay 0 seconds
- Lessons 2–5: Time delay 4 seconds

Activity directions
Use the sounds you learned to sound out some words. I'll say a word, and you sound it out.

Teaching moment

✔ To help the student segment all of the sounds in the word, hold up a finger for each sound the student needs to find. Remember to hold up fingers for sounds, not letters (e.g., the word *hutch* has 3 sounds but 5 letters; the word *wing* has 3 sounds but 4 letters; the word *rink* has 4 sounds and 4 letters).

✔ Or if the student needs help, divide the dry-erase board into sections based on the number of sounds in the word. Have the student sound out the word by choosing one sound at a time on the software screen, while you write the letter/sound the student chooses on the dry-erase board (one sound per section).

✔ If the student chooses an incorrect response, give a reminder to not guess but to wait and you will help. Add to the directions, **If you are not sure of the answer, don't guess. Wait for me to help you.**

✔ If the student makes an error on even one sound, have the student listen as you segment **all** the sounds in the word in the correct sequence. Then restate to touch the sounds in the word.

Cue	Student's independent response	If student needs help
Sound out the word <u>sing</u>.	Touches <u>s</u>, <u>i</u>, and <u>ng</u> for the sounds /<u>s</u>/, /<u>ɪ</u>/, and /<u>ŋ</u>/.	If no response after 4 seconds or an incorrect response, say, **Listen, /<u>s</u>/ /<u>ɪ</u>/ /<u>ŋ</u>/. Touch the sounds in <u>sing</u>.** If still no response or an incorrect response, model segmenting the word by touching each letter and saying each sound. Then say, **Your turn. Touch the sounds in <u>sing</u>.** If still no response or an incorrect response, say, **Let's touch the sounds in <u>sing</u>.** Then physically guide the student to touch each sound while you say it.

Repeat with the <u>content</u> for each lesson; see **Level 20 Content** on p. 217.

ERSB Teacher's Guide ■ Level 20

Decoding

Objective 5
Decode CVC, CVCC, and CCVC words and identify their meanings.
Pronunciation: /ŋ/ as in sa<u>ng</u>, /ɪ/ as in s<u>i</u>ng

Prompting
- Lesson 1: Time delay 0 seconds
- Lessons 2–5: Time delay 4 seconds

Activity directions
Now, use the sounds and letters you learned to read a word and find its picture.

Teaching moment
✔ Be certain the student knows the name of each picture.

✔ Students may need you to continue to demonstrate how to sound out/decode the word. To sound out the word, prolong each letter sound as you say it. Then say the word (blending the sounds together); find the picture representing it. Be sure to follow this demonstration with independent responding by the student.

Cue	Student's independent response	If student needs help
First, let's hear each picture's name.	Listens as each picture is named.	
Say, **Your turn. Read the word and find the picture.**	Finds the picture of <u>ring</u>.	If no response after 4 seconds, point to the word and say, **This is /<u>r</u>/ /<u>ɪ</u>/ /<u>ŋ</u>/**. Then touch the picture and say, **Here is <u>ring</u>**. the student's hand if needed.
		If an incorrect response, point to the letters in the word as you say, **This says <u>ring</u>**. Touch the picture and say, **Here is the picture of <u>ring</u>**. Remove your finger and say, **Now you read <u>ring</u> and find the picture**. Physically guide the student's hand if needed.

Repeat with the <u>content</u> for each lesson; see **Level 20 Content** on p. 217.

ERSB Teacher's Guide ■ Level 20

Sight words

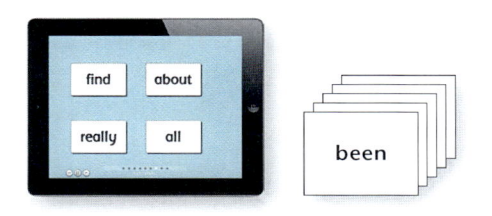

Objective 6
Read 6 new sight words.

Prompting
- Lesson 1: Time delay 0 seconds
- Lessons 2–5: Time delay 4 seconds

Activity directions
Sight words are tricky because you can't sound them out. You have to remember what they look like. Find the word.

Teaching moment
✔ The pace between the presentation of words is purposely rapid to keep the student motivated.

✔ Use the sight word flashcards to provide extra practice of sight word reading. Provide up to 4 response options for students to choose from.

✔ Note that the words *long* and *song* are included as sight words because though students can read the /ŋ/, they have not yet learned /ɔ/, the diphthong in these words.

✔ If the student chooses an incorrect response, give a reminder to not guess but to wait and you will help. You can also add to the directions, **If you are not sure of the answer, don't guess. Wait for me to help you.**

Cue	Student's independent response	If student needs help
Find the word been.	Finds the word been.	If no response after 4 seconds or an incorrect response, model finding the word and say, **This is been. You touch it.** Physically guide the student to find the word if needed.

Repeat with the new sight words and review sight words, words required for reading the story for this level; see **Level 20 Content** on p. 217.

Reading text / Comprehension questions

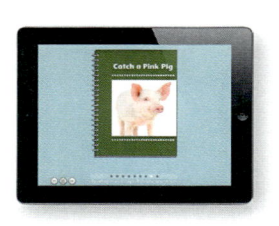

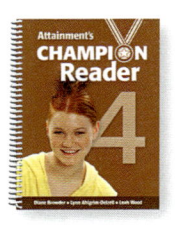

Objective 7 / Objective 8
Read connected text. / Answer comprehension questions about connected text.

Prompting
Least intrusive prompt

Activity directions
Now that you know how to read words, you can read a page from the story. Today you will read about Beth, Sloan, and Tam at a fair.

Teaching moment
✔ One page of the story is read during each lesson, followed by the comprehension questions.

✔ Use **Champion Reader 4** to give students additional reading practice. The comprehension questions that could be asked if not using the software and possible response options are listed in the **Level 20 Content** on p. 217. Write response options on the dry-erase board for students to read.

Cue	Student's independent response	If student needs help
Say, **Read this story silently in your head.** Do not read to the student or point to the words.	Reads the sentences silently.	

(Table continues)

Cue	Student's independent response	If student needs help
After the student reads the sentences on the page, say, **Let's answer some questions about the story. Where did the girls go to get cash?**	Chooses the word <u>bank</u>.	If no response or an incorrect response, say, **Read this sentence again.** Point to each word in the sentence that has the answer, then ask the question again.
		If still no response or an incorrect response, read the sentence with the answer to the student, **They first went to the bank to get cash**. Then ask, **Where did the girls go to get cash?**
		If still no response or an incorrect response, physically guide the student to find <u>bank</u>, and say, **The bank. The girls went to the bank to get cash.**

Repeat with the <u>content</u> for each lesson; see **Level 20 Content** on p. 217.

Closing /Writing activity

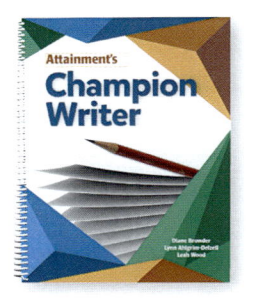

Objective 9
Write responses to activities that review level objectives.

Activity directions
Your lesson is over. GREAT reading today! Let's complete a page in your Champion Writer.

Teaching moment
✔ In order to keep the lesson from becoming too long, consider completing the writing activity at another time of the day.

✔ Some students may need adaptations to complete the writing page in **Champion Writer**; see p. 20 for ideas.

✔ Use the dry-erase board and an erasable marker to give the student practice in writing/forming sight words and words containing the letter/sounds of this level.

LEVEL 21

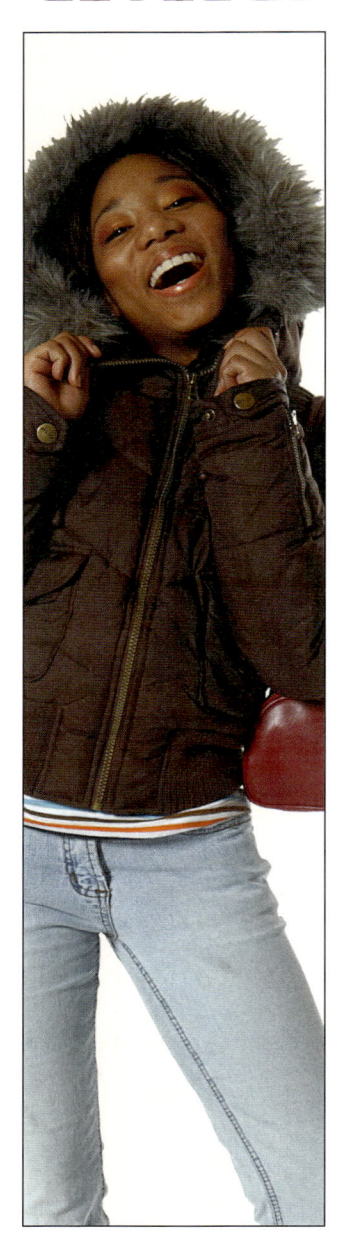

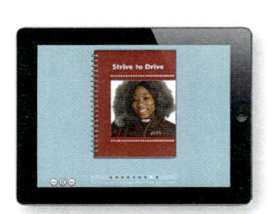

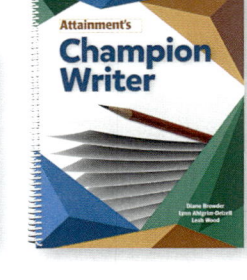

Focus
R-controlled vowels—er, ur, ir, or, ar

Phonemic awareness
- Blend sounds for CVr, CVrC, CVrCC, CCVrC, and CCVr words
- Segment middle sounds in words
- Segment sounds in CVrC, CVr, CCVrC, and CVrCC words

Phonics
- Sounds /ɝ/ and /ɑr/ corresponding to graphemes er, ur, ir, or, and ar
- Decode VrC, CVrC, CVr, and CCVrC words

Sight words
purse, buy, over, some, sure, took, mall, curve

Generalization words
hurt, dirt, yard, start, hard, fern, down, wow, someday, driveway

Connected text
- ATOS level = 1.8
- Lexile level = 330L

Objectives
1. Identify er, ur, ir, or, and ar when given the sounds /ɝ/ and /ɑr/.
2. Blend sounds to form CVr, CVrC, CVrCC, CCVrC, and CCVr words.
3. Segment the middle sounds in words.
4. Segment the sounds in CVrC, CVr, CCVrC, and CVrCC words.
5. Decode VrC, CVrC, CVr, and CCVrC words and identify their meanings.
6. Read 8 new sight words.
7. Read connected text.
8. Answer comprehension questions about connected text.
9. Write responses to activities that review level objectives.

Teaching notes
This level teaches r-controlled vowels. An r-controlled vowel refers to an r following a vowel. The vowel and the r are usually in the same syllable, so the r sound affects how the vowel sound is pronounced. Together they make their own sound.

Level 21 Content

	Lesson 1	Lesson 2	Lesson 3	Lesson 4	Lesson 5
Letter/sound identification	**New**: er, ur, ir, or, ar **Review**: nk, ng, tch				
Blending	park, burn, cart, star, card, fur	Optional demo: arm park, turn, fern, mark, fur	Optional demo: arm bird, bark, car, smart, firm	Optional demo: arm burn, farm, harm, burst, firm	Optional demo: arm barb, card, bark, shirt, star
Segmenting I	Listen for the *middle* sound: fern, park, turn, furs, mark, third	Listen for the *middle* sound: Optional demo: worm bird, turn, cart, fern, curve	Listen for the *middle* sound: Optional demo: worm shirt, farm, harm, turn, turf	Listen for the *middle* sound: Optional demo: worm purse, cart, start, fern, turn	Listen for the *middle* sound: Optional demo: worm burn, harm, start, third, purse
Segmenting II	worm, bird, bark, car, smart, part	Optional demo: first burn, farm, harm, burst, shirt	Optional demo: first farm, cart, star, card, park	Optional demo: first park, turn, fur, fern, arm	Optional demo: first car, turn, star, bird, shirt
Decoding	star, shirt, burn, farm, barn, park	Optional demo: star park, bird, worm, card, surf	Optional demo: star fern, skirt, shirt, barn, arm	Optional demo: star worm, bird, car, barn, park	Optional demo: star barn, arm, worm, skirt, burn
Sight Words	**New**: purse, buy, over, some, sure, took, mall, curve **Review**: come, where, school, door, find, today, one, head, happy, done, alone				
Comprehension questions (correct response in **bold**)	Where does Jess want to drive someday? (**school**, shelf, farm, took) Where do Jess and Mom go first? (tank, **bank**, bed, mall)	What does Jess start? (cart, star, **car**, seat) Who is in the seat next to Jess? (Dad, Tam, **Mom**, Ron) What does the car hit? (car, **curb**, crab, dirt) What does Mom say to be? (sad, smell, happy, **smart**)	Where does Jess drive first? (tank, barn, **bank**, sun) What does Jess get at the bank? (car, **cash**, trash, park) What does Jess want to buy at the mall? (smart, mall, socks, **skirt**) What does Jess do just fine? (pick, buy, **park**, hurt)	What does Jess buy? (**skirt**, dirt, yard, skid) What does Jess find to match the skirt? (scream, socks, **shirt**, shine) What was the cat chasing? (**bird**, boat, barn, curve) Where does the car end up after it slid? (bird, safe, **yard**, harm)	What does Jess take too fast? (bird, **curve**, yard, smart) Where does the cat run to? (**barn**, fern, bend, car) How does Jess drive the rest of the way home? (fast, slime, **slow**, sleep) Where does Jess safely make it to? (hill, some, slide, **home**)

Letter/sound identification

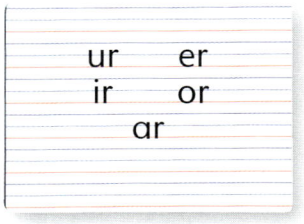

Objective 1
Identify er, ur, ir, or, and ar when given the sounds /ɜ/ and /ɑr/.
Pronunciation: /ɜ/ as in h<u>er</u>, /ɑr/ as in st<u>ar</u>

Prompting
- Lesson 1: Time delay 0 seconds
- Lessons 2–5: Time delay 4 seconds

Activity directions
I'll say a sound, and you find the letters that makes that sound.

Teaching moment
✔ Introduce the concept of r-controlled vowels, **Today we are going to read words that have vowels followed by the letter r. For these vowels, the r is kind of controlling and bossy and it changes the vowel sound.**

✔ Point to the tile on the software screen showing the er, ir, or, and ur, or write and point to them on the dry-erase board and tell students that all of these r-controlled vowels say /ɜ/.

✔ Point to the tile on the software screen showing the ar or write and point to ar on the dry-erase board and tell students that this r-controlled vowel says /ɑr/.

✔ If the student chooses an incorrect response, give a reminder to not guess but to wait and you will help. You can also add to the directions, **If you are not sure of the answer, don't guess. Wait for me to help you.**

Cue	Student's independent response	If student needs help
What letters says /<u>ar</u>/?	Finds the letters <u>ar</u> to make the /<u>ar</u>/ sound.	If no response after 4 seconds or an incorrect response, model finding the letter/sound, and continue pointing to it until the student finds it. If needed, physically guide the student to find the letter and say, **This is /<u>ar</u>/. You touch it.**

Repeat with er, ur, ir, and or and Level 20 review: ng, nk, and tch.

Blending

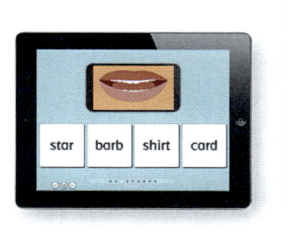

Objective 2
Blend sounds to form CVr, CVrC, CVrCC, CCVrC, and CCVr words.
Pronunciation: /ɑr/ as in st<u>ar</u>

Prompting
- Lesson 1: Time delay 0 seconds
- Lessons 2–5: Time delay 4 seconds

Activity directions
I'll say some sounds. You blend the sounds together and find the word they make.

Teaching moment
✔ Prolong or emphasize the sounds at the beginning, middle, or end to help the student identify the word.

✔ Provide a one-second pause between the sounds to help students process the sounds.

Cue	Student's independent response	If student needs help
/p/ /ɑr/ /k/. Which word am I saying?	Finds the word park.	If no response after 4 seconds or an incorrect response, model finding the word and say, **This is park. You touch it.** Continue pointing to it until the student finds it. If needed, physically guide the student to find the word.

Repeat with /ɝ/ words and the content for each lesson; see **Level 21 Content** on p. 227.

ERSB Teacher's Guide ■ Level 21

Segmenting I

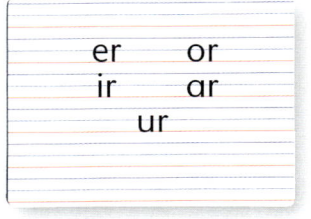

er   or
ir   ar
  ur

Objective 3
Segment the middle sounds in words.
Pronunciation: /ɝ/ as in h<u>er</u>, /ɑr/ as in st<u>ar</u>

Prompting
- Lesson 1: Time delay 0 seconds
- Lessons 2–5: Time delay 4 seconds

Activity directions
I'll say a word. You show me the middle sound you hear in the word.

Teaching moment
✔ To practice without the software, provide more words with /ɝ/ and /ɑr/ in the middle.

✔ Pause for one second between the direction ("What is the middle sound in") and the target word to prepare the student for the target word.

✔ To make it easier for the student, emphasize or prolong the middle sound in the word, which is the r-controlled vowel.

✔ If the student chooses an incorrect response, give a reminder to not guess but to wait and you will help. You can also add to the directions, **If you are not sure of the answer, don't guess. Wait for me to help you.**

Cue	Student's independent response	If student needs help
What is the middle sound in <u>fern</u>?	Finds <u>er</u> to say /ɝ/.	If no response after 4 seconds or an incorrect response, model finding <u>er</u>. Say, **The middle sound is /ɝ/. You touch it.** If needed, physically guide the student to find /ɝ/.

Repeat with /ɑr/ words and the <u>content</u> for each lesson; see **Level 21 Content** on p. 227.

Segmenting II

w	or	m

Objective 4
Segment the sounds in CVrC, CVr, CCVrC, and CVrCC words.
Pronunciation: /ɜ˞/ as in as in h<u>er</u>

Prompting
- Lesson 1: Time delay 0 seconds
- Lessons 2–5: Time delay 4 seconds

Activity directions
Use the sounds you learned to sound out some words. I'll say a word, and you sound it out.

Teaching moment
✔ To help the student segment all of the sounds in the word, hold up a finger for each sound the student needs to find. Remember to hold up fingers for sounds, not letters (e.g., the word *worm* has 3 sounds but 4 letters).

✔ Or if the student needs help, divide the dry-erase board into sections based on the number of sounds in the word. Have the student sound out the word by choosing one sound at a time on the software screen, while you write the letter/sound the student chooses on the dry-erase board (one sound per section).

✔ If the student chooses an incorrect response, give a reminder to not guess but to wait and you will help. Add to the directions, **If you are not sure of the answer, don't guess. Wait for me to help you.**

✔ If the student makes an error on even one sound, have the student listen as you segment **all** the sounds in the word in the correct sequence. Then restate to touch the sounds in the word.

Cue	Student's independent response	If student needs help
Sound out the word <u>worm</u>.	Touches <u>w</u>, <u>or</u>, and <u>m</u> for the sounds /w/, /ɜ˞/, and /m/.	If no response after 4 seconds or an incorrect response, say, **Listen, /<u>w</u>/ /<u>ɜ˞</u>/ /<u>m</u>/. Touch the sounds in <u>worm</u>.**
		If still no response or an incorrect response, model segmenting the word by touching each letter and saying each sound. Then say, **Your turn. Touch the sounds in <u>worm</u>.**
		If still no response or an incorrect response, say, **Let's touch the sounds in <u>worm</u>.** Then physically guide the student to touch each sound while you say it.

Repeat with the <u>content</u> for each lesson; see **Level 21 Content** on p. 227.

Decoding

Objective 5
Decode VrC, CVrC, CVr, and CCVrC words and identify their meanings.
Pronunciation: /ar/ as in st<u>ar</u>

Prompting
- Lesson 1: Time delay 0 seconds
- Lessons 2–5: Time delay 4 seconds

Activity directions
Now, use the sounds and letters you learned to read a word and find its picture.

> **Teaching moment**
> ✔ Be certain the student knows the name of each picture.
> ✔ If students need help decoding, sound out the word by prolonging each letter sound as you say it. Then say the word (blending the sounds together); find the picture representing it. Be sure to follow this demonstration with independent responding by the student.

Cue	Student's independent response	If student needs help
First, let's hear each picture's name.	Listens as each picture is named.	
Say, **Your turn. Read the word and find the picture.**	Finds the picture of <u>star</u>.	If no response after 4 seconds, point to the word and say, **This is /<u>st</u>/ /<u>ar</u>/.** Then touch the picture and say, **Here is <u>star</u>. Now you read <u>star</u> and find the picture.** Physically guide the student's hand if needed.

Repeat with the <u>content</u> for each lesson; see **Level 21 Content** on p. 227.

Sight words

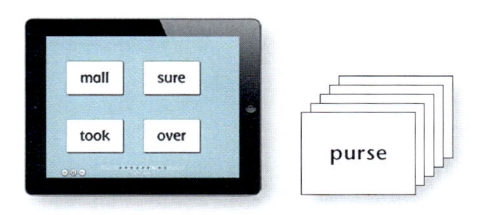

Objective 6
Read 8 new sight words.

Prompting
- Lesson 1: Time delay 0 seconds
- Lessons 2–5: Time delay 4 seconds

Activity directions
Sight words are tricky because you can't sound them out. You have to remember what they look like. Find the word.

Teaching moment
✔ The pace between the presentation of words is purposely rapid to keep the student motivated.

✔ Use the sight word flashcards to provide extra practice of sight word reading. Provide up to 4 response options for students to choose from.

✔ Note that words including the r-controlled vowels are included as sight words since students have not learned a rule for the silent e following r-controlled vowels (e.g., *purse, curve*).

✔ If the student chooses an incorrect response, give a reminder to not guess but to wait and you will help. You can also add to the directions, **If you are not sure of the answer, don't guess. Wait for me to help you.**

Cue	Student's independent response	If student needs help
Find the word purse.	Finds the word purse.	If no response after 4 seconds or an incorrect response, model finding the word and say, **This is purse. You touch it.** Physically guide the student to find the word if needed.

Repeat with the new sight words and review sight words, words required for reading the story for this level; see **Level 21 Content** on p. 227.

Reading text / Comprehension questions

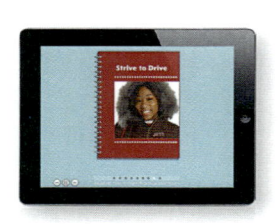

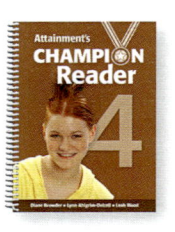

school
shelf
farm
took

Objective 7 / Objective 8
Read connected text. / Answer comprehension questions about connected text.

Prompting
Least intrusive prompt

Activity directions
Now that you know how to read words, you can read a page from the story. Today you will read about Sloan and her first driving experiences.

> ### Teaching moment
> ✓ One page of the story is read during each lesson, followed by the comprehension questions.
>
> ✓ Compound words are embedded in this level's story. Remind students that these words are made of two smaller words and they can read them by breaking the larger word apart.
>
> ✓ Use **Champion Reader 4** to give students additional reading practice. The comprehension questions that could be asked if not using the software and possible response options are listed in the **Level 21 Content** on p. 227. Write response options on the dry-erase board for students to read.

Cue	Student's independent response	If student needs help
Say, **Read this story silently in your head.** Do not read to the student or point to the words.	Reads the sentences silently.	

(Table continues)

ERSB Teacher's Guide ■ Level 21

Cue	Student's independent response	If student needs help
After the student reads the sentences on the page, say, **Let's answer some questions about the story, Where does Jess want to drive someday?**	Chooses the word school.	If no response or an incorrect response, say, **Read this sentence again**. Point to each word in the sentence that has the answer, then ask the question again. If still no response or an incorrect response, read the sentence with the answer to the student, **Someday, I may get to drive the car to school alone.** Then ask, **Where does Jess want to drive someday?** If still no response or an incorrect response, physically guide the student to find school, and say, **School. Someday Jess wants to drive to school.**

Repeat with the content for each lesson; see **Level 21 Content** on p. 227.

Closing /Writing activity

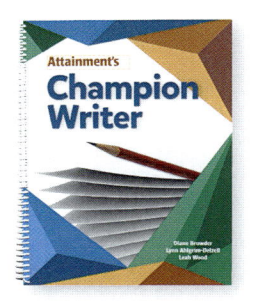

school
park
surf
bird

Objective 9
Write responses to activities that review level objectives.

Activity directions
Your lesson is over. GREAT reading today! Let's complete a page in your Champion Writer.

Teaching moment

✔ In order to keep the lesson from becoming too long, consider completing the writing activity at another time of the day.

✔ Some students may need adaptations to complete the writing page in **Champion Writer**; see p. 20 for ideas.

✔ Use the dry-erase board and an erasable marker to give the student practice in writing/forming sight words and words containing the letter/sounds of this level.

LEVEL 22

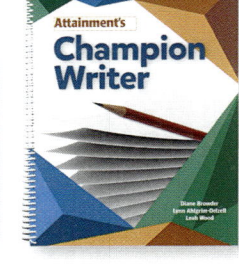

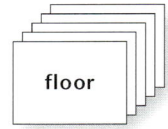

Focus
R-controlled vowel—or; silent first letters—kn, wr

Phonemic awareness
- Blend sounds for CV, CVr, CVrC, CVC, CVCC, and CVCe words
- Segment first, middle, and last sounds in words
- Segment sounds in CV, CVr, CVrC, CVC, CVCe, and CVCC words

Phonics
- Sounds /or/, /r/, and /n/ corresponding to graphemes or, wr, and kn
- Decode CVr, CVrC, CVCC, and CVCe words and identify their meanings

Sight words
floor, knew, watch, bore

Generalization words
form, wrote, knee, know, friendship, bracelets

Connected text
- ATOS level = 2.9
- Lexile level = 410L

Objectives
1. Identify or, wr, and kn when given the sounds /ɔr/, /r/, and /n/.
2. Blend sounds to form CV, CVr, CVrC, CVC, CVCC, and CVCe words.
3. Segment the first, middle, and last sounds in words.
4. Segment the sounds in CV, CVr, CVrC, CVC, CVCe, and CVCC words.
5. Decode CVr, CVrC, CVCC, and CVCe words and identify their meanings.
6. Read 4 new sight words.
7. Read connected text.
8. Answer comprehension questions about connected text.
9. Write responses to activities that review level objectives.

Teaching notes
This level teaches another r-controlled vowel: or. An r-controlled vowel refers to an r following a vowel. This level also focuses on silent first letters: kn and wr. Since kn makes /n/, it is placed on the n tile. And wr says /r/, so it is placed on the r tile.

Level 22 Content

	Lesson 1	Lesson 2	Lesson 3	Lesson 4	Lesson 5
Letter/sound identification	**New**: or, kn (on the n tile), wr (on the r tile) **Review**: or, er, ir, ur, ar				
Blending	born, knit, farm, for, knock, wrist	**Optional demo**: form fern, knock, wrist, cork, knob	**Optional demo**: form fort, knife, wrap, for, wreck	**Optional demo**: form knock, wrap, pork, knob, fort	**Optional demo**: form fern, wrist, pork, knife, born
Segmenting I	Listen for the *first* sound in each word: knock, wrap, wrong, knit, write, knob	Listen for the *last* sound in each word: **Optional demo**: far floor, car, more, stir, purr	Listen for the *middle* sound in each word: **Optional demo**: mark fort, park, fern, turn, porch	Listen for the *first* sound in each word: **Optional demo**: art orange, arch, urge, orca, knob	Listen for the *first* sound in each word: **Optional demo**: art arch, wrap, irk, wrong, knock
Segmenting II	knit, fort, knife, wrap, farm, wreck	**Optional demo**: knit knock, wrap, pork, knob, hurt	**Optional demo**: knit knack, farm, knock, wrist, cart	**Optional demo**: knit fern, knock, wrist, knob, wren	**Optional demo**: knit knock, wrap, cork, farm, knack
Decoding	fork, cork, knock, wrist, worm, knob	**Optional demo**: fork knob, knife, wrap, wreck, worm	**Optional demo**: fork car, knock, wrap, knob, hurt	**Optional demo**: fork knock, farm, corn, knife, wrist	**Optional demo**: fork worm, wrap, corn, knock, wreck
Sight Words	**New**: floor, knew, watch, bore **Review**: from, pretty, said, text, their, took, door, all, more				
Comprehension questions (correct response in **bold**)	Where were Jean and Jane sitting? (flag, **floor**, steps, door) Who was at the door? (**Sloan**, Tim, Mom, Slim) What is on the floor? (beds, park, are, **beads**)	Where did Sloan sit? (**chair**, chase, bore, chin) What did Sloan take out? (fine, **phone**, beef, dark) Who wants to teach Sloan how to make a bracelet? (Jon, Gus, **Jean**, Mom) What did Sloan send on her phone? (that, both, **text**, chat)	What did Jean use to cut the string? (fine, **knife**, knack, wrong) Where did Jean take the knife from? (cut, when, cat, **cork**) What did Jane make with her beads? (**star**, step, stand, bird) What was one of the colors Jane used in her bracelet? (**white**, red, yellow, green)	Who will get bracelets? (frog, **friends**, phone, Mom) How did Jean and Jane place the bracelets they made? (two, **row**, floor, phone) What did Jean think the bracelet would match? (skirt, phone, **shirt**, bank) Where did Jean put the bracelet for Sloan to see? (**knee**, wrap, knock, head)	What did Sloan do to pick up the bracelet? (**bent**, sat, sing, bud) Where did Jean say to wrap the bracelet? (**wrist**, wrap, rip, wrong) Who will Sloan give her bracelet to? (**Wren**, Knack, Wrong, Star) What will last longer than the text on Sloan's phone? (pretty, batch, bead, **bracelet**)

Letter/sound identification

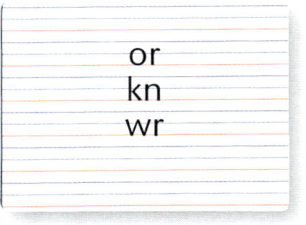

Objective 1
Identify or, wr, and kn when given the sounds /ɔr/, /r/, and /n/. Pronunciation: /ɔr/ as in <u>or</u>

Prompting
- Lesson 1: Time delay 0 seconds
- Lessons 2–5: Time delay 4 seconds

Activity directions
I'll say a sound, and you find the letters that make that sound.

Teaching moment

✔ Remind students about r-controlled vowels, **Today we are going to learn another r-controlled vowel: or. Remember, for these vowels, the r is kind of controlling and bossy and it changes the vowel sound.**

✔ Point to the tile on the software screen showing the or or write and point to it on the dry-erase board and tell students or says /ɔr/.

✔ Point to the tile on the software screen showing the kn, which is added to the n tile, or write and point to kn on the dry-erase board. Tell students, **When kn starts a word, the k is silent and kn says /n/, like n.**

✔ Point to the tile on the software screen showing the wr, which is added to the r tile, or write and point to wr on the dry-erase board. Tell students, **When wr starts a word, the w is silent and wr says /r/, like r.**

✔ If the student chooses an incorrect response, give a reminder to not guess but to wait and you will help. You can also add to the directions, **If you are not sure of the answer, don't guess. Wait for me to help you.**

Cue	Student's independent response	If student needs help
What letters say /ɔr/?	Finds the letters <u>or</u> to make the /<u>or</u>/ sound.	If no response after 4 seconds or an incorrect response, model finding the letter/sound, and continue pointing to it until the student finds it. If needed, physically guide the student to find the letter and say, **This is /ɔr/. You touch it.**

Repeat with wr and kn and Level 21 review: er, ur, ir, or, and ar.

Blending

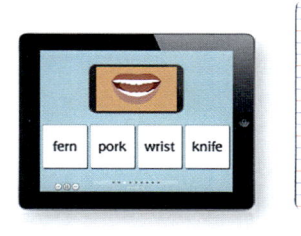

Objective 2
Blend sounds to form CV, CVr, CVrC, CVC, CVCC, and CVCe words.
Pronunciation: /ɔr/ as in or

Prompting
- Lesson 1: Time delay 0 seconds
- Lessons 2–5: Time delay 4 seconds

Activity directions
I'll say some sounds. You blend the sounds together and find the word they make.

Teaching moment
✔ Prolong or emphasize the sounds at the beginning, middle, or end to help the student identify the word.

✔ Provide a one-second pause between the sounds to help students process the sounds.

Cue	Student's independent response	If student needs help
/b/ /ɔr/ /n/. Which word am I saying?	Finds the word born.	If no response after 4 seconds or an incorrect response, model finding the word and say, **This is born. You touch it.** Continue pointing to it until the student finds it. If needed, physically guide the student to find the word.

Repeat with the content for each lesson; see **Level 22 Content** on p. 237.

Segmenting I

Objective 3
Segment the first, middle, and last sounds in words.
Pronunciation: /ɔr/ as in or

Prompting
- Lesson 1: Time delay 0 seconds
- Lessons 2–5: Time delay 4 seconds

Activity directions
I'll say a word. You show me the first/middle/last sound you hear in the word.

Teaching moment
✔ To practice without the software, provide more words with /or/ in the middle or /n/ and /r/ at the beginning of the words.

✔ Pause for one second between the direction ("What is the first/last/middle sound in") and the target word to prepare the student for the target word.

✔ To make it easier for the student, emphasize or prolong the first/last/middle sound in the word.

✔ If the student chooses an incorrect response, give a reminder to not guess but to wait and you will help. You can also add to the directions, **If you are not sure of the answer, don't guess. Wait for me to help you.**

Cue	Student's independent response	If student needs help
(Lessons 1, 4, and 5) **What is the first sound in knock?**	Finds kn to say /n/.	If no response after 4 seconds or an incorrect response, model finding kn. Say, **The first sound is /n/. You touch it.** If needed, physically guide the student to find /n/.
(Lesson 2) **What is the last sound in more?**	Finds or to say /ɔr/.	If no response after 4 seconds or an incorrect response, model finding or. Say, **The last sound is /ɔr/. You touch it.** If needed, physically guide the student to find /ɔr/.
(Lesson 3) **What is the middle sound in fort?**	Finds or to say /ɔr/.	If no response after 4 seconds or an incorrect response, model finding or. Say, **The middle sound is /ɔr/. You touch it.** If needed, physically guide the student to find /ɔr/.

Repeat with the content for each lesson; see **Level 22 Content** on p. 237.

Segmenting II

kn	i	t

Objective 4
Segment the sounds in CV, CVr, CVrC, CVC, CVCe, and CVCC words.
Pronunciation: /ɪ/ as kn<u>i</u>t

Prompting
- Lesson 1: Time delay 0 seconds
- Lessons 2–5: Time delay 4 seconds

Activity directions
Use the sounds you learned to sound out some words. I'll say a word, and you sound it out.

Teaching moment
✔ To help the student segment all of the sounds in the word, hold up a finger for each sound the student needs to find. Remember to hold up fingers for sounds, not letters (e.g., the word *knit* has 3 sounds but 4 letters)

✔ Or if the student needs help, divide the dry-erase board into sections based on the number of sounds in the word. Have the student sound out the word by choosing one sound at a time on the software screen, while you write the letter/sound the student chooses on the dry-erase board (one sound per section).

✔ If the student chooses an incorrect response, give a reminder to not guess but to wait and you will help. Add to the directions, **If you are not sure of the answer, don't guess. Wait for me to help you.**

✔ If the student makes an error on even one sound, have the student listen as you segment **all** the sounds in the word in the correct sequence. Then restate to touch the sounds in the word.

Cue	Student's independent response	If student needs help
Sound out the word <u>knit</u>.	Touches <u>kn</u>, <u>i</u>, and <u>t</u> for the sounds /<u>n</u>/, /<u>ɪ</u>/, and /<u>t</u>/.	If no response after 4 seconds or an incorrect response, say, **Listen, /<u>n</u>/ /<u>ɪ</u>/ /<u>t</u>/. Touch the sounds in <u>knit</u>.**
		If still no response or an incorrect response, model segmenting the word by touching each letter and saying each sound. Then say, **Your turn. Touch the sounds in <u>knit</u>.**
		If still no response or an incorrect response, say, **Let's touch the sounds in <u>knit</u>.** Then physically guide the student to touch each sound while you say it.

Repeat with the <u>content</u> for each lesson; see **Level 22 Content** on p. 237.

Decoding

Objective 5
Decode CVr, CVrC, CVCC, and CVCe words and identify their meanings.
Pronunciation: /ɔr/ as in or

Prompting
- Lesson 1: Time delay 0 seconds
- Lessons 2–5: Time delay 4 seconds

Activity directions
Now, use the sounds and letters you learned to read a word and find its picture.

Teaching moment
✔ Be certain the student knows the name of each picture.

✔ Students may need you to continue to demonstrate how to sound out/decode the word. To sound out the word, prolong each letter sound as you say it. Then say the word (blending the sounds together); find the picture representing it. Be sure to follow this demonstration with independent responding by the student.

Cue	Student's independent response	If student needs help
First, let's hear each picture's name.	Listens as each picture is named.	
Say, **Your turn. Read the word and find the picture.**	Finds the picture of <u>fork</u>.	If no response after 4 seconds, point to the word and say, **This is /f/ /ɔr/ /k/.** Then touch the picture and say, **Here is <u>fork</u>. Now you read <u>fork</u> and find the picture.** Physically guide the student's hand if needed.
		If an incorrect response, point to the letters in the word as you say, **This says <u>fork</u>.** Touch the picture and say, **Here is the picture of <u>fork</u>.** Remove your finger and say, **Now you read <u>fork</u> and find the picture.** Physically guide the student's hand if needed.

Repeat with the <u>content</u> for each lesson; see **Level 22 Content** on p. 237.

Sight words

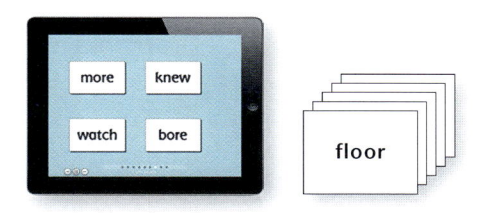

Objective 6
Read 4 new sight words.

Prompting
- Lesson 1: Time delay 0 seconds
- Lessons 2–5: Time delay 4 seconds

Activity directions
Sight words are tricky because you can't sound them out. You have to remember what they look like. Find the word.

Teaching moment
✔ The pace between the presentation of words is purposely rapid to keep the student motivated.

✔ Use the sight word flashcards to provide extra practice of sight word reading. Provide up to 4 response options for students to choose from.

✔ Note that words including or and kn are included as sight words since students have not learned a rule for the silent e following r-controlled vowel or (e.g., bore, more), double oor (door), and ew (knew).

✔ If the student chooses an incorrect response, give a reminder to not guess but to wait and you will help. You can also add to the directions, **If you are not sure of the answer, don't guess. Wait for me to help you.**

Cue	Student's independent response	If student needs help
Find the word floor.	Finds the word floor.	If no response after 4 seconds or an incorrect response, model finding the word and say, **This is floor. You touch it.** Physically guide the student to find the word if needed.

Repeat with the new sight words and review sight words, words required for reading the story for this level; see **Level 22 Content** on p. 237.

ERSB Teacher's Guide ■ Level 22

Reading text / Comprehension questions

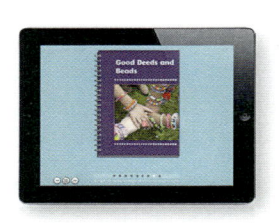

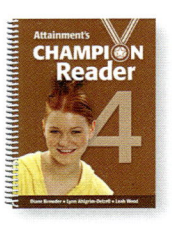

flag
floor
steps
door

Objective 7 / Objective 8
Read connected text. / Answer comprehension questions about connected text.

Prompting
Least intrusive prompt

Activity directions
Now that you know how to read words, you can read a page from the story. In this story, Jane and Jean make beaded jewelry for their friends.

Teaching moment
✓ One page of the story is read during each lesson, followed by the comprehension questions.

✓ Compound words are embedded in this level's story. Remind students that these words are made of two smaller words and they can read them by breaking the larger word apart.

✓ Use **Champion Reader 4** to give students additional reading practice. The comprehension questions that could be asked if not using the software and possible response options are listed in the **Level 22 Content** on p. 237. Write response options on the dry-erase board for students to read.

Cue	Student's independent response	If student needs help
Say, **Read this story silently in your head.** Do not read to the student or point to the words.	Reads the sentences silently.	

(Table continues)

ERSB Teacher's Guide ■ **Level 22**

Cue	Student's independent response	If student needs help
After the student reads the sentences on the page, say, **Let's answer some questions about the story. Where were Jean and Jane sitting?**	Chooses the word <u>floor</u>.	If no response or an incorrect response, say, **Read this sentence again.** Point to each word in the sentence that has the answer, then ask the question again. If still no response or an incorrect response, read the sentence with the answer to the student, **Jean and Jane sat on the floor**. Then ask, **Where were Jean and Jane sitting?** If still no response or an incorrect response, physically guide the student to find <u>floor</u>, and say, **Floor. Jean and Jane sat on the floor.**

Repeat with the <u>content</u> for each lesson; see **Level 22 Content** on p. 237.

Closing /Writing activity

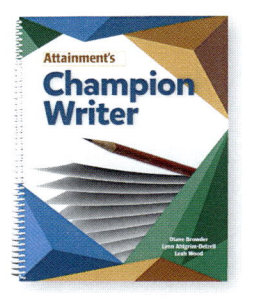

cork
knit
wren

Objective 9
Write responses to activities that review level objectives.

Activity directions
Your lesson is over. GREAT reading today! Let's complete a page in your Champion Writer.

Teaching moment

✔ In order to keep the lesson from becoming too long, consider completing the writing activity at another time of the day.

✔ Some students may need adaptations to complete the writing page in **Champion Writer**; see p. 20 for ideas.

✔ Use the dry-erase board and an erasable marker to give the student practice in writing/forming sight words and words containing the letter/sounds of this level.

LEVEL 23

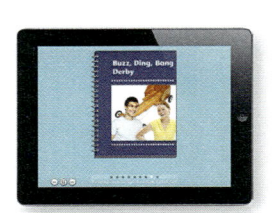

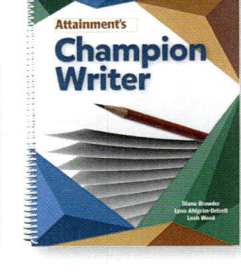

Focus
Diphthongs—oi, oy, aw, au, o

Phonemic awareness
- Blend sounds for CV, CVC, CCV, VvC, CVvC, CVrC, and CCCV words
- Segment first, middle, and last sounds in words
- Segment sounds in CV, CVC, CCV, VvC, CVvC, and CCCV words

Phonics
- Sounds /ɔɪ/ and /ɔ/ corresponding to graphemes oi, oy and aw, au, o
- Decode CV, CVC, CCV, VvC, CVvC, and CCCV words and identify their meanings

Sight words
cause, derby, down, loud, who, whoa, noise

Generalization words
dawn, yawns, join, points, lawn, boys, fault, draw, soapbox

Connected text
- ATOS level = 2.5
- Lexile level = 380L

Objectives
1. Identify oi, oy and aw, au, o when given the sounds /ɔɪ/ and /ɔ/.
2. Blend sounds to form CV, CVC, CCV, VvC, CVvC, CVrC, and CCCV words.
3. Segment the first, middle, and last sounds in words.
4. Segment the sounds in CV, CVC, CCV, VvC, CVvC, and CCCV words.
5. Decode CV, CVC, CCV, VvC, CVvC, and CCCV words and identify their meanings.
6. Read 7 new sight words.
7. Read connected text.
8. Answer comprehension questions about connected text.
9. Write responses to activities that review level objectives.

Teaching notes
This level introduces diphthongs oi, oy, au, and aw. A diphthong is a sound that begins with one vowel sound and gradually changes to another vowel sound within the same syllable. Note that the letter o is included with au and aw because sometimes o says aw (as in dog).

Level 23 Content

	Lesson 1	Lesson 2	Lesson 3	Lesson 4	Lesson 5
Letter/sound identification	**New:** oi, oy, aw, au, o **Review:** or, kn, wr				
Blending	coin, coil, cork, paw, straw, caw	**Optional demo:** soil hawk, toy, straw, saw, coil	**Optional demo:** soil jaw, oil, law, caw, coin	**Optional demo:** soil caw, saw, haw, bawl, straw	**Optional demo:** soil straw, caw, hawk, oil, coin
Segmenting I	**Listen for the *first* sound in each word:** oil, awful, awkward, oink, awesome, oyster	**Listen for the *middle* sound in each word:** **Optional demo:** coin boil, cause, haul, sauce, toil	**Listen for the *last* sound in each word:** **Optional demo:** raw caw, toy, boy, claw, straw	**Listen for the *middle* sound in each word:** **Optional demo:** toil sauce, toys, cause, coin, haul	**Listen for the *first* sound in each word:** **Optional demo:** owl oil, awful, ointment, awkward, oyster
Segmenting II	caw, saw, coin, haul, bawl, boil	**Optional demo:** coil coin, oil, paw, saw, toy	**Optional demo:** coil hawk, toy, straw, bawl, coin	**Optional demo:** coil jaw, soil, law, oil, caw	**Optional demo:** coil hawk, joy, soil, jaw, caw
Decoding	raw, hawk, toy, straw, saw, oil	**Optional demo:** raw oil, jaw, soil, paw, haul	**Optional demo:** raw boil, paw, toy, haul, bawl	**Optional demo:** raw coin, coil, haul, paw, toy	**Optional demo:** raw haul, paw, boil, oil, bawl
Sight Words	**New:** cause, derby, down, loud, who, whoa, noise **Review:** from, knew, about				
Comprehension questions (correct response in **bold**)	What did Mike do so early in the morning? (**yawn,** soap, saw, yes) What did Mike hear? (**noise,** cause, nine, dawn) What did Sloan make? (**car,** saw, cart, coil)	What did Sloan ask Mike to hand to her? (**oil,** noise, bench, boil) Where was the oil? (back, chair, **bench,** join) What did Sloan and Mike put the car in? (track, cluck, train, **truck**)	Where did Mike and Sloan push the car to? (yawn, dirt, **lawn,** lace) How did Sloan say to drive? (sale, great, sad, **safe**) Where did the man tell Sloan to write her name? (fire, box, flip, **form**) What did the racers flip to see who went first? (coil, drive, **coin,** car)	What happened to Jen's car? (red, wren, **wreck,** hill) Who beat the two boys and a girl? (Sam, **Sloan,** Slim, Tim) Where on Jen was a red mark from the crash? (arm, raw, mark, **jaw**) Whose said the wreck was her fault? (Ben, **Jen,** Sloan, Dad)	Who is racing against Sloan in the last heat? (Mim, **Ben,** Tim, Ron) What lane does Sloan get? (rich, right, live, **left**) Who is the champ of the race? (Slim, **Sloan,** Sam, Ben)

Letter/sound identification

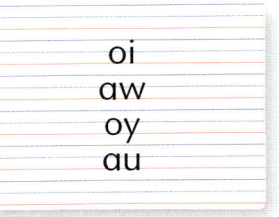

oi
aw
oy
au

Objective 1
Identify oi, oy, and aw, au, and o when given the sounds /ɔɪ/ and /ɔ/.
Pronunciation: /ɔɪ/ as in c<u>oi</u>n, /ɔ/ as in str<u>aw</u>

Prompting
- Lesson 1: Time delay 0 seconds
- Lessons 2–5: Time delay 4 seconds

Activity directions
I'll say a sound, and you find the letter that makes that sound.

Teaching moment
✔ Introduce the diphthong /ɔɪ/, **Today we are going to read words that have a sound made by two vowels together. For these sounds, the two vowels glide together.**

✔ Point to the tile on the software screen showing the oi, oy tile or write and point to them on the dry-erase board. Tell students, **These vowels together say /ɔɪ/.**

✔ Point to the tile on the software screen showing the aw, au, o or write and point to aw and au on the dry-erase board. Tell students, **These vowels together say /ɔ/.**

✔ If the student chooses an incorrect response, give a reminder to not guess but to wait and you will help. You can also add to the directions, **If you are not sure of the answer, don't guess. Wait for me to help you.**

Cue	Student's independent response	If student needs help
What letters say /ɔɪ/?	Finds the letters <u>oi</u> to make the /ɔɪ/ sound.	If no response after 4 seconds or an incorrect response, model finding the letter/sound, and continue pointing to it until the student finds it. If needed, physically guide the student to find the letter and say, **This is /ɔɪ/. You touch it.**

Repeat with aw, au, o and Level 22 review: or, kn, and wr.

Blending

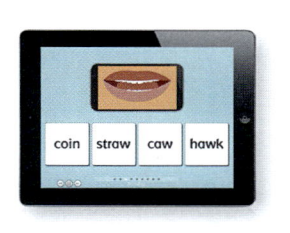

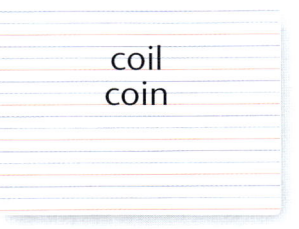

Objective 2
Blend sounds to form CV, CVC, CCV, VvC, CVvC, CVrC, and CCCV words.
Pronunciation: /ɔɪ/ as in c<u>oi</u>n

Prompting
- Lesson 1: Time delay 0 seconds
- Lessons 2–5: Time delay 4 seconds

Activity directions
I'll say some sounds. You blend the sounds together and find the word they make.

> **Teaching moment**
> ✔ Prolong or emphasize the sounds at the beginning, middle, or end to help the student identify the word.
> ✔ Provide a one-second pause between the sounds to help students process the sounds.

Cue	Student's independent response	If student needs help
/k/ /ɔɪ/ /n/. **Which word am I saying?**	Finds the word <u>coin</u>.	If no response after 4 seconds or an incorrect response, model finding the word and say, **This is <u>coin</u>. You touch it.** Continue pointing to it until the student finds it. If needed, physically guide the student to find the word.

Repeat with the <u>content</u> for each lesson; see **Level 23 Content** on p. 247.

Segmenting I

Objective 3
Segment the first, middle, and last sounds in words.
Pronunciation: /ɔɪ/ as in c<u>oi</u>n, /ɔ/ as in str<u>aw</u>

Prompting
- Lesson 1: Time delay 0 seconds
- Lessons 2–5: Time delay 4 seconds

Activity directions
I'll say a word. You show me the first/middle/last sound you hear in the word.

Teaching moment
✔ To practice without the software, provide more words with /ɔɪ/ and /ɔ/ at the beginning, middle, or end of words.

✔ Pause for one second between the direction ("What is the first/middle/last sound in") and the target word to prepare the student for the target word.

✔ To make it easier for the student, emphasizie or slightly prolong the first/middle/last sound in the word.

✔ If the student chooses an incorrect response, give a reminder to not guess but to wait and you will help. You can also add to the directions, **If you are not sure of the answer, don't guess. Wait for me to help you.**

Cue	Student's independent response	If student needs help
(Lessons 1 and 5) **What is the first sound in <u>oi</u>l?**	Finds <u>oi</u> to say /ɔɪ/.	If no response after 4 seconds or an incorrect response, model finding <u>oi</u>. Say, **The first sound is /ɔɪ/. You touch it.** If needed, physically guide the student to find /ɔɪ/.
(Lessons 2 and 4) **What is the middle sound in s<u>au</u>ce?**	Finds <u>au</u> to say /ɔ/.	If no response after 4 seconds or an incorrect response, model finding <u>au</u>. Say, **The middle sound is /ɔ/. You touch it.** If needed, physically guide the student to find /ɔ/.
(Lesson 3) **What is the last sound in r<u>aw</u>?**	Finds <u>aw</u> to say /ɔ/.	If no response after 4 seconds or an incorrect response, model finding <u>aw</u>. Say, **The last sound is /ɔ/. You touch it.** If needed, physically guide the student to find /ɔ/.

Repeat with the <u>content</u> for each lesson; see **Level 23 Content** on p. 247.

Segmenting II

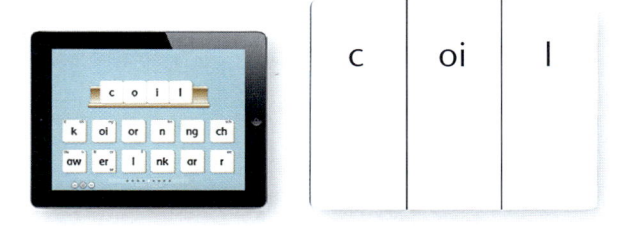

| c | oi | l |

Objective 4
Segment the sounds in CV, CVC, CCV, VvC, CVvC, and CCCV words.
Pronunciation: /ɔɪ/ as in c<u>oi</u>n

Prompting
- Lesson 1: Time delay 0 seconds
- Lessons 2–5: Time delay 4 seconds

Activity directions
Use the sounds you learned to sound out some words. I'll say a word, and you sound it out.

Teaching moment

✔ To help the student segment all of the sounds in the word, hold up a finger for each sound the student needs to find. Remember to hold up fingers for sounds, not letters (e.g., the word *coil* has 3 sounds but 4 letters; the word *saw* has 2 sounds but 3 letters).

✔ Or if the student needs help, divide the dry-erase board into sections based on the number of sounds in the word. Have the student sound out the word by choosing one sound at a time on the software screen, while you write the letter/sound the student chooses on the dry-erase board (one sound per section).

✔ If the student chooses an incorrect response, give a reminder to not guess but to wait and you will help. Add to the directions, **If you are not sure of the answer, don't guess. Wait for me to help you.**

✔ If the student makes an error on even one sound, have the student listen as you segment **all** the sounds in the word in the correct sequence. Then restate to touch the sounds in the word.

Cue	Student's independent response	If student needs help
Sound out the word <u>coil</u>.	Touches <u>c</u>, <u>oi</u>, and <u>l</u> for the sounds /k/, /ɔɪ/, and /l/.	If no response after 4 seconds or an incorrect response, say, **Listen, /k/ /ɔɪ/ /l/. Touch the sounds in <u>coin</u>.** If still no response or an incorrect response, model segmenting the word by touching each letter and saying each sound. Then say, **Your turn. Touch the sounds in <u>coin</u>.** If still no response or an incorrect response, say, **Let's touch the sounds in <u>coil</u>.** Then physically guide the student to touch each sound while you say it.

Repeat with the <u>content</u> for each lesson; see **Level 23 Content** on p. 247.

ERSB Teacher's Guide ■ Level 23

251

Decoding

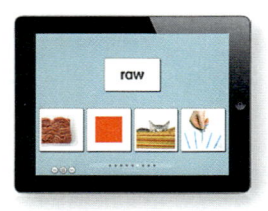

Objective 5
Decode CV, CVC, CCV, VvC, CVvC, and CCCV words and identify their meanings.
Pronunciation: /ɔ/ as in str<u>aw</u>

Prompting
- Lesson 1: Time delay 0 seconds
- Lessons 2–5: Time delay 4 seconds

Activity directions
Now, use the sounds and letters you learned to read a word and find its picture.

> **Teaching moment**
> ✔ Be certain the student knows the name of each picture.
> ✔ If students need help decoding, sound out the word by prolonging each letter sound as you say it. Then say the word (blending the sounds together); find the picture representing it. Be sure to follow this demonstration with independent responding by the student.

Cue	Student's independent response	If student needs help
First, let's hear each picture's name.	Listens as each picture is named.	
Say, **Your turn. Read the word and find the picture.**	Finds the picture of <u>raw</u>.	If no response after 4 seconds, point to the word and say, **This is /r/ /ɔ/**. Then touch the picture and say, **Here is <u>raw</u>. Now you read <u>raw</u> and find the picture.** Physically guide the student's hand if needed.
		If an incorrect response, point to the letters in the word as you say, **This says <u>raw</u>**. Touch the picture and say, **Here is the picture of <u>raw</u>**. Remove your finger and say, **Now you read <u>raw</u> and find the picture.** Physically guide the student's hand if needed.

Repeat with the <u>content</u> for each lesson; see **Level 23 Content** on p. 247.

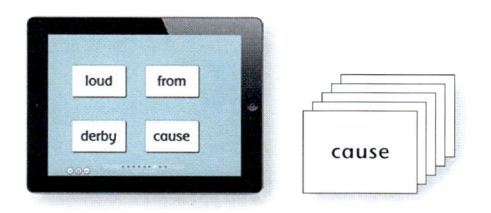

Sight words

Objective 6
Read 7 new sight words.

Prompting
- Lesson 1: Time delay 0 seconds
- Lessons 2–5: Time delay 4 seconds

Activity directions
Sight words are tricky because you can't sound them out. You have to remember what they look like. Find the word.

Teaching moment
✔ The pace between the presentation of words is purposely rapid to keep the student motivated.

✔ Use the sight word flashcards to provide extra practice of sight word reading. Provide up to 4 response options for students to choose from.

✔ Note that words including au and oi are included as sight words since students have not learned a rule for the silent e following them (e.g., cause, noise).

✔ If the student chooses an incorrect response, give a reminder to not guess but to wait and you will help. You can also add to the directions, **If you are not sure of the answer, don't guess. Wait for me to help you.**

Cue	Student's independent response	If student needs help
Find the word cause.	Finds the word cause.	If no response after 4 seconds or an incorrect response, model finding the word and say, **This is cause. You touch it.** Physically guide the student to find the word if needed.

Repeat with the new sight words and review sight words, words required for reading the story for this level; see **Level 23 Content** on p. 247.

ERSB Teacher's Guide ■ **Level 23**

Reading text / Comprehension questions

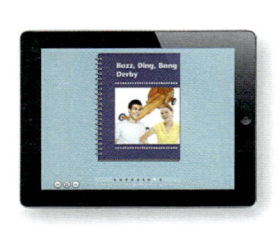

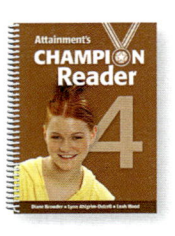

Objective 7 / Objective 8

Read connected text. / Answer comprehension questions about connected text.

Prompting

Least intrusive prompt

Activity directions

Now that you know how to read words, you can read a page from the story. In today's story, Mike, Ben, and Sloan are in a soapbox derby.

Teaching moment

✓ One page of the story is read during each lesson, followed by the comprehension questions.

✓ Compound words are embedded in this level's story. Remind students that these words are made of two smaller words and they can read them by breaking the larger word apart.

✓ Help students know what a soapbox derby is by finding more images on the web. Explain what the words *dawn* and *nose-to-nose* mean in the story.

✓ Use **Champion Reader 4** to give students additional reading practice. The comprehension questions that could be asked if not using the software and possible response options are listed in the **Level 23 Content** on p. 247. Write response options on the dry-erase board for students to read.

Cue	Student's independent response	If student needs help
Say, **Read this story silently in your head.** Do not read to the student or point to the words.	Reads the sentences silently.	

(Table continues)

ERSB Teacher's Guide ■ Level 23

Cue	Student's independent response	If student needs help
After the student reads the sentences on the page, say, **Let's answer some questions about the story. What did Mike do so early in the morning?**	Chooses the word yawn.	If no response or an incorrect response, say, **Read this sentence again.** Point to each word in the sentence that has the answer, then ask the question again.
		If still no response or an incorrect response, read the sentence with the answer to the student, **It was dawn. Mike yawns.** Then ask, **What did Mike do so early in the morning?**
		If still no response or an incorrect response, physically guide the student to find yawn, and say, **Yawn. Mike yawns.**

Repeat with the content for each lesson; see **Level 23 Content** on p. 247.

Closing /Writing activity

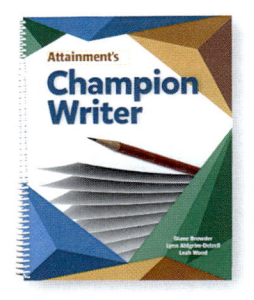

Objective 9
Write responses to activities that review level objectives.

Activity directions
Your lesson is over. GREAT reading today! Let's complete a page in your Champion Writer.

Teaching moment

✔ In order to keep the lesson from becoming too long, consider completing the writing activity at another time of the day.

✔ Some students may need adaptations to complete the writing page; see p. 20 for ideas.

✔ Use the dry-erase board and an erasable marker to give the student practice in writing/forming sight words and words containing the letter/sounds of this level.

LEVEL 24

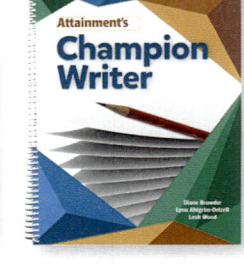

Focus
Digraphs—long o͞o, ew; ing

Phonemic awareness
- Blend sounds for CV, CVC, CCV, CVCC, CCCV, CCVC, and CVC+ing words
- Segment middle and last sounds in words
- Segment sounds in CV, CVC, CCV, CCVC, CVCC, CVrC, CCV+ing, and CVC+ing words

Phonics
- Sounds /u/ and /ɪŋ/ corresponding to graphemes oo, ew, and ing
- Decode CVC, CCV, CCCV, CVCC, CCVC, CVC+ing, CCV+ing, VvC+ing, CVvC+ing, CCVCC+ing words and identify their meanings

Sight words
ball, people, fence, tight, using

Generalization words
brings, digging, getting, grew, growing, loose, spool, shoots, roots, helping, picking, feeding

Connected text
- ATOS level = 2.7
- Lexile level = 400L

Objectives
1. Identify o͞o, ew, and ing when given the sounds /u/ and /ɪŋ/.
2. Blend sounds to form CV, CVC, CCV, CVCC, CCCV, CCVC, and CVC+ing words.
3. Segment the middle and last sounds in words.
4. Segment the sounds in CV, CVC, CCV, CCVC, CVCC, CVrC, CCV+ing, and CVC+ing words.
5. Decode CVC, CCV, CCCV, CVCC, CCVC, CVC+ing, CCV+ing, VvC+ing, CVvC+ing, CCVCC+ing words and identify their meanings.
6. Read 5 new sight words.
7. Read connected text.
8. Answer comprehension questions about connected text.
9. Write responses to review the level objectives.

Teaching notes
This level introduces the digraph o͞o its long form. It also introduces ew, which makes the same sound. A digraph is a sound represented by two letters (e.g., oo). In addition, although students have already been introduced to the /ŋ/ sound, this level adds /ɪ/ to /ŋ/ to add new dimension to reading. Now, students will read action verbs with ing. This level only briefly discusses how ing can change the spelling of the verb.

Level 24 Content

	Lesson 1	Lesson 2	Lesson 3	Lesson 4	Lesson 5
Letter/sound identification	New: oo, ew, ing Review: oi, oy, aw, au, o				
Blending	tools, stew, chew, zoo, threw, running	Optional demo: zoo screw, joking, spoon, stool, making	Optional demo: zoo raking, sing, soon, new, stew	Optional demo: zoo room, running, meeting, flew, loon	Optional demo: zoo raking, joking, boots, tools, room
Segmenting I	Listen for the *middle* sound in each word: loop, tool, coil, fork, card	Listen for the *last* sound/two sounds in each word: Optional demo: dancing threw, crew, flew, stew, stepping	Listen for the *last* sound/two sounds in each word: Optional demo: dancing pulling, screw, flew, winding, walking	Listen for the *last* sound/two sounds in each word: Optional demo: dancing wing, sing, joking, drew, stew	Listen for the *middle* sound in each word: Optional demo: stoop food, choose, room, loop, tool
Segmenting II	stoop, new, soon, loon, boots, think	Optional demo: flew running, boots, stew, sing, park	Optional demo: flew room, crew, ring, fling, making	Optional demo: flew pork, new, food, wing, spoon	Optional demo: flew playing, pork, fling, boots, spoon
Decoding	food, boots, screw, planting, stew, eating	Optional demo: boots tools, food, reading, stew, eating	Optional demo: tools stew, planting, boots, tooth, eating	Optional demo: boots food, playing, screw, planting, stool	Optional demo: tools playing, screw, boots, tooth, stew
Sight Words	New: ball, people, fence, tight, using Review: who, put, after, use, says				
Comprehension questions (correct response in **bold**)	Who is the girl? (**Wren**, Wrist, Write, Red) What does Wren work on? (crib, truck, **crew**, stew) What will the crew make with the food? (stem, feed, **stew**, stoop)	What does the crew put on? (socks, **boots**, hats, bats) What is the crew making? (**fence**, door, boots, dirt) What tool does Liv bring? (drip, nail, **drill**, dig)	What is fun for the crew? (**planting**, sleeping, pulling, sitting) What does the crew sit on? (**knees**, knocks, hands, beds) What does the crew make room for? (**seeds**, food, weeds, seats) What does the crew dig? (worms, **holes**, down, hills)	What did Wren and Liv watch for? (parts, **plants**, play, whoa) What does Liv see? (chill, shine, **shoots**, see) What is white and in the dirt? (red, **roots**, white, toots) What are the roots helping the plants get? (fort, road, **food**, bean)	What does Wren pick? (**beans**, been, weeds, leaf) What is Liv doing with the peas? (**eating**, throwing, waving, digging) What does the crew make? (step, new, **stew**, crew) Where will the crew be taking the stew? (**room**, broom, booth, food) What will the crew be doing with the people? (planting, walking, **feeding**, making)

ERSB Teacher's Guide ■ Level 24

Letter/sound identification

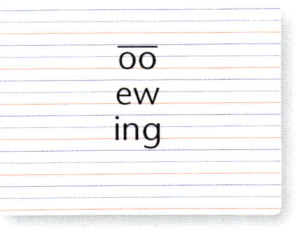

Objective 1
Identify oo, ew, and ing when given the sounds /u/ and /ɪŋ/.
Pronunciation: /u/ as in b<u>oo</u>t, st<u>ew</u>; /ɪŋ/ as in runn<u>ing</u>

Prompting
- Lesson 1: Time delay 0 seconds
- Lessons 2–5: Time delay 4 seconds

Activity directions
I'll say a sound, and you find the letter that makes that sound.

Teaching moment
✔ Introduce /u/. **Today we are going to read words that have a sound made by two vowels together .** Point to the tile on the software screen showing oo and ew or write and point to them on the dry-erase board. Tell students, **These vowels together say /u/.**

✔ Point to the tile on the software screen showing ing or write and point to ing on the dry-erase board. Tell students, **These sounds together say /ɪŋ/. You already learned the /ŋ/ sound. Now you will learn how to read ing when it is added to action words.**

✔ If the student chooses an incorrect response, give a reminder to not guess but to wait and you will help. You can also add to the directions, **If you are not sure of the answer, don't guess. Wait for me to help you.**

Cue	Student's independent response	If student needs help
What letters says /u/?	Finds the letters oo and ew to make the /u/ sound.	If no response after 4 seconds or an incorrect response, model finding the letter/sound, and continue pointing to it until the student finds it. If needed, physically guide the student to find the letter and say, **This is /u/. You touch it.**

Repeat with ing and Level 23 review: oi, oy and aw, au, o.

Blending

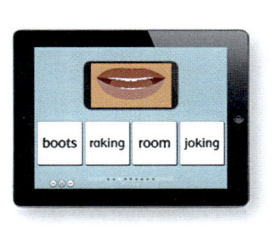

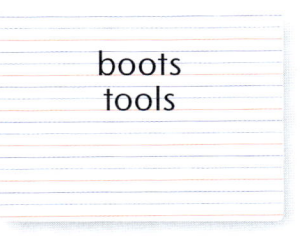

Objective 2
Blend sounds to form CV, CVC, CCV, CVCC, CCCV, CCVC, and CVC + ing words.
Pronunciation: /u/ as in b<u>oo</u>t, st<u>ew</u>; /ɪŋ/ as in runn<u>ing</u>; /t/ as in <u>t</u>ools; /l/ as in too<u>l</u>s; /z/ as in tool<u>s</u>

Prompting
- Lesson 1: Time delay 0 seconds
- Lessons 2–5: Time delay 4 seconds

Activity directions
I'll say some sounds. You blend the sounds together and find the word they make.

Teaching moment
✔ Prolong or emphasize the sounds at the beginning, middle, or end to help the student identify the word.

✔ Provide a one-second pause between the sounds to help students process the sounds.

✔ Point out on screen to students that, **Sometimes the ending ing adds another letter to a word, like run to running.**

✔ Point out on screen to students that, **Sometimes the ending ing replaces the silent e, like joke to joking.**

✔ Note that the consonant blend <u>thr</u> is included in blending as students should be able to generalize the sounds learned (/θ/ and /r/) to blends.

Cue	Student's independent response	If student needs help
/t/ /u/ /l/ /z/. Which word am I saying?	Finds the word <u>tools</u>.	If no response after 4 seconds or an incorrect response, model finding the word and say, **This is <u>tools</u>. You touch it.** Continue pointing to it until the student finds it. If needed, physically guide the student to find the word.

Repeat with the <u>content</u> for each lesson; see **Level 24 Content** on p. 257.

ERSB Teacher's Guide ■ Level 24

Segmenting I

Objective 3
Segment the middle and last sounds in words.
Pronunciation: /u/ as in b<u>oo</u>t, /ɪŋ/ as in runn<u>ing</u>

Prompting
- Lesson 1: Time delay 0 seconds
- Lessons 2–5: Time delay 4 seconds

Activity directions
I'll say a word. You show me the middle/last/last two sounds you hear in the word.

Teaching moment
✔ To practice without the software, provide more words with /u/ in the middle and /ɪŋ/ at the end.

✔ Pause for one second between the direction ("What is the middle/last sound/two sounds in") and the target word to prepare the student for the target word.

✔ To make it easier for the student, emphasize or prolong the middle sound or the last sound(s). Note that ing is two sounds (the ng is one sound) not three.

✔ If the student chooses an incorrect response, give a reminder to not guess but to wait and you will help. You can also add to the directions, **If you are not sure of the answer, don't guess. Wait for me to help you.**

Cue	Student's independent response	If student needs help
(Lessons 1 and 5) **What is the middle sound in loop?**	Finds <u>oo</u> to say /<u>u</u>/.	If no response after 4 seconds or an incorrect response, model finding <u>oo</u>. Say, **The middle sound is /u/. You touch it**. If needed, physically guide the student to find /u/.
(Lessons 2, 3, and 4) **What is the last sound in threw?**	Finds <u>ew</u> to say /<u>u</u>/.	If no response after 4 seconds or an incorrect response, model finding <u>ew</u>. Say, **The last sound is /u/. You touch it**. If needed, physically guide the student to find /u/.
(Lessons 2, 3, and 4) **What are the last two sounds in dancing?**	Finds <u>ing</u> to say /ɪŋ/.	If no response after 4 seconds or an incorrect response, model finding <u>ing</u>. Say, **The last two sounds are /ɪŋ/. You touch it**. If needed, physically guide the student to find /ɪŋ/.

Repeat with the <u>content</u> for each lesson; see **Level 24 Content** on p. 257.

Segmenting II

| s | t | oo | p |

Objective 4
Segment the sounds in CV, CVC, CCV, CCVC, CVCC, CVrC, CCV+ing, and CVC+ing words.
Pronunciation: /u/ as in b<u>oo</u>t

Prompting
- Lesson 1: Time delay 0 seconds
- Lessons 2–5: Time delay 4 seconds

Activity directions
Use the sounds you learned to sound out some words. I'll say a word, and you sound it out.

Teaching moment

✔ To help the student segment all of the sounds in the word, hold up a finger for each sound the student needs to find. Remember to hold up fingers for sounds, not letters (e.g., the word *stoop* has 4 sounds but 5 letters; the word *pulling* has 5 sounds and 5 letters).

✔ Or if the student needs help, divide the dry-erase board into sections based on the number of sounds in the word. Have the student sound out the word by choosing one sound at a time on the software screen, while you write the letter/sound the student chooses on the dry-erase board (one sound per section).

✔ If the student chooses an incorrect response, give a reminder to not guess but to wait and you will help. Add to the directions, **If you are not sure of the answer, don't guess. Wait for me to help you.**

✔ If the student makes an error on even one sound, have the student listen as you segment **all** the sounds in the word in the correct sequence. Then restate to touch the sounds in the word.

Cue	Student's independent response	If student needs help
Sound out the word <u>stoop</u>.	Touches <u>st</u>, oo, and <u>p</u> for the sounds /st/, /u/, and /p/.	If no response after 4 seconds or an incorrect response, say, **Listen, /st/ /u/ /p/. Touch the sounds in <u>stoop</u>.** If still no response or an incorrect response, model segmenting the word by touching each letter and saying each sound. Then say, **Your turn. Touch the sounds in <u>stoop</u>.** If still no response or an incorrect response, say, **Let's touch the sounds in <u>stoop</u>.** Then physically guide the student to touch each sound while you say it.

Repeat with the <u>content</u> for each lesson; see **Level 24 Content** on p. 257.

Decoding

Objective 5
Decode CVC, CCV, CCCV, CVCC, CCVC, CVC+ing, CCV+ing, VvC+ing, CVvC+ing, CCVCC+ing words and identify their meanings.
Pronunciation: /u/ as in b<u>oo</u>t

Prompting
- Lesson 1: Time delay 0 seconds
- Lessons 2–5: Time delay 4 seconds

Activity directions
Now, use the sounds and letters you learned to read a word and find its picture.

Teaching moment
✔ Be certain the student knows the name of each picture.

✔ If students need help decoding, sound out the word by prolonging each letter sound as you say it. Then say the word (blending the sounds together); find the picture representing it. Be sure to follow this demonstration with independent responding by the student.

Cue	Student's independent response	If student needs help
First, let's hear each picture's name.	Listens as each picture is named.	
Say, **Your turn. Read the word and find the picture.**	Finds the picture of <u>boots</u>.	If no response after 4 seconds, point to the word and say, **This is /<u>b</u>/ /<u>u</u>/ /<u>t</u>/ /<u>s</u>/.** Then touch the picture and say, **Here is <u>boots</u>. Now you read <u>boots</u> and find the picture.** Physically guide the student's hand if needed. If an incorrect response, point to the letters in the word as you say, **This says <u>boots</u>.** Touch the picture and say, **Here is the picture of a <u>boots</u>.** Remove your finger and say, **Now you read <u>boots</u> and find the picture.** Physically guide the student's hand if needed.

Repeat with the <u>content</u> for each lesson; see **Level 24 Content** on p. 257.

Sight words

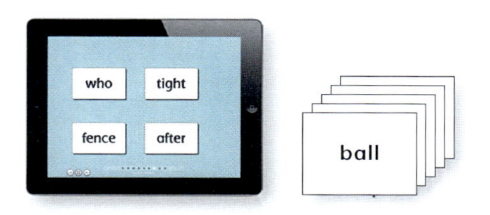

Objective 6
Read 5 new sight words.

Prompting
- Lesson 1: Time delay 0 seconds
- Lessons 2–5: Time delay 4 seconds

Activity directions
Sight words are tricky because you can't sound them out. You have to remember what they look like. Find the word.

Teaching moment
✔ The pace between the presentation of words is purposely rapid to keep the student motivated.

✔ Use the sight word flashcards to provide extra practice of sight word reading. Provide up to 4 response options for students to choose from.

✔ Note that words including ing are included as sight words since students have not learned a rule for deleting the silent e (e.g., using).

✔ If the student chooses an incorrect response, give a reminder to not guess but to wait and you will help. You can also add to the directions, **If you are not sure of the answer, don't guess. Wait for me to help you.**

Cue	Student's independent response	If student needs help
Find the word ball.	Finds the word for ball.	If no response after 4 seconds or an incorrect response, model finding the word and say, **This is ball. You touch it.** Physically guide the student to find the word if needed.

Repeat with the new sight words and review sight words, words required for reading the story for this level; see **Level 24 Content** on p. 257.

Reading text /Comprehension questions

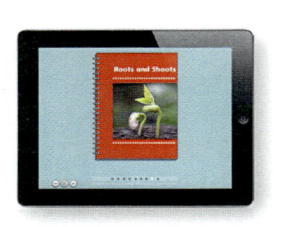

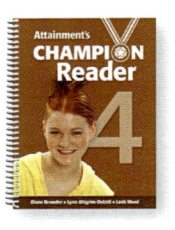

Wren
Wrist
Write
Red

Objective 7 / Objective 8
Read connected text. / Answer comprehension questions about connected text.

Prompting
Least intrusive prompt

Activity directions
Now that you know how to read words, you can read a page from the story. In this story, Wren and Liz plant a garden.

Teaching moment
✓ One page of the story is read during each lesson, followed by the comprehension questions.

✓ Compound words are embedded in this level's story. Remind students that these words are made of two smaller words and they can read them by breaking the larger word apart.

✓ Use **Champion Reader 4** to give students additional reading practice. The comprehension questions that could be asked if not using the software and possible response options are listed in the **Level 24 Content** on p. 257. Write response options on the dry-erase board for students to read.

Cue	Student's independent response	If student needs help
Say, **Read this story silently in your head.** Do not read to the student or point to the words.	Reads the sentences silently.	
After the student reads the sentences on the page, say, **Let's answer some questions about the story. Who is the girl?**	Chooses the word Wren.	If no response or an incorrect response, say, **Read this sentence again**. Point to each word in the sentence that has the answer, then ask the question again. If still no response or an incorrect response, read the sentence with the answer to the student, **Wren is a girl**. Then ask, **Who is the girl?** If still no response or an incorrect response, physically guide the student to find Wren, and say, **Wren. Wren is the girl.**

Repeat with the content for each lesson; see **Level 24 Content** on p. 257.

Closing /Writing activity

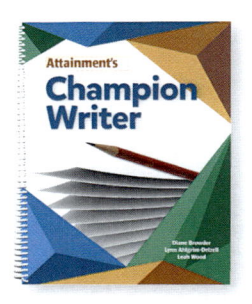

screw
room
pulling

Objective 9
Write responses to activities that review level objectives.

Activity directions
Your lesson is over. GREAT reading today! Let's complete a page in your Champion Writer.

Teaching moment
✔ In order to keep the lesson from becoming too long, consider completing the writing activity at another time of the day.

✔ Some students may need adaptations to complete the writing page; see p. 20 for ideas.

✔ Use the dry-erase board and an erasable marker to give the student additional practice in writing/forming sight words and words containing the letter/sounds of this level.

LEVEL 25

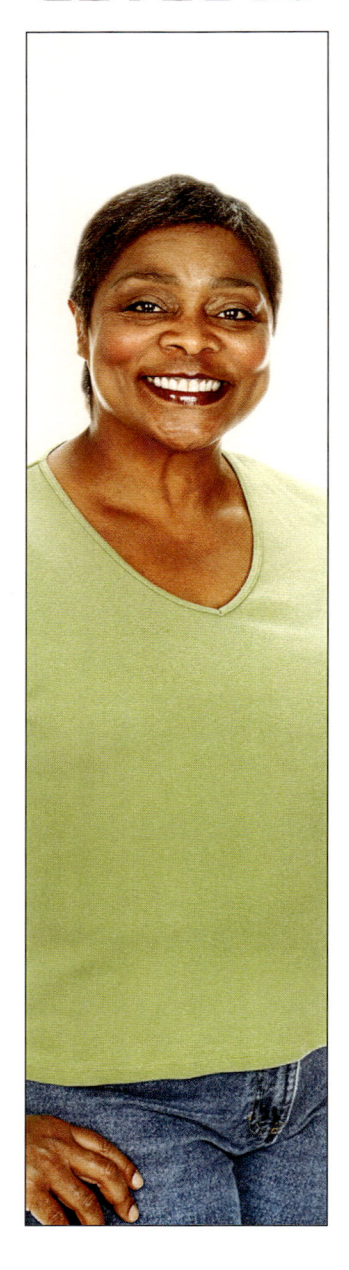

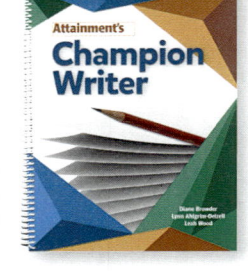

Focus
Diphthongs—ow, ou, y (long ē)

Phonemic awareness
- Blend sounds for VC, VCCCV, CV, CVCe, CCVC, CVCC, CVCV, CCVCC, CCVCV, CCVCCV, and CVrCCV words
- Segment middle and last sounds in words
- Segment sounds in VC, VCV, VCCV, CV, CVC, CCVC, CVCC, CVCV, and CCVCV words

Phonics
- Sounds /aʊ/ and /i/ corresponding to graphemes ow, ou, and y (long ē)
- Decode VC, VCCVCe, CV, CVC, CCVC, CVCV, CVCC, CVCCV, CCVCC, CCVCV, CVCC+ing, and compound words and identify their meanings

Sight words
cook, hour, tall, hear

Generalization words
scouts, proud, south, sound, howl, growl, chow, lucky, plenty, sticky

Connected text
- ATOS level = 2.3
- Lexile level = 450L

Objectives
1 Identify ow, ou, and y (long ē) when given the sounds /aʊ/ and /i/.
2 Blend sounds to form VC, VCCCV, CV, CVCe, CCVC, CVCC, CVCV, CCVCC, CCVCV, CCVCCV, and CVrCCV words.
3 Segment the middle and last sounds in words.
4 Segment the sounds in VC, VCV, VCCV, CV, CVC, CCVC, CVCC, CVCV, and CCVCV words.
5 Decode VC, VCCVCe, CV, CVC, CCVC, CVCV, CVCC, CVCCV, CCVCC, CCVCV, CVCC+ing, and compound words and identify their meanings.
6 Read 4 new sight words.
7 Read connected text.
8 Answer comprehension questions about connected text.
9 Write responses to review the level objectives.

Teaching notes
This level introduces the diphthongs ow and ou and introduces y (long ē). A diphthong is a sound that begins with one vowel sound and gradually changes to another vowel sound within the same syllable. In this level the students learn that y has another sound; y as the long ē sound.

ERSB Teacher's Guide ■ Level 25

Level 25 Content

	Lesson 1	Lesson 2	Lesson 3	Lesson 4	Lesson 5
Letter/sound identification	**New**: ow, ou, y (on the ē tile) **Review**: o͞o, ew, ing				
Blending	our, sour, out, ground, brown, flour	**Demo**: flour penny, frowns, shortly, bow, empty	**Demo**: flour out, pound, happy, ouch, quickly	**Demo**: flour sloppy, owl, crunchy, hour, messy	**Demo**: flour frowns, quickly, owl, ouch, out
Segmenting I	**Listen for the *middle* sound in each word:** frown, choose, sour, chewed, gown, house	**Listen for the *last* sound in each word:** **Optional demo**: sadly wing, quickly, plow, bow, messy	**Listen for the *middle* sound in each word:** **Optional demo**: clown cause, gown, beet, town, house	**Listen for the *last* sound in each word:** **Optional demo**: sadly cow, empty, blue, happy, thing	**Listen for the *last* sound in each word:** **Optional demo**: sadly empty, glue, messy, cow, sing
Segmenting II	bow, frown, funny, spout, dog, fully	**Optional demo**: fussy town, sour, happy, owl, icky	**Optional demo**: fussy gowns, puppy, logs, round, bow	**Optional demo**: fussy stout, sour, frown, smelly, couch	**Optional demo**: stout oddly, puppy, fussy, icky, town
Decoding	town, outside, tent, round, cow, hotdog	**Optional demo**: couch spout, owl, happy, candy, town	**Optional demo**: owl cow, couch, gowns, spout, ground	**Optional demo**: couch candy, ouch, outside, camping, penny	**Optional demo**: couch round, hotdog, camping, owl, candy
Sight Words	**New**: cook, hour, tall, hear	**Review**: one, ball, like, soon, two, from, have			
Comprehension questions (correct response in **bold**)	What are Sloan and Liv? (**scouts**, skid, scowl, cats) Where will Liv and Sloan go? (sledding, **camping**, singing, snowing) In how many hours will Liv and Sloan leave? (five, two, **one**, three)	What does Liv use to get a bag from the top shelf? (stem, **stool**, school, smile) What did Sloan pack? (stool, foot, **gowns**, frowns) What does Liv set on the ground? (mat, boots, **pack**, gowns)	What does Sloan want to do? (bike, side, cry, **hike**) What does Mom make when she hears all the screaming? (cow, smile, **frown**, out)? What do the campers have to set up quickly? (**tent**, then, proud, bike) What is Liv proud of? (**house**, help, gown, funny)	Where do the girls go? (howl, **hike**, swim, lake) What do the girls see? (pound, **path**, pat, south) What does Liv say she heard? (grime, chow, **growl**, green) What does Sloan say she heard? (toot, hug, him, **hoot**) What is in the tree? (**owl**, chow, cow, mud)	What does Mom call camp food? (cub, chime, **chow**, owl) What do the girls place down on the ground? (bogs, **logs**, limes, dogs) What did Mom say the girls could have after they ate? (**treat**, train, trick, happy) What is one word that describes the treat? (muddy, quietly, fussy, **sticky**) What do the girls think is fun? (**camping**, sleeping, chow, singing)

Letter/sound identification

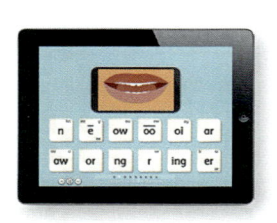

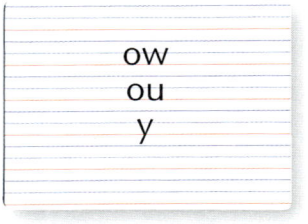

ow
ou
y

Objective 1
Identify ow, ou, and y (long ē) when given the sounds /aʊ/ and /i/.
Pronunciation: /aʊ/ as in c<u>ow</u>, /i/ as in quickl<u>y</u>

Prompting
- Lesson 1: Time delay 0 seconds
- Lessons 2–5: Time delay 4 seconds

Activity directions
I'll say a sound, and you find the letter(s) that makes that sound.

Teaching moment

✓ Introduce /aʊ/, **Today we are going to read words that have another sound made by two vowels together.** Point to the tile on the software screen showing ow and ou or write and point to them on the dry-erase board. Tell students, **These vowels together say /aʊ/.**

✓ Introduce y as /i/. Point to the y in the corner of the long ē tile on the software screen or write and point to it on the dry-erase board. Tell students, **Sometimes y says /i/. Here it is on the long ē tile.**

✓ If the student chooses an incorrect response, give a reminder to not guess but to wait and you will help. You can also add to the directions, **If you are not sure of the answer, don't guess. Wait for me to help you.**

Cue	Student's independent response	If student needs help
What letters say /a<u>ʊ</u>/?	Finds the letters <u>ow</u> to make the /a<u>ʊ</u>/ sound.	If no response after 4 seconds or an incorrect response, model finding the letter/sound, and continue pointing to it until the student finds it. If needed, physically guide the student to find the letter and say, **This is /a<u>ʊ</u>/. You touch it.**

Repeat with y and Level 24 review: oo, ew, and ing.

Blending

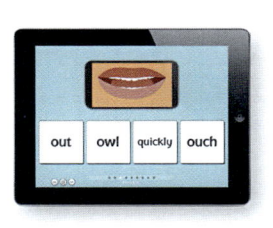

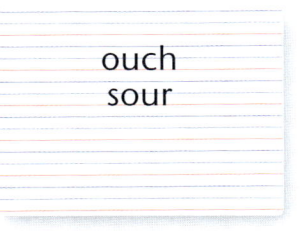

Objective 2
Blend sounds to form VC, VCCCV, CV, CVCe, CCVC, CVCC, CVCV, CCVCC, CCVCV, CCVCCV, and CVrCCV words.
Pronunciation: /aʊ/ as in cow

Prompting
- Lesson 1: Time delay 0 seconds
- Lessons 2–5: Time delay 4 seconds

Activity directions
I'll say some sounds. You blend the sounds together and find the word they make.

Teaching moment
✔ Prolong or emphasize the sounds at the beginning, middle, or end to help the student identify the word.

✔ Provide a one-second pause between the sounds to help students process the sounds.

Cue	Student's independent response	If student needs help
/s/ /aʊ/ /ɝ/. Which word am I saying?	Finds the word sour.	If no response after 4 seconds or an incorrect response, model finding the word and say, **This is sour. You touch it.** Continue pointing to it until the student finds it. If needed, physically guide the student to find the word.

Repeat with the content for each lesson; see **Level 25 Content** on p. 267.

ERSB Teacher's Guide ■ Level 25

Segmenting I

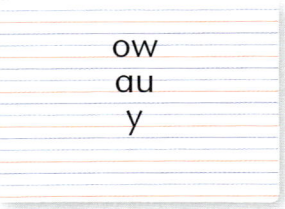

ow
au
y

Objective 3
Segment the middle and last sounds in words.
Pronunciation: /aʊ/ as in c<u>ow</u>, /i/ as in quickl<u>y</u>

Prompting
- Lesson 1: Time delay 0 seconds
- Lessons 2–5: Time delay 4 seconds

Activity directions
I'll say a word. You show me the middle/last sound you hear in the word.

Teaching moment
✔ To practice without the software, provide more words with /ow/ in the middle and y pronounced as /i/ at the end of the word.

✔ Pause for one second between the direction ("What is the middle/last sound in") and the target word to prepare the student for the target word.

✔ To make it easier for the student, emphasize or prolong the middle/last sound in the word.

✔ If the student chooses an incorrect response, give a reminder to not guess but to wait and you will help. You can also add to the directions, **If you are not sure of the answer, don't guess. Wait for me to help you.**

Cue	Student's independent response	If student needs help
(Lessons 1 and 3) **What is the middle sound in frown?**	Finds <u>ow</u> to say /aʊ/.	If no response after 4 seconds or an incorrect response, model finding <u>ow</u>. Say, **The middle sound is /aʊ/. You touch it.** If needed, physically guide the student to find /aʊ/.
(Lessons 2, 4, and 5) **What is the last sound in sadly?**	Finds y to say /i/.	If no response after 4 seconds or an incorrect response, model finding <u>y</u>. Say, **The last sound is /i/. You touch it.** If needed, physically guide the student to find /i/.

Repeat with the <u>content</u> for each lesson; see **Level 25 Content** on p. 267.

Segmenting II

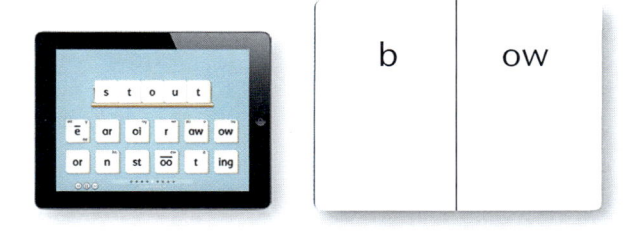

Objective 4
Segment the sounds in VC, VCV, VCCV, CV, CVC, CCVC, CVCC, CVCV, and CCVCV words.
Pronunciation: /aʊ/ as in c<u>ow</u>

Prompting
- Lesson 1: Time delay 0 seconds
- Lessons 2–5: Time delay 4 seconds

Activity directions
Use the sounds you learned to sound out some words. I'll say a word, and you sound it out.

Teaching moment

✔ Remember the students are choosing the letters to correspond to the sounds they hear. When the software responds to students' choices, it will automatically add additional letters where appropriate. You can explain this to the student, **Sometimes when y is added to the end of a word, an extra letter is added in the middle, like in funny and fully.**

✔ To help the student segment all of the sounds in the word, hold up a finger for each sound the student needs to find. Remember to hold up fingers for sounds, not letters (e.g., the word *funny* has 4 sounds but 5 letters, the word *bow* has 2 sounds but 3 letters).

✔ If the student makes an error on even one sound, have the student listen as you segment **all** the sounds in the word in the correct sequence. Then restate to touch the sounds in the word.

✔ If the student chooses an incorrect response, give a reminder to not guess but to wait and you will help. Add to the directions, **If you are not sure of the answer, don't guess. Wait for me to help you.**

Cue	Student's independent response	If student needs help
Sound out the word <u>bow</u>.	Touches <u>b</u> and <u>ow</u> for the sounds /b/ and /aʊ/.	If no response after 4 seconds or an incorrect response, say, **Listen, /b/ /aʊ/. Touch the sounds in <u>bow</u>.** If still no response or an incorrect response, model segmenting the word by touching each letter and saying each sound. Then say, **Your turn. Touch the sounds in <u>bow</u>.** If still no response or an incorrect response, say, **Let's touch the sounds in <u>bow</u>.** Then physically guide the student to touch each sound while you say it.

Repeat with the <u>content</u> for each lesson; see **Level 25 Content** on p. 267.

Decoding

Objective 5
Decode VC, VCCVCe, CV, CVC, CCVC, CVCV, CVCC, CVCCV, CCVCC, CCVCV, CVCC+ing, and compound words and identify their meanings.
Pronunciation: /aʊ/ as in c<u>ow</u>

Prompting
- Lesson 1: Time delay 0 seconds
- Lessons 2–5: Time delay 4 seconds

Activity directions
Now, use the sounds and letters you learned to read a word and find its picture.

Teaching moment
✔ Be certain the student knows the name of each picture.

✔ If students need help decoding, sound out the word by prolonging each letter sound as you say it. Then say the word (blending the sounds together); find the picture representing it. Be sure to follow this demonstration with independent responding by the student.

✔ Also when a compound word is onscreen, remind students how to read a compound word. Say, **Remember, compound words are two short words that go together to make a new larger word. Break the large word into two smaller words to read it.**

Cue	Student's independent response	If student needs help
First, let's hear each picture's name.	Listens as each picture is named.	
Say, **Your turn. Read the word and find the picture.**	Finds the picture of <u>town</u>.	If no response after 4 seconds, point to the word and say, **This is /t/ /aʊ/ /n/.** Then touch the picture and say, **Here is <u>town</u>. Now you read <u>town</u> and find the picture.** Physically guide the student's hand if needed. If an incorrect response, point to the letters in the word as you say, **This says <u>town</u>.** Touch the picture and say, **Here is the picture of <u>town</u>.** Remove your finger and say, **Now you read <u>town</u> and find the picture.** Physically guide the student's hand if needed.

Repeat with the <u>content</u> for each lesson; see **Level 25 Content** on p. 267.

Sight words

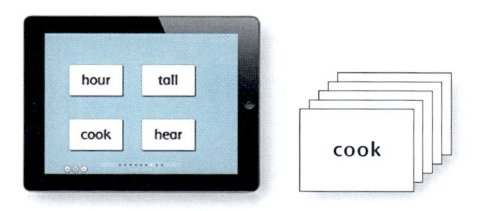

Objective 6
Read 4 new sight words.

Prompting
- Lesson 1: Time delay 0 seconds
- Lessons 2–5: Time delay 4 seconds

Activity directions
Sight words are tricky because you can't sound them out. You have to remember what they look like. Find the word.

Teaching moment
✔ The pace between the presentation of words is purposely rapid to keep the student motivated.

✔ Use the sight word flashcards to provide extra practice of sight word reading. Provide up to 4 response options for students to choose from.

✔ Note that words including oo are included as sight words since students have not learned how to read oo as a short sound (e.g., cook).

✔ If the student chooses an incorrect response, give a reminder to not guess but to wait and you will help. You can also add to the directions, **If you are not sure of the answer, don't guess. Wait for me to help you.**

Cue	Student's independent response	If student needs help
Find the word cook.	Finds the word for cook.	If no response after 4 seconds or an incorrect response, model finding the word and say, **This is cook. You touch it.** Physically guide the student to find the word if needed.

Repeat with the new sight words and review sight words, words required for reading the story for this level; see **Level 25 Content** on p. 267.

ERSB Teacher's Guide ■ Level 25

Reading text / Comprehension questions

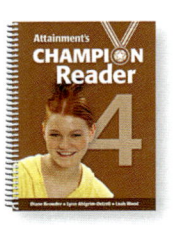

scouts
skid
scowl
cats

Objective 7 / Objective 8
Read connected text. / Answer comprehension questions about connected text.

Prompting
Least intrusive prompt

Activity directions
Now that you know how to read words, you can read a page from the story. Today you will read about Sloan and Liv's camping adventure.

Teaching moment
✔ One page of the story is read during each lesson, followed by the comprehension questions.

✔ Compound words are embedded in this level's story. Remind students that these words are made of two smaller words and they can read them by breaking the larger word apart.

✔ Use **Champion Reader 4** to give students additional reading practice. The comprehension questions that could be asked if not using the software and possible response options are listed in the **Level 25 Content** on p. 267. Write response options on the dry-erase board for students to read.

Cue	Student's independent response	If student needs help
Say, **Read this story silently in your head.** Do not read to the student or point to the words.	Reads the sentences silently.	

(Table continues)

ERSB Teacher's Guide ■ Level 25

Cue	Student's independent response	If student needs help
After the student reads the sentences on the page, say, **Let's answer some questions about the story. What are Sloan and Liv?**	Chooses the word <u>scouts</u>.	If no response or an incorrect response, say, **Read this sentence again**. Point to each word in the sentence that has the answer, then ask the question again. If still no response or an incorrect response, read the sentence with the answer to the student, **Sloan and Liv are scouts**. Then ask, **What are Sloan and Liv?** If still no response or an incorrect response, physically guide the student to find <u>scouts</u>, and say, **Scouts. Sloan and Liv are scouts**.

Repeat with the <u>content</u> for each lesson; see **Level 25 Content** on p. 267.

Closing /Writing activity

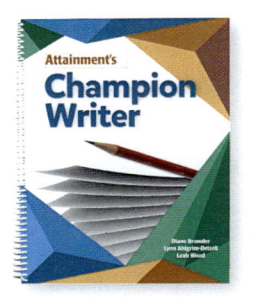

ground
frowned
empty

Objective 9
Write responses to activities that review level objectives.

Activity directions
Your lesson is over. GREAT reading today! Let's complete a page in your Champion Writer.

Teaching moment

✔ In order to keep the lesson from becoming too long, consider completing the writing activity at another time of the day.

✔ Some students may need adaptations to complete the writing page in **Champion Writer**; see p. 20 for ideas.

✔ Use the dry-erase board and an erasable marker to give the student practice in writing/forming sight words and words containing the letter/sounds of this level.

LEVEL 26

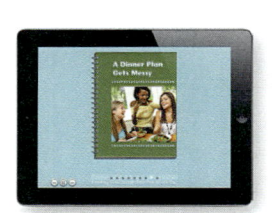

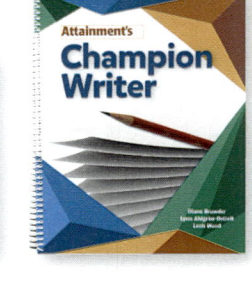

Focus
Digraph—oo (short); past tense marker—ed

Phonemic awareness
- Blend sounds for CVC, CVCC, CCVC, and CCVCC words
- Segment middle and last sounds in words
- Segment sounds in CVC, CVCC, CCVC, CCVCC, CCVrC, and CVCCC words

Phonics
- Sounds /ʊ/, /ɛd/, /d/, and /t/ corresponding to graphemes oo (short), ed, d, or t
- Decode CVC, CVCC, CCVC, CCVCC, CVCCC, CCVrC words, and compound words and identify their meanings

Sight words
give, old, read (pronounced red), wanted

Generalization words
few, whoosh, stood, needed, started, patted, baked, melted, asked, helped, thanks

Connected text
- ATOS level = 2.6
- Lexile level = 490L

Objectives
1. Identify oo (short), and past tense markers ed, d, or t when given the sounds /ʊ/, /ɛd/, /d/, and /t/.
2. Blend sounds to form CVC, CVCC, CCVC, and CCVCC words.
3. Segment the middle and last sounds in words.
4. Segment the sounds in CVC, CVCC, CCVC, CCVCC, CCVrC, and CVCCC words.
5. Decode CVC, CVCC, CCVC, CCVCC, CVCCC, CCVrC words, and compound words and identify their meanings.
6. Read 4 new sight words.
7. Read connected text.
8. Answer comprehension questions about connected text.
9. Write responses to review level objectives.

Teaching notes
This final level introduces the digraph oo its short form. It also adds the past tense marker ed to the student's reading repertoire. This is the first level to use phrases as response options for the comprehension questions. Students should now be able to read end of first grade text.

Level 26 Content

	Lesson 1	Lesson 2	Lesson 3	Lesson 4	Lesson 5
Letter/sound identification	**New:** oo (short), ed (on the d tile), ed (on the t tile), ed for /ɛd/ **Review:** ow, ou, y (long ē)				
Blending	looked, cook, smiled, hood, stepped, wool	**Optional demo:** stepped took, frowned, hooked, foot, grabbed	**Optional demo:** stepped stirred, Brook, matted, grabbed, shook	**Optional demo:** stepped chopped, cleaned, wood, hopped, treated	**Optional demo:** stepped chopped, took, frowned, cooked, book
Segmenting I	**Listen for the *last* sound in each word:** cleaned, stirred, sticky, danced, bring, runner	**Listen for the *middle* sound in each word:** **Optional demo:** foot Brook, shook, took, pound, hood	**Listen for the *last* sound in each word:** **Optional demo:** cleaned standing, girls, frowned, taking, smiled	**Listen for the *middle* sound in each word:** **Optional demo:** foot bake, cook, boys, tool, book	**Listen for the *last* sound in each word:** **Optional demo:** danced sticky, cleaned, taking, runner, smiled
Segmenting II	cooked, Brook, danced, foot, hoped, took	**Optional demo:** stepped hopped, cook, stirred, wood, book	**Optional demo:** stepped cleaned, took, chopped, hood, wool	**Optional demo:** stepped cooked, grabbed, Brook, look, raked	**Optional demo:** stepped cook, chopped, hoped, Brook, liked
Decoding	frowned, cookbook, stepped, Brook, raked, hook	**Optional demo:** hook cook, stirred, smiled, wood, cookbook	**Optional demo:** hook book, chopped, frowned, danced, wool	**Optional demo:** hook smiled, cook, Brook, hopped, mopped	**Optional demo:** hook Brook, frowned, cookbook, wool, raked
Sight Words	**New:** give, old, read (pronounced red), wanted **Review:** oh, my, them, were, have, here, there				
Comprehension questions (correct response in **bold**)	What does Brook have? (funny dogs, **good friends**, bad friends, big friends) When did Brook's dinner plan take place? (**last week**, this week, never, today) What do Brook's friends make her do? (sleep, **smile**, cry, smell)	What did Brook take down from the shelf? (outside, old book, **cookbook**, fun book) What did Brook want to make? (far, book, hood, **food**) What did Brook want her friends to be doing when they were done eating? (messy, smelly, **smiling**, sleeping)	How did Brook get to the food? (**drove car**, walked, took bus, rode bike) What did Brook pay for? (**food**, book, car, took) What was it time to do? (**cook food**, clean house, eat dinner, huge mound)	What did Brook stir into the meat? (**milk and eggs**, candy and nuts, flour and water, melted cheese) What fell to the ground? (**pan**, fan, pie, pat) Where did the food fly? (on friends, **all over**, on the car, in sunshine) What does Brook want to give her friends? (good water, **good food**, bad food, sunny day)	Who came to visit? (dogs, **friends**, frogs, funny) What did the friends look at? (door, **floor**, flood, helped) What did they friends clean up? (messy milk, a bird, **messy food**, a cat) What did Brook say to her friends? (go away, see you, **thank you**, no thanks)

Letter/sound identification

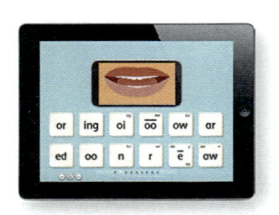

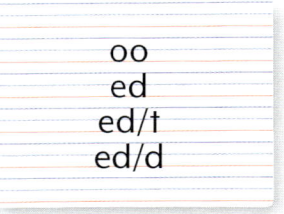

oo
ed
ed/t
ed/d

Objective 1
Identify oo (short), and past tense markers ed, d, or t when given the sounds /ʊ/, /ɛd/, /d/, and /t/.
Pronunciation: /ʊ/ as in f<u>oo</u>t, /ɛd/ as in patt<u>ed</u>

Prompting
- Lesson 1: Time delay 0 seconds
- Lessons 2–5: Time delay 4 seconds

Activity directions
I'll say a sound, and you find the letter(s) that makes that sound.

Teaching moment

✔ Introduce /ʊ/. **Today we are going to read words that have the /ʊ/ sound. You already learned that oo says /u/ but oo can be a short sound and then it says /ʊ/.** Point to the tile on the software screen showing the oo tile or write and point to it on the dry-erase board. Tell students, **These two vowels together say /ʊ/.**

✔ Introduce ed. Point to the ed in the corner of the /t/ tile and the /d/ tile on the software screen and the new tile with ed on it; or write and point to them on the dry-erase board. Tell students, **Notice the letters ed on this tile, and on the d and the t tile. Sometimes ed says /ɛd/, like in patted, but sometimes ed just says /d/, like in smiled. Ed can also say /t/, like in helped. Ed is added to the end of action words to talk about action that happened in the past.**

✔ If the student chooses an incorrect response, give a reminder to not guess but to wait and you will help. You can also add to the directions, **If you are not sure of the answer, don't guess. Wait for me to help you.**

Cue	Student's independent response	If student needs help
What letters say /ʊ/?	Finds the letters <u>oo</u> to make the /ʊ/ sound.	If no response after 4 seconds or an incorrect response, model finding the letter/sound, and continue pointing to it until the student finds it. If needed, physically guide the student to find the letters and say, **This says /ʊ/. You touch it.**

Repeat with ed and Level 25 review: ow, ou, and y (long ē).

Blending

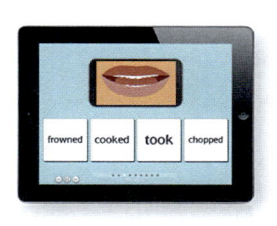

Objective 2
Blend sounds to form CVC, CVCC, CCVC, and CCVCC words.
Pronunciation: /ʊ/ as in f<u>oo</u>t

Prompting
- Lesson 1: Time delay 0 seconds
- Lessons 2–5: Time delay 4 seconds

Activity directions
I'll say some sounds. You blend the sounds together and find the word they make.

Teaching moment
✔ Prolong or emphasize the sounds at the beginning, middle, or end to help the student identify the word.

✔ If the student seems confused by the double consonants in words like *stepped* and *matted*, explain, **Sometimes when ed is added to a word, an extra letter is added, like in** *stepped***.**

✔ Provide a one-second pause between the sounds to help students process the sounds.

Cue	Student's independent response	If student needs help
/l/ /ʊ/ /k/ /t/. **Which word am I saying?**	Finds the word <u>looked</u>.	If no response after 4 seconds or an incorrect response, model finding the word and say, **This is <u>looked</u>. You touch it.** Continue pointing to it until the student finds it. If needed, physically guide the student to find the word.

Repeat with the <u>content</u> for each lesson; see **Level 26 Content** on p. 277.

Segmenting I

Objective 3
Segment the middle and last sounds in words.
Pronunciation: /ʊ/ as in foot

Prompting
- Lesson 1: Time delay 0 seconds
- Lessons 2–5: Time delay 4 seconds

Activity directions
I'll say a word. You show me the middle/last sound you hear in the word.

Teaching moment
✔ To practice without the software, provide more words with /ʊ/ in the middle and more words ending in ed.

✔ Pause for one second between the direction ("What is the middle/last sound in") and the target word to prepare the student for the target word.

✔ To make it easier for the student, emphasize or prolong the middle/last sound in the word.

✔ If the student chooses an incorrect response, give a reminder to not guess but to wait and you will help. You can also add to the directions, **If you are not sure of the answer, don't guess. Wait for me to help you.**

Cue	Student's independent response	If student needs help
(Lessons 2 and 4) **What is the middle sound in Brook?**	Finds oo to say /ʊ/.	If no response after 4 seconds or an incorrect response, model finding oo. Say, **The middle sound is /ʊ/. You touch it.** If needed, physically guide the student to find /ʊ/.
(Lessons 1, 3, and 5) **What is the last sound in cleaned?**	Finds ed to say /d/.	If no response after 4 seconds or an incorrect response, model finding ed. Say, **The last sound is /d/. You touch it.** If needed, physically guide the student to find /d/.

Repeat with the content for each lesson; see **Level 26 Content** on p. 277.

Segmenting II

c	oo	k	ed

Objective 4
Segment the sounds in CVC, CVCC, CCVC, CCVCC, CCVrC, and CVCCC words.
Pronunciation: /ʊ/ as in f<u>oo</u>t

Prompting
- Lesson 1: Time delay 0 seconds
- Lessons 2–5: Time delay 4 seconds

Activity directions
Use the sounds you learned to sound out some words. I'll say a word, and you sound it out.

Teaching moment

✔ To help the student segment all of the sounds in the word, hold up a finger for each sound the student needs to find. Remember to hold up fingers for sounds, not letters (e.g., the word *danced* has 5 sounds but 6 letters, *foot* has 3 sounds but 4 letters).

✔ Or if the student needs help, divide the dry-erase board into sections based on the number of sounds in the word. Have the student sound out the word by choosing one sound at a time on the software screen, while you write the letter/sound the student chooses on the dry-erase board (one sound per section).

✔ If the student chooses an incorrect response, give a reminder to not guess but to wait and you will help. Add to the directions, **If you are not sure of the answer, don't guess. Wait for me to help you.**

✔ If the student makes an error on even one sound, have the student listen as you segment all the sounds in the word in the correct sequence. Then restate to touch the sounds in the word.

Cue	Student's independent response	If student needs help
Sound out the word <u>cooked</u>.	Touches <u>c</u>, <u>oo</u>, <u>k</u>, and <u>d</u> for the sounds /k/, /ʊ/, /k/, and /t/.	If no response after 4 seconds or an incorrect response, say, **Listen, /k/ /ʊ/ /k/ /t/. Touch the sounds in <u>cooked</u>.** If still no response or an incorrect response, model segmenting the word by touching each letter and saying each sound. Then say, **Your turn. Touch the sounds in <u>cooked</u>.** If still no response or an incorrect response, say, **Let's touch the sounds in <u>cooked</u>.** Then physically guide the student to touch each sound while you say it.

Repeat with the <u>content</u> for each lesson; see **Level 26 Content** on p. 277.

Decoding

Objective 5
Decode CVC, CVCC, CCVC, CCVCC, CVCCC, and CCVrC words, and compound words and identify their meanings.
Pronunciation: /ʊ/ as in f<u>oo</u>t

Prompting
- Lesson 1: Time delay 0 seconds
- Lessons 2–5: Time delay 4 seconds

Activity directions
Now, use the sounds and letters you learned to read a word and find its picture.

Teaching moment
✔ Be certain the student knows the name of each picture.

✔ Students may need you to continue to demonstrate how to sound out/decode the word. To sound out the word, prolong each letter sound as you say it. Then say the word (blending the sounds together); find the picture representing it. Be sure to follow this demonstration with independent responding by the student.

✔ Also when a compound word is onscreen, remind students how to read a compound word. Say, **Remember, compound words are two short words that go together to make a new larger word. Break the large word into two smaller words to read it.**

Cue	Student's independent response	If student needs help
First, let's hear each picture's name.	Listens as each picture is named.	
Say, **Your turn. Read the word and find the picture.**	Finds the picture of <u>hook</u>.	If no response after 4 seconds, point to the word and say, **This is /<u>h</u>/ /<u>ʊ</u>/ /<u>k</u>/.** Then touch the picture and say, **Here is <u>hook</u>. Now you read <u>hook</u> and find the picture.** Physically guide the student's hand if needed. If an incorrect response, point to the letters in the word as you say, **This says <u>hook</u>.** Touch the picture and say, **Here is the picture of <u>hook</u>.** Remove your finger and say, **Now you read <u>hook</u> and find the picture.** Physically guide the student's hand if needed.

Repeat with the <u>content</u> for each lesson; see **Level 26 Content** on p. 277.

Sight words

Objective 6
Read 4 new sight words.

Prompting
- Lesson 1: Time delay 0 seconds
- Lessons 2–5: Time delay 4 seconds

Activity directions
Sight words are tricky because you can't sound them out. You have to remember what they look like. Find the word.

Teaching moment

✔ The pace between the presentation of words is purposely rapid to keep the student motivated.

✔ Use the sight word flashcards to provide extra practice of sight word reading. Provide up to 4 response options for students to choose from.

✔ Note that the word *wanted* is included as a sight word since students have not learned a rule for reading the a in wanted.

✔ If the student chooses an incorrect response, give a reminder to not guess but to wait and you will help. You can also add to the directions, **If you are not sure of the answer, don't guess. Wait for me to help you.**

Cue	Student's independent response	If student needs help
Find the word give.	Finds the word give.	If no response after 4 seconds or an incorrect response, model finding the word and say, **This is give. You touch it.** Physically guide the student to find the word if needed.

Repeat with the new sight words and review sight words, words required for reading the story for this level; see **Level 26 Content** on p. 277.

ERSB Teacher's Guide ■ Level 26

Reading text / Comprehension questions

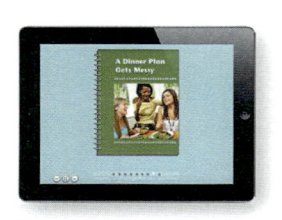

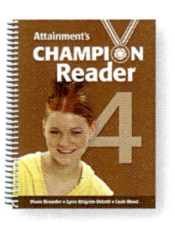

funny dogs
good friends
bad friends
big friends

Objective 7 / Objective 8
Read connected text. / Answer comprehension questions about connected text.

Prompting
Least intrusive prompt

Activity directions
Now that you know how to read words, you can read a page from the story. Today you will read about Brook and her friends.

Teaching moment

✔ One page of the story is read during each lesson, followed by the comprehension questions.

✔ Compound words are embedded in this level's story. Remind students that these words are made of two smaller words and they can read them by breaking the larger word apart.

✔ Use **Champion Reader 4** to give students additional reading practice. The comprehension questions that could be asked if not using the software and possible response options are listed in the **Level 26 Content** on p. 277. Write response options on the dry-erase board for students to read. This is the first level where students are given phrases as response options.

Cue	Student's independent response	If student needs help
Say, **Read this story silently in your head.** Do not read to the student or point to the words.	Reads the sentences silently.	

(Table continues)

Cue	Student's independent response	If student needs help
After the student reads the sentence(s) on the page, say, **Let's answer some questions about the story. What does Brook have?**	Chooses the phrase good friends.	If no response or an incorrect response, say, **Read this sentence again**. Point to each word in the sentence that has the answer, then ask the question again.
		If still no response or an incorrect response, read the sentence with the answer to the student, **My name is Brook and I have good friends**. Then ask, **What does Brook have?**
		If still no response or an incorrect response, physically guide the student to find good friends, and say, **Good friends. Brook has good friends**.

Repeat with the content for each lesson; see **Level 26 Content** on p. 277.

Closing/Writing activity

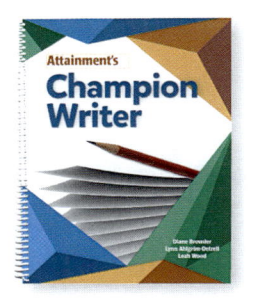

Objective 9
Write responses to activities that review level objectives.

Activity directions
Your lesson is over. GREAT reading today! Let's complete a page in your Champion Writer.

cooked
hooked
looking

Teaching moment

✔ In order to keep the lesson from becoming too long, consider completing the writing activity at another time of the day.

✔ Some students may need adaptations to complete the writing page in **Champion Writer**; see p. 20 for ideas.

✔ Use the dry-erase board and an erasable marker to give the student practice in writing/forming sight words and words containing the letter/sounds of this level.

Appendixes

Appendix A: Decision Tree

The following basic skills are needed for ERSB:

- Print concepts: knowing text goes from top to bottom and left to right, orienting a book, distinguishing between pictures and words, knowing some reading terms (letter, word, beginning, first, middle, end, last)
- Beginning stages of phonological awareness (rhyme, syllable segmentation)
- Listening comprehension (at least for literal recall)
- Some sight words

Each area of need can be addressed individually, but if more than one skill needs instruction, consider using ELSB.

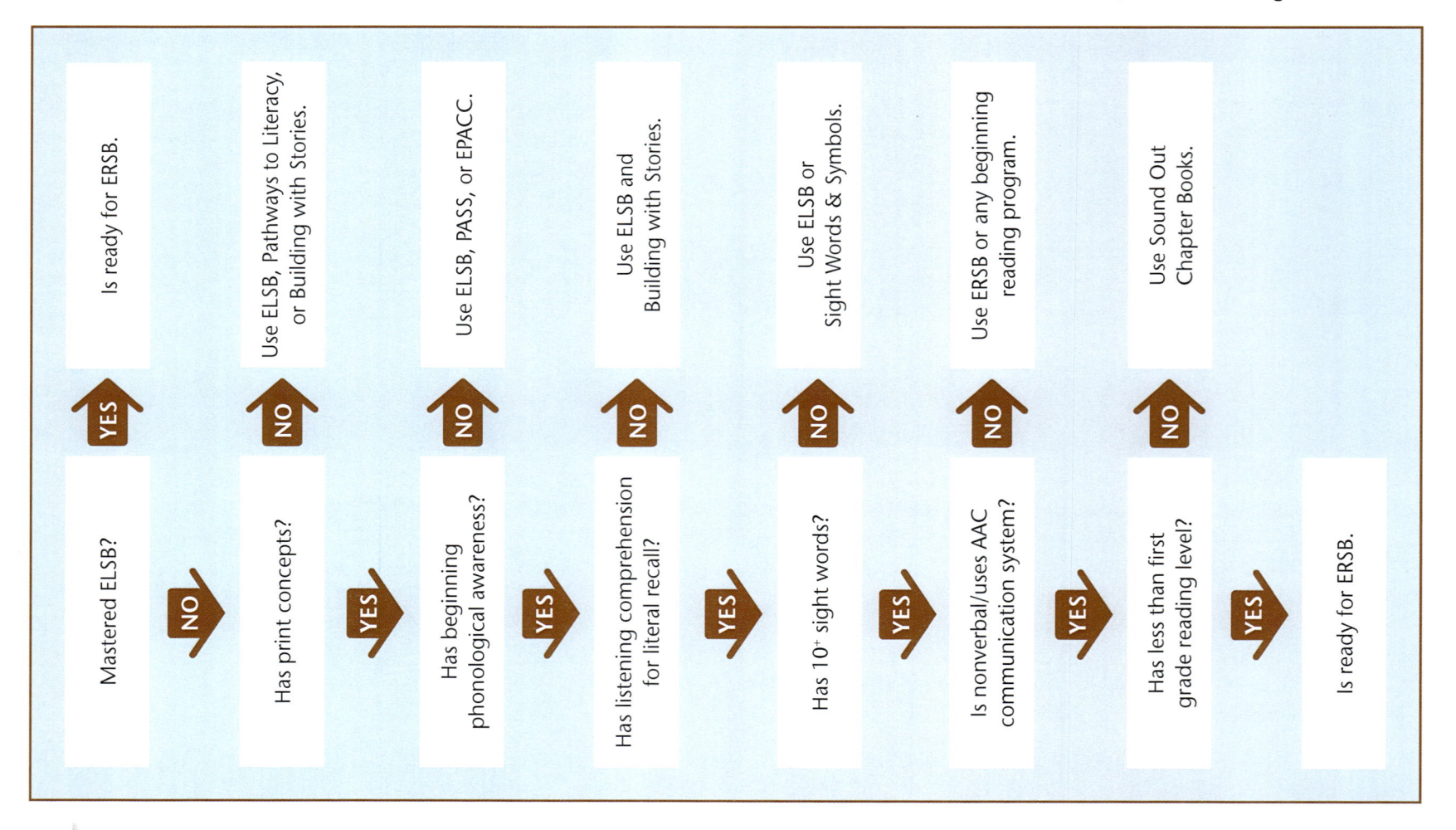

Question	Answer	Action
Mastered ELSB?	YES	Is ready for ERSB.
Mastered ELSB?	NO → Has print concepts?	
Has print concepts?	NO	Use ELSB, Pathways to Literacy, or Building with Stories.
Has print concepts?	YES → Has beginning phonological awareness?	
Has beginning phonological awareness?	NO	Use ELSB, PASS, or EPACC.
Has beginning phonological awareness?	YES → Has listening comprehension for literal recall?	
Has listening comprehension for literal recall?	NO	Use ELSB and Building with Stories.
Has listening comprehension for literal recall?	YES → Has 10+ sight words?	
Has 10+ sight words?	NO	Use ELSB or Sight Words & Symbols.
Has 10+ sight words?	YES → Is nonverbal/uses AAC communication system?	
Is nonverbal/uses AAC communication system?	NO	Use ERSB or any beginning reading program.
Is nonverbal/uses AAC communication system?	YES → Has less than first grade reading level?	
Has less than first grade reading level?	NO	Use Sound Out Chapter Books.
Has less than first grade reading level?	YES	Is ready for ERSB.

Appendix B: How to Complete ERSB Activities without the Software

Letter/sound identification

1. Practice producing single sounds by listening to how the narrator in the software says each.
2. Use the alphabet cards or the dry-erase board to present the alphabet letters to the student.
3. Provide Lesson 1 at 0-seconds time delay. Provide Lessons 2–5 at 4-seconds time delay.
4. Say the sound for the student. Follow the script in the lesson plan.
5. Provide specific praise.
6. Assist the student using the prompts described.

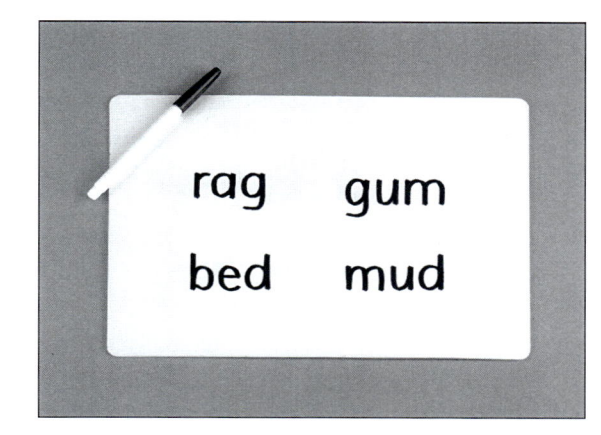

Blending

1. Practice segmenting words by listening to how the narrator in the software segments words.
2. Write response options on the dry-erase board.
3. Provide Lesson 1 at 0-seconds time delay. Provide Lessons 2–5 at 4-seconds time delay.
4. Say the segmented word for the student. Follow the script in the lesson plan.
5. Provide specific praise.
6. Assist the student using the prompts described in the lesson plan.

Segmenting I

1. Practice stretching/saying a word by listening to how the narrator says it in the software.
2. Use the alphabet cards or the dry-erase board to present the alphabet letters to the student. Use the same letters used in the letter/sound identification activity.
3. Provide Lesson 1 at 0-seconds time delay. Provide Lessons 2–5 at 4-seconds time delay.
4. Say the word for the student. Follow the script in the lesson plan.
5. Provide specific praise.
6. Assist the student using the prompts described in the lesson plan.

ERSB Teacher's Guide ■ Appendix B

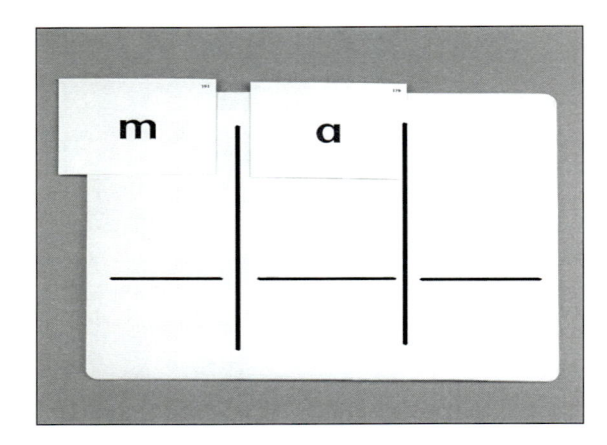

Segmenting II

1. Practice saying a word by listening to how the narrator says it in the software.
2. Use the alphabet cards or the dry-erase board to present the alphabet letters to the student. Use the same letters used in the letter/sound identification activity.
3. Provide Lesson 1 at 0-seconds time delay. Provide Lessons 2–5 at 4-seconds time delay.
4. Say the word for the student. Follow the script in the lesson plan.
5. Provide specific praise.
6. Assist the student using the prompts described in the lesson plan.

Decoding

1. Prepare pictures cards for this activity by printing the Decoding Photos file found on the CD.
2. Provide 4 response options for the student: the correct response, one picture beginning with the same sound, one ending with the same sound or one having the same middle sound, and one obviously wrong response.
3. Provide Lesson 1 at 0-seconds time delay. Provide Lessons 2–5 at 4-seconds time delay.
4. Follow the script in the lesson plan.
5. Provide specific praise.
6. Assist the student using the prompts described in the lesson plan.

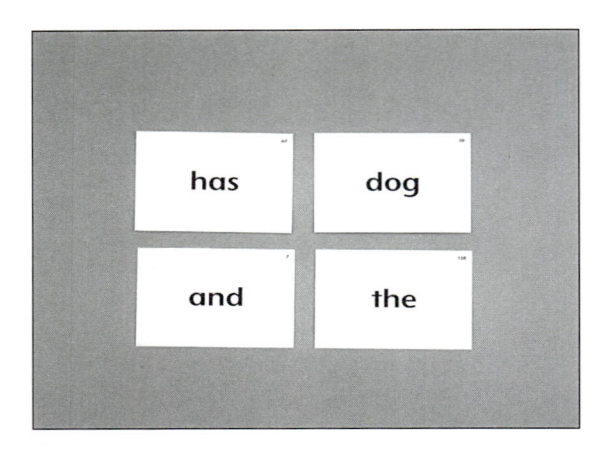

Sight words

1. Use the sight word flashcards.
2. Set 4 response options in front of the student: the correct response and three others. Shuffle before giving another word.
3. Provide Lesson 1 at 0-seconds time delay. Provide Lessons 2–5 at 4-seconds time delay.
4. Follow the script in the lesson plan.
5. Provide specific praise.
6. Assist the student using the prompts described in the lesson plan.

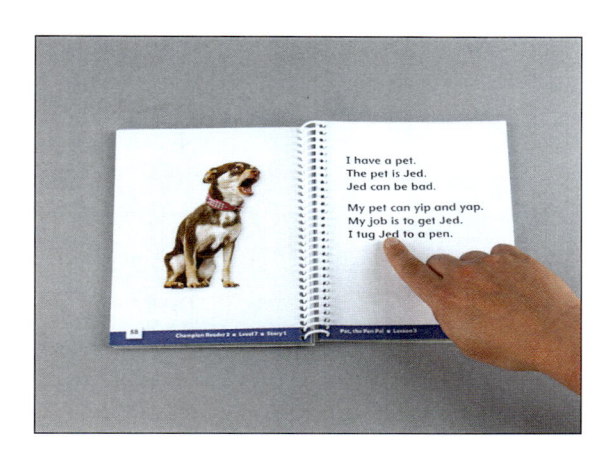

Reading connected text

1 Use the Champion Reader to have the student read the appropriate page.

2 Prompt the student as described in the lesson plan.

Comprehension questions

1 Refer to the Level Content chart at the start of each level for suggested comprehension questions and responses options.

2 Write response options on the dry-erase board.

3 Ask the comprehension question after the student has read all of the text on the page. Do not read the response options.

4 Follow the prompting script in the lesson plan.

5 Provide specific praise.

6 Assist the student using the prompts described in the lesson plan.

ERSB Teacher's Guide ■ Appendix B

Appendix C: Guide to Pronunciation of Phonemes Using the International Phonetic Alphabet

consonants		vowels	dipthongs	r-controlled vowels
/b/ as in bat	/r/ as in rat	/ɪ/ as in pin	/ʊ/ as in book	/ɝ/ as in bird
/d/ as in duck	/s/ as in ice and sip	/æ/ as in cat	/aʊ/ as in ouch	/ɑr/ as in card
/f/ as in fun	/t/ as in tent	/ɛ/ as in pet	/ɔɪ/ as in toy	/ɔr/ as in fort
/g/ as in goat	/v/ as in van	/ɑ/ as in cot	/u/ as in zoo	
/h/ as in hat	/w/ as in wet	/ʌ/ as in up	/ɔ/ as in haul and ball	
/dʒ/ as in jam	/z/ as in zip and nose	/aɪ/ as in line		
/k/ as in duck	/θ/ as in thin	/i/ as in bee		
/l/ as in lime	/ʃ/ as in shine	/eɪ/ as in pane		
/m/ as in moon	/tʃ/ as in cheese	/o/ as in go		
/n/ as in nose	/j/ as in yarn	/ju/ cute		
/p/ as in Pat	/ŋ/ as in wing			

Appendix D: Characters by Name

Ben		Gus		Jess's mom		Pat		Tim's dad	
Beth		Jake		Kim		Ron		Tom	
Beth's mom		Jane		Liv		Sam		Ty	
Brad		Jean		Liv's mom		Sloan		Ty's dad	
Brook		Jed		Mike		Ty's mom		Wren	
Dane		Jen		Mike's mom		Tam		Yum	
Dane's mom		Jess		Mim		Tim		Zack	

Appendix E: Data Collection Form

ERSB Data Collection Form

Name _____ Date _____

Level _____ Lesson 2 3 4 5 Instructor _____

Scoring: + = Independently correct response   M = Model prompt provided
P = Physical prompt provided

Letter/sound identification (List the level's letters/sounds and review letters/sounds. Write response options on the dry-erase board. Say the sound; have the student touch its letter.)

1.	4.
2.	5.
3.	6.

Correct, independent responses: Score _____ / _____   _____ %

Comments/notes: _____

Blending (List the words whose sounds you will segment for the student to blend. Write response options on the dry-erase board.)

1.	4.
2.	5.
3.	6.

Correct, independent responses: Score _____ / _____   _____ %

Comments/notes: _____

Segmenting I (List the words the you will say and indicate whether the student is to listen for the initial (I), medial (M), or final (F) sound in the word. Write response options on the dry-erase board.)

1.	4.
2.	5.
3.	6.

Correct, independent responses: Score _____ / _____   _____ %

Comments/notes: _____

Segmenting II (List the words you will say to the student. Write letter/sound response options on the dry-erase board.)

1.	4.
2.	5.
3.	6.

Correct, independent responses: Score _____ / _____   _____ %

Comments/notes: _____

ERSB Data Collection Form (continued)

Decoding (List the words you will provide to students for decoding. Write response options on the dry-erase board. Prepare picture choices using the file provided on the CD.)

1.	4.
2.	5.
3.	6.

Correct, independent responses: Score _____ / _____ _____%

Comments/notes: _____

Sight Words (List the new and review sight words for the student. Use the sight word flashcards for this activity.)

1.	7.
2.	8.
3.	9.
4.	10.
5.	11.
6.	12.

Correct, independent responses: Score _____ / _____ _____%

Comments/notes: _____

Reading Connected Text (Use the spiral-bound books for reading practice. Follow the student's reading with comprehension questions.)

Comments/notes: _____

Comprehension Questions (Write response options on the dry-erase board. Refer to the Level Content chart at the start of each level.)

1.	4.
2.	5.
3.	6.

Correct, independent responses: Score _____ / _____ _____%

Comments/notes: _____

References

Adams, M. J. (1990). *Beginning to read: Thinking and learning about print.* Cambridge, MA: The MIT Press.

Ahlgrim-Delzell, L., Browder, D. M., & Wood, L. (2014). Effects of systematic instruction and an augmentative communication device on phonics skills acquisition for students with moderate intellectual disability who are nonverbal. *Education and Training in Autism and Developmental Disabilities, 49,* 517–532.

Ahlgrim-Delzell, L., Browder, D., Wood, L., Preston, A., & Kemp-Inman, A. (2014). *Systematic instruction of phonics using an iPad for students who are nonverbal.* Manuscript in preparation.

Alberto, P. A., Waugh, R. E., & Fredrick, L. D. (2010). Teaching the reading of connected text through sight-word instruction to students with moderate intellectual disabilities. *Research in Developmental Disabilities, 31,* 1467–1474.

Allor, J., Mathes, P., Roberts, J., Jones, F., & Champlin, T. (2010). Teaching students with moderate intellectual disabilities to read: An experimental examination of a comprehensive reading intervention. *Education and Training in Autism and Developmental Disabilities, 45,* 3–22.

Armbruster, B. B., Fehr, F., & Osborn, J. (2003). *Put reading first: The research building blocks for teaching children to read.* Washington, DC: National Institute for Literacy.

Attainment Company. (2014). *Sound out chapter books* [software]. Verona, WI: Author.

Bradford, S., Shippen, M. E., Alberto, P. A., Houchins, D. E., & Flores, M. M. (2006). Using systematic instruction to teach decoding skills to middle school students with moderate intellectual disabilities. *Education and Training in Developmental Disabilities, 41,* 323–324.

Browder, D. M., Ahlgrim-Delzell, L., Spooner, F., Mims, P. J., & Baker, J. (2009). Using time delay to teach literacy to students with severe developmental disabilities. *Exceptional Children, 74,* 343–363.

Browder, D. M., Ahlgrim-Delzell, L., Flowers, C., & Baker, J. N. (2012). An evaluation of a multicomponent early literacy program for students with severe developmental disabilities. *Remedial and Special Education, 33,* 237–246.

Browder, D. M., Gibbs, S., Ahlgrim-Delzell, L., Courtade, G., & Lee, A. (2007). *Early literacy skills builder (ELSB).* Verona, WI: Attainment Company.

Browder, D. M., Hudson, M. E., & Wood, L. (2013). Teaching students with moderate intellectual disability who are emergent readers to comprehend passages of text. *Exceptionality, 21,* 191–206.

Browder, D. M., Trela, K., & Jimenez, B. (2007). Training teachers to follow a task analysis to engage middle school students with moderate and severe developmental disabilities in grade-appropriate literature. *Focus on Autism and Other Developmental Disabilities, 22,* 206–219.

Browder, D.M., Wakeman, S., Spooner, F., Ahlgrim-Delzell, L., & Algozzine, B. (2006). Research on reading instruction for individuals with significant cognitive disabilities. *Exceptional Children, 72,* 392–408.

Bus, A. G., van IJzendoorn, M. H., & Pellegrini, A. D. (1995). Joint book reading makes for success in learning to read: A meta-analysis on intergenerational transmission of literacy. *Review of Educational Research, 65*(1), 1–21.

Carnine, D., Silbert, J., & Kameʼenui, E., & Tarver, S. (2004). *Direct instruction reading* (3rd ed.). Columbus, OH: Merrill.

Elam, S. (2007). *Phonics primer.* Manassas Par, VA: National Right to Read Foundation.

Engelmann, S., & Bruner, E. C. (2003). *Reading mastery.* Columbus, OH: SRA/McGraw-Hill.

Engelmann, S., Carnine, L., & Johnson, G. (1988). *Corrective reading: Word-attack basics* (Level A). Columbus, OH: Macmillan/McGraw-Hill.

Gibbs, S. L., Campbell, M. L., Helf, S, & Cooke, N. (2007) *Early reading tutor.* Columbus, OH: SRA/McGraw-Hill.

High Noon Books. (2005). *Sound out chapter books.* Novato, CA: author.

Justice, L. M., McGinty, A. S., Piasta, S. B., Kaderavek, J. N., & Fan, X. (2010). Print-focused read alouds in preschool classrooms: Intervention effectiveness and moderators of child outcomes. *Language, Speech, and Hearing Services in Schools, 41*(4), 504–520.

Kliewer, C., Biklen, D., & Kasa-Hendrickson, C. (2006). Who may be literate? Disability and resistance to the cultural denial of competence. *American Educational Research Journal, 43*(2), 163–192.

Mathes, P.G., & Torgesen, J. K. (2005). *Early interventions in reading.* Columbus, OH: SRA/McGraw-Hill.

MetaMetrics. (2014, October). *The Lexile framework for reading.* Retrieved from www.metametricsinc.com

Mims, P. J., Hudson, M. E., & Browder, D. M. (2012). Using read-alouds of grade-level biographies and systematic prompting to promote comprehension for students with moderate and severe developmental disabilities. *Focus on Autism and Other Developmental Disabilities, 27,* 67–80.

Mims, P., Lee, A., Zakas, T., & Browder, D. (2013). *Teaching to standards: English language arts.* Verona, WI: Attainment Company.

National Reading Panel. (2000). *Teaching children to read: An evidence-based assessment of the scientific research literature on reading and its implications for reading instruction* (NIH Publication No. 00-4769). Washington, DC: U.S. Government Printing Office.

No Child Left Behind Act. (2001). *Statement of purpose.* H.R. 1-16(9). Washington, DC: 107th Congress of the United States.

Presseley, M. (2005). *Dolch professional development guide.* Columbus, OH: SRA.

Renaissance Learning. (2014, October). *ATOS analyzer.* Retrieved from www.renaissance.com

Skotko, B. G., Koppenhaver, D. A., & Erickson, K. A. (2004). Parent reading behaviors and communication outcomes in girls with Rett Syndrome. *Exceptional Children, 70,* 145–166.

Spooner, F., Knight, V. F., Browder, D. M., & Smith, B. R. (2012). Evidence-based practice for teaching academics to students with severe developmental disabilities. *Remedial and Special Education, 33,* 374–387.

Wolery, M., Bailey, D. B., & Sugai, G. M. (1988). *Effective teaching: Principles and procedures of applied behavior analysis with exceptional students.* Boston: Allyn & Bacon.

Zakas, T., & Schreiber, L. (2010). *Building with stories.* Verona, WI: Attainment Company.